Gro

Wo

SAGE SOURCEBOOKS FOR THE HUMAN SERVICES SERIES

Series Editors: ARMAND LAUFFER and CHARLES GARVIN

Recent Volumes in This Series

Urania Glassman
Len Kates

Group
Work

A Humanistic
Approach

SAGE SOURCEBOOKS FOR THE HUMAN SERVICES SERIES 13

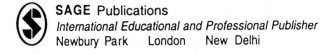

SAGE Publications
International Educational and Professional Publisher
Newbury Park   London   New Delhi

We dedicate this book to our spouses, Ron and Susan, who love the value of the humanistic group, cherish democracy, and share our hope that the world can become more humane. And to our children—Jennifer, Julie, Amy, Danny, Asa, and Alex—we hope that you carry on with efforts to develop humanistic and democratic milieus.

For information address:

SAGE Publications, Inc.
2111 West Hillcrest Drive
Newbury Park, California 91320
E-mail: order@sagepub.com

SAGE Publications Ltd.
28 Banner Street
London EC1Y 8QE
England

SAGE Publications India Pvt. Ltd.
M-32 Market
Greater Kailash I
New Delhi 110 048 India

Printed in the United States of America

Library of Congress Cataloging-in-Publication Data

Glassman, Urania.
   Group work : a humanistic approach / by Urania Glassman, Len
Kates.
      p.   cm. — (Sage sourcebooks for the human services series ;
   v. 13)
   Includes bibliographical references (p. 275).
   ISBN 0-8039-3453-X. — ISBN 0-8039-3454-8 (pbk.)
   1. Social group work. I. Kates, Len. II. Title. III. Series.
HV45.G56   1990
361.4—dc20   90-8225
                                                             CIP

96 97 98 99 00 01 02 10 9 8 7 6 5

Sage Production Editor: Susan McElroy

CONTENTS

ACKNOWLEDGMENTS

The culture and the spirit, as well as the membership, of the Association for the Advancement of Social Work with Groups, and the planners and participants of the Annual Symposia, have spawned and shaped this work. This book could not have been written without that context of friends and colleagues who provided the arena in which to test our ideas.

Thank you, with deep affection and gratitude, to our special colleagues—Charles Garvin, Catherine Papell, and Beulah Rothman—who have been constant sources of intellectual and emotional sustenance. We cherish your support.

We thank our Adelphi colleagues, Sylvia Aron and Marty Seitz, who have given us their perspectives on group work method, and who have used our work to teach group work.

It is with great sadness that we acknowledge the memory of the late Helene Fishbein, who supported and encouraged our vision.

We are forever indebted to the people who have been our students at the Adelphi University School of Social Work and the City College of the City University of New York, who experienced our ideas and shared their viewpoints.

We recognize the members of our groups and of our colleagues' groups who have responded with vigor and effectiveness to the processes of the democratic humanistic method.

We have written this book in the legacies and framework of Saul Bernstein and William Schwartz, as well as those of our learned colleagues James Garland, Hubert Jones, Ralph Kolodny, Alex Gitterman, and Lawrence Shulman. We thank Norma Lang who has broadened our minds and souls with her intellectual clarity, especially about the democratic group. We pay tribute to Jerome Gold of the City College House Plan Association for daring to create a multifaceted group work milieu that has spawned so many group workers. House Plan was indeed a laboratory for life. We give thanks to Marvin Parnes and Jane Hassinger for their faith and belief in our work.

With fondness we acknowledge the confidence in us shown by friends Bruce Brown, Kay Davidson, and Ellen Sue Mesbur.

PREFACE

The humanistic method of social work with groups embodies the values and practices of social group work's heritage as well as those of the social work profession. As a group approach, the humanistic method may be used to assist clients with their preventive, rehabilitative, treatment, and social action agendas and goals. The humanistic group work method may be employed by allied human service professionals—activities therapists, nurses, psychiatrists, psychologists, residential care staff, and special educators—who assist people in attaining effectiveness, satisfaction, and change in their interpersonal relationships and circumstances.

We have written this book on values, norms, and techniques in humanistic group work to share our experiences and approaches with other group practitioners who also wish to continue to develop an appreciation of the potency of the professionally guided small group. It is written for those who appreciate and savor the supportive effects that social responsibility, caring, mutual aid, and respect for individual uniqueness have on the group member.

We have also written this book in continual support of the human spirit as well as the humanistic visions of our teachers, students, and colleagues as we all champion personal and social change through the combined effects of self-determination and collective effort.

We have written this book to join with those who are violated and enraged by the existence, nature, and activities of authoritarian groups that develop social and professional situations for controlling social milieus and individuals, and for suppressing differences. Such groups arbitrarily attempt to change people in order to meet narrowly derived and selfishly defined ideological and pseudoprofessional objectives. We wish to bear symbolic witness to the memory and the plights of victims of authoritarianism.

In this work we have set out to present and explicate the special features of the humanistic group work method and process, which is used to develop a unique social form for assisting people in their efforts to change themselves and their circumstances (Lang, 1981). Our experiences as members and practitioners in a variety of types of groups have led us to the following conviction: The small face-to-face group may be developed into a special productive milieu within which members can feel belonging and acceptance, friendship and comfort, challenge and support, and feel it to be a place to develop social goals and actions in order to enhance the quality of life.

Contemporary forms of racism, classism, ethnocentrism, sexism, and stigmatization, as well as the repression of humanistic mores by cybernetic systems, bring about an urgency to focus on social work professional activities for developing humanistic groups. We cannot forget the totalitarian and destructive events in Jonestown. We are deeply concerned that to this day, in the face of the lessons of the Nazi debacle, people are still damaged and repressed by political and professional demagogues who use power to distort people's humanity, spirit, and relationships with loved ones and communities. Unhappily, in the last decade or so, we have lost sight of the significant personal and social gains that accrue for people in humanistically oriented, professionally guided groups.

It is most satisfying to remember camping groups, youngsters in residential care for whom participation in group life is a corrective opportunity that counters despair and isolation, and women in the postmastectomy groups our colleagues tell us about with the excitement of new explorers at a frontier. Included in this are the many programs run by groups for themselves and others: the members and workers in groups for the blind, for campers, for city dwellers, the groups for the very frail and forgetful elderly who were helped out of isolation and loneliness, the members and practitioners in groups for people who are retarded, groups for the chronically mentally ill, for the homeless. All of these groupings receive applause for their bonds of mutuality.

There are groups in school settings run by social workers trying to help youngsters cope with family instability, feelings of fragmentation, loneliness, and academic underachievement, as well as a variety of disabilities. There are groups for sobriety, groups for persons with AIDS, and for homeless persons; these groups are for self-help along with social action. Groups spring up everywhere in hospital settings—in neonatal, pediatric, oncology, medicine, spinal cord, pulmonary, dialysis, and psychiatric units.

The humanistic group work method in this book is presented to assist in evolving a group practice for personal, interpersonal, and situational growth by means of the unique values and norms of social group work. This humanistic group work method has significant utility in both clinical and community settings. It can be used for prevention, treatment, remediation, and collective action. The method and its theories are drawn from several psychosocial frames of reference, including ego psychology, symbolic interactionism, and social institutional theory (Berger & Luckmann, 1966), as well as T-group theory and research (Bennis & Shepard, 1962). The context is humanistic; the method is democratic.

This book describes an art and its technology of expression through techniques of group work practice. These techniques emanate from the special values, objectives, and unique experiences of clinical and community groups assisted by social group work practitioners and other like-minded facilitators. The book is centered on the role of the group practitioner, using group work methods to contribute to the personal and political empowerment of group members in their community and institutional contexts.

—Urania Glassman
Len Kates

INTRODUCTION

The humanistic group developed through the humanistic group work method is similar to other small group forms that have been developed and studied. It exhibits the universal characteristics of small groups. It has norms, a culture, face to face interaction, affective bonds, and cohesion. It also reflects the various themes of group life that revolve around closeness (Garland, Jones, & Kolodny, 1973) and the dynamics of power and love (Bennis & Shepard, 1962).

The humanistic group aims to develop and sustain a particular kind of small face-to-face group that is built on selected values which link its members to each other through a distinct set of affective bonds; these affects include trust, care, respect, acceptance, and anger. These values and feelings are used to develop and intensify members' individual and interpersonal potentials in the context of their needs and interests. Not all small group experiences have as an outcome people's growth, nor connect them with ways of developing their capabilities within their individual and collective capacities. Some group experiences, while providing affective bonds, inhibit members' growth. This occurs because the group's standards for behavior violate, or do not support, individuation or difference.

The humanistic group method is rooted in the history and traditions of humanism and democracy. Humanism is built on particular values that cast people in society as responsible for and to one another; democracy is defined by particular standards of interaction that yield equality in relation to power, position, and resources. The aim of the humanistic method is the development of effective behavior for the group and the members, within the group's milieu and its external social environment. The method's objectives are designed to assist the members with their interactional and problem-solving processes. The unique process of this method is denoted by a culture of humanistic values and democratic norms that shape the interactions of the members and the practitioner.

Humanistic values shape people's stances and attitudes about themselves and others in the group. Humanistic values for social group work were stated by Gisela Konopka (1963). They have stood the test of time as fundamental means for the development of group experiences. This set of values takes the following positions: (1) individuals are of inherent worth; (2) people are mutually responsible for each other; and (3) people have the fundamental right to experience mental health brought about by social and political conditions that support their fulfillment.

Democratic norms are the specific standards that develop the patterns and qualities of the members' behaviors. Democratic norms chart pathways for cooperative interaction and fluid distribution of position, power, and resources; they motivate the change efforts of the members in the humanistic group (White & Lippitt, 1968).

These values and norms, through the leadership behaviors they sanction, celebrate each member and the practitioner as participants who actively create and sustain this experiment for social living characterized by trial and error, give and take, and considerable efforts to bring about change in their collective and individual experiences.

Members seek enhanced social interactions in the group, as well as in their formal and informal relationships outside of it. The latter include family, couple, peer, and work relationships; they also include the situations that come about through members' voluntary and involuntary participation in health, education, and social welfare programs. The group members have related needs for effectiveness and change in their social environments that provide the arena for achieving the group's purpose. The group members may or may not know one another. They may be patients in a hospital for the chronically ill, single parents, prisoners, adolescent gang members, clients in an outpatient mental health clinic, elderly people living alone, mothers receiving economic and social welfare entitlements, children in residential care, homeless persons, married couples, or relatives of dying loved ones.

Another important principle that defines the humanistic group is the principle of "externality" (Papell & Rothman, 1980b). In this frame of reference, the members develop experiences in relating that reach beyond the boundaries of the meeting time itself into their actual community. Members are encouraged to build social networks with each other, by using the time between sessions to support and enhance one another's interpersonal and environmental goals. Members also are encouraged to include significant others from their external networks into the group's experiences to the extent that this involvement enhances the group as a viable organism. The group develops programs, experiential situations, and activities for all concerned to provide alternative avenues for socialization, experimentation, and for exposure to circumstances that have the power to affect the well-being of the members.

The humanistic group work method takes into account that people have different capacities to take care of themselves. Some can, because they have had family, cultural, socioeconomic, and life experiences that provide the means to live effectively and with satisfaction. Others might have difficulty because the necessary conditions of society and economics have prevented and continue to prevent their caring for themselves and others. Still others may have severe physical or emotional inabilities which prevent them from being fully able to take care of themselves and others. The thesis of humanistic group work is antithetical to blaming the victim. While some physically or mentally unable people have been born into circumstances that provide emotional and social sustenance for them to contribute to their peers, others have not been involved in these necessary conditions. Consequently, they are very much less able to express their abilities and contribute to others; they have been in conditions that barely meet their needs or respect their rights.

The practitioner in the humanistic group joins with or forms a small face-to-face group in which members are assisted to participate and interact genuinely and undefensively. The practitioner consciously uses humanistic values and democratic norms, as well as derivative practice techniques, in a human and connected way. He or she has developed understanding, appreciation, and acceptance of the humanistic values and democratic standards of interaction. The practitioner can signify attitudes and actions that represent a democratic humanistic process. This process propels the group and provides perspective for members' evaluations of the values, norms, and processes that exist in the situations which have brought them together. The group worker's activities are ethically employed to assist the members in forming and using the group experience for effectiveness and change in their external situations.

Driven by its values, norms, and practitioner stances, the humanistic group work method is experiential, experimental, existential, and interactional.

It is experiential primarily because it creates a social organism that has the capacity for externality (Papell & Rothman, 1980b), which lives in and affects the social, political, and economic environments of the members. Members experience themselves and their caring abilities in situations with one another and significant others. They enact their desires, they reflect upon these actions, and they act again with one another as well as in important situations.

The method is experimental because the members are encouraged to try out different ways of interacting within the group's meeting environment and in the social milieu. Driven by its ethos, members are not encouraged to try out all behaviors, but rather those that are in keeping with values that respect human dignity and the worth of self and others. Emotionally and socially unethical behaviors, as well as those that are harmful, are not encouraged.

Humanistic group work is existential, because in the process members develop their own values and assume personal responsibility for their own behavior and future actions as they integrate the values and norms provided by the practitioner in their intersubjective relationships with the members. It is existential because the group process is in a perpetual state of engagement and growth, providing opportunities for change and self-actualization for each member.

Because it is an interactional method, humanistic group work focuses on and supports efforts toward developing satisfying interpersonal situations. Self-expression is examined within the group's interpersonal relations, and in other significant settings. The viewpoint of the humanistic method includes the intrapsychic as a unit of attention in the helping or belonging process. Through the group's experiences within its environment and in social situations, persons express themselves both as members and as individuals, simultaneously changing their interpersonal and inner selves. (In the group psychotherapy experience, persons express themselves as individuals changing their inner selves. Interpersonal change in group therapy is assumed to be a by-product of the treatment of psychological and emotional difficulties within the self.)

In sum, there are several essentials that comprise this book's thesis. First, humanistic group work makes a philosophical, political, and experiential statement about the conditions that most helpfully govern human intersubjectivity. It affirms the dignity and worth of individuals; it affirms those values that foster striving for mutual fulfillment of people, while at the same time negating values based on elitism, dominance, and disrespect for human relations. It seeks to establish a milieu of caring and belonging that symbolizes an enlightened form of human interaction and social order. The values and norms it espouses have broad implications for the well-being not only of the group members themselves, but of society at large as well.

It places a positive value on the development of the goodness of people rather than their destructiveness; it affirms that the individual strives for positive growth, quality of life, and interpersonal connection, rather than destructiveness and isolation.

In this affirmation of values, humanistic group method may go against prevailing social values, and even certain prevailing practices in the helping professions. Nonetheless, humanistic group work espouses these values because it is built on a vision and conviction growing out of experience; it is not built on a position of neutrality about the stance and attitude of the practitioner with the group.

Second, the humanistic method of group work is built on a set of behaviors the practitioner uses to operationalize its values and norms. Not all practitioner strategies in groups build humane social milieus. Within the context of humanistic values and democratic norms the group work practitioner sees domination, submission, exclusion, isolation, scapegoating, and destructiveness as attitudes and acts carried out when people are fearful and anxious, often about their own survival. These interactions breed variations of disregard and repression that do harm.

Through these beliefs the group practitioner uses empathic relationships, group work techniques, and a range of derivative knowledge to help members deal with and overcome interpersonal obstacles. The group work techniques help members develop abilities, while at the same time affecting significant others as well. In fact, group work techniques may represent not only what the practitioner does in humanistic group work practice, but effective ways in which members can interact with one another toward self-development and role enhancement in and out of the group experience.

Third, humanistic group work strives to empower persons who might have been victimized by dint of disability or lower status in the society at large. From this perspective the group practitioner engages the members in a process that focuses and assists them all in their entitlement to a range of social, economic, and political conditions that insure survival and satisfaction.

The effort of this book is to make a statement about a particular value base upon which social group work has been established in its history and traditions, and to delineate practice approaches and techniques for the group worker that are in direct consonance with these values. In addition, the effort of this treatise is to recognize and affirm that group life can be a powerful corrective experience for the member when the practitioner operates within a framework of humanistic values. It is also an effort that attests to the importance of democratic actions in the practitioner's use of self as a safeguard for the member against demagoguery in group life that will sow the seeds of destructiveness and do violence to the human spirit. And finally, it is the hope that not only the practitioner, but the member, too, of a humanistic group will utilize many of the behaviors that emanate from its values.

Part I

DIMENSIONS OF THE
HUMANISTIC APPROACH

Chapter 1

HUMANISTIC VALUES AND DEMOCRATIC NORMS

A FOUNDATION OF HUMANISTIC VALUES

Membership in a humanistic group that values the individual, and fosters responsibility for others, supports and enhances social and mental health by creating a little pocket of humanistic egalitarian life that is realistic and healing. Caring, mutual aid, cooperation, inclusivity, open participation, nonelitism, and respect for differences are types of interactions that are necessary for the creation of this kind of milieu (Glassman & Kates, 1986b). One need only have lived under totalitarian regimes from Argentina to Greece and South Africa (Theodorakis, 1973; Timerman, 1981), or heard about them from refugees (Glassman & Skolnik, 1984) or political prisoners, to sustain the conviction that a democratic humanistic group is a fundamental means for achieving enhanced mental and social health.

The timeless nature of these ethics is well stated in the words of Neva Boyd (1971), originally written half a century ago:

Social group work is the promotion and leadership . . . of mutual participation groups in which the members participate collectively in the feeling, thinking, and action involved in carrying out communal interests. The psychological essence of such experience for the participants is psychological intimacy. (p. 141)

Mutual participant groups reveal a possible gradation from those characterized by individuation to those characterized by collectivism.... The group that is responsible for its own destiny is forced to solve its own problems; hence everything that concerns any aspect of it becomes a group responsibility. This is a type of democratic collectivism in which the rights of the individual are neither exercised at the sacrifice of those of the group, nor subordinated to them, but are preserved as an essential part of the whole. (p. 148)

Expression of humanistic values and democratic norms reveals the practitioner's basic convictions about the members' and other people's worth. These attitudes and actions are messages to the members about how they may connect to and challenge one another meaningfully and productively. The practitioner's ability to own and express humanistic values and democratic norms is essential for achieving humanistic and democratic processes in the social work group. The ability to own and use these is as important, if not more important, than the practitioner's ability to use techniques. Techniques without values and norms are dangerous. They may lead to control, domination, and coercion without respect for human nature and members' rights to determine their own processes and goals.

Furthermore, practitioners' lack of appreciation of the qualities of humanistic values and democratic norms may give rise to elitist attitudes. Using knowledge of human behavior and development that is devoid of values may effect an aloof image that does not permit the members to hold the practitioner accountable for his or her attempts to influence the members. By contrast, the group practitioner who uses the humanistic form represents its democratic standards by example, as well as by engaging with the members fully as the group evolves its experiences. The practitioner explicitly invokes sanctions against acts of physical violence, emotional violation, character assassination, acts of stereotyping, stigmatizing, scapegoating, and other forms of subjective assumptions. All else in the process—a full range of emotions and activities—is grist for the mill, for interaction, learning, and change.

HISTORICAL OVERVIEW OF DEMOCRATIC PRINCIPLES

Social group workers have contributed to the effort to understand the helpful and dangerous aspects of small groups. They have played an important part in the development of democratic practices in group process. Writings in group work in the last 50 years by Bernstein (1973), Coyle (1948/1978), Klein (1953), Konopka (1963, 1978), Schwartz (1961), and Trecker (1972) focus on a historical commitment to motivating and sustaining an ethical and humane social system. These practitioner-scholars have used the small face-to-face group to educate members for citizenship, and to expand members' economic and educational opportunities. Group workers have traditionally used the small group to educate, remediate, and empower members to meet their needs in their communities, whether these are their natural social situations or institutional ones. Groups are formed in child guidance clinics, geriatric centers, medical centers, on the street with the homeless, and in mental health settings—in locked units and aftercare programs. These group experiences represent efforts to maximize participation and empowerment for people who are economically deprived and socially ostracized.

Efforts to define what is uniquely social group work have been made by contemporary theoreticians and practitioners such as Garland, Jones, and Kolodny (1973); Garvin (1987); Gitterman and Shulman (1987); Lang (1972, 1981); and Papell and Rothman (1980b). These colleagues have presented models including practice principles and skills that embrace humanistic values and democratic standards for the group's milieu. These efforts underline the necessity of learning technologies of practice, as well as empathetically expressing the values of the group work method to develop a democratic system as a milieu within which the members meet their needs.

VALUES OF THE HUMANISTIC GROUP

The values that comprise the nature of the humanistic approach to group work practice are the following:

Humanistic Value 1: *People have inherent worth and capacities regardless of race, class, status, age, and gender, as well as physical and psychological condition.*

Humanistic Value 2: *People are responsible for and to one another because social life is a natural and necessary human characteristic.*

Humanistic Value 3: *People have a right to belong and to be included.*

Humanistic Value 4: *People, having emotional and intellectual voices that are essential to their existence, have a right to take part and to be heard.*

Humanistic Value 5: *People have the right to freedom of speech, and freedom of expression.*

Humanistic Value 6: *Differences among members are enriching to one another.*

Humanistic Value 7: *People have a right to freedom of choice, to determine their own destinies.*

Humanistic Value 8: *People have the right to question and challenge those professionals who have sanction to guide and direct their lives.*

These humanistic values are fundamental and indisputable in group work. Evolving and sustaining them requires effort and conviction. The professional group worker must be willing to struggle with the group in order to have these emotional, social, and philosophical frames of reference bring about processes that lead the members to hold these values as uppermost. Acceptance of these values is but the first step in the process. The members will have to express these values through their actions and in the quality of their interactions with one another.

DEMOCRATIC NORMS AS VALUES IN ACTION

The roots of a democratic culture do not lie in its theories and conceptions, but rather in conduct and its satisfactions. (Lindeman, 1980)

Group norms are the implicit and explicit standards developed in the members' transactions that guide their behavior. Norms develop in groups in a variety of complex ways. They develop through the planned, as well as unplanned, efforts of the participants; they also develop through the power and influence of those, including the practitioner, who are exerting leadership. There are no guarantees that a group's norms will be humane and democratic. Group norms that are based on the domination of others by a powerful clique, or that foster exclusion, can develop all too easily. By contrast, democratic norms are those standards that operationalize humanistic values, the substance of the social group work process.

Having a set of humanistic values without the capacity to follow through in behavior can be an empty gesture. Humanistic values and democratic standards are too important to the enabling process of social group work to be left to develop by chance. Without a planned and concerted effort by the practitioner to express these, there are no assurances that the humanistic democratic culture will come about.

There also are no assurances that members will hear the person with unique characteristics, or that they will make decisions that respect the positions of the members in the minority. Furthermore, there are no guarantees that members will reach out to connect to others without aggression. The practitioner has a fundamental ethical obligation and all-important practice role to play in affecting how the members value and interact with one another. The practitioner is pivotal through expressing the humanistic values and democratic norms so that these will shape the members' behaviors. The practitioner must be the most active proponent of this milieu until the members demonstrate their abilities to sustain it.

This section will examine humanistic values 1, 2, 3, and 4 as they are expressed by the practitioner. How each value is enacted through a set of democratic norms that set standards for humanistic relationships among members will be presented. The role of the practitioner will be delineated and demonstrated through practice illustrations. (See Table 1.1 at the end of this chapter for a summary of values, norms, and practitioner roles.) In Chapter 2, humanistic values 5, 6, 7, and 8 will be similarly presented (see Table 2.1 in the next chapter for a further summary).

Humanistic Value 1:
People Have Inherent Worth and Capacities
Regardless of Race, Class, Status, Age, and Gender,
as Well as Physical and Psychological Condition

This value underlies all others in the formation of the humanistic group. It places emphasis on the individual as a being with a unique spirit and energy. Incorporating this value in the group sets the stage for subsequent ways in which members perceive, help, and work with one another. It helps the members develop an egalitarian milieu, rather than an elitist one that would undermine the efforts and strivings of the members.

Democratic Norm 1:
The Group Protects Each Member's Right to
Contribute to and Receive From the Group

The values that accompany membership in an egalitarian group do not lead to the denigration of the positions, contributions, and potentials of people. Members possessing more knowledge, prior experience, higher social status, or economic class cannot use these as reasons for defaming or subjugating others. Members in the humanistic group are responsible for developing continual awareness of their elitist and prejudicial approaches toward others; and they work toward changing these attitudes and actions.

Adherence to this norm does not result in homogenization of members and denial of their distinctive qualities. Group members are called upon to develop ways of presenting and taking pride in their participation and contributions. Members are called upon to acknowledge the significance and quality of the contributions of other members without comparison with their own or to others. Members develop approaches to dealing with their own lack of knowledge as they review each others' special expertise and resources.

Practitioner role. The practitioner stresses the value of each member to the life and process of the group. The practitioner explicitly states that each member's contribution sets a direction for the group's process and experience. The group worker indicates that each member and the practitioner have cultural and psychological differences. The practitioner engages attitudes, perceptions, and actions divisive to this norm by actively intervening in the group's process.

Illustration. The parents of nursery school children have been meeting regularly concerning the effects of the program on their children. They also consider the special aspects of parenting nursery-school-age children. One mother, Denise, is quite upset because the children are not given alphabet-recognition or reading readiness skills. Several parents respond by talking about the need to build social skills first. None feel particularly expert in their knowledge.

Maude insists that her older child has done quite well in this program and will learn to read in the first grade where it is more appropriate. Matt wonders if Doris, who has majored in child development in college, could enlighten the group. Doris hesitates. One parent jumps in, saying she doesn't think book learning could provide the answer. A discussion ensues about the value of book learning versus experience; Doris still has not responded.

The practitioner, Yvonne, asks the group how it is going to allow for the unique skill and knowledge of each member to be part of their process, pointing out that excluding ideas might put everyone in the situation of making a decision based on the opinion of one or two members. More discussion follows, centering on how to integrate members' feelings and experiences regardless of whether these come from book learning or intuition. Dave turns his attention back to Doris, asking her once again, "Come on, I want to know what you know about this age group. Do you think they should be taught to read now?" Other members chime in, saying they want to hear from Doris, and others too. Doris begins by telling the group that she does feel that social skills come first, and that children will eventually be more open and ready to read when they feel good with each other and are also read to by the teacher and their parents. Dave points out to Denise that the teacher does do a lot of reading to the kids and they seem totally absorbed in it; more talk ensues.

Discussion. A fundamental error made by group practitioners who are overly concerned about individuals' feelings, rather than with their roles as group members, is to probe the individual member's feelings and opinions. Instead, the practitioner should first encourage the members to look at how all of them can contribute to the group process.

The practitioner in this illustration responded to the group issue by focusing on how each member would contribute to the group, rather than to feelings about the special inclusion of Doris or about having Dave's question answered.

If Doris had answered the question without the prior discussion of how expertise and knowledge would be used by the group, differences concerning book learning in relation to experience would have gone underground. Fixed subgroups could have emerged, creating a tug of war between Doris' views and Denise's. Had the member (Doris) immediately answered the question, the practitioner should have encouraged discussion about how to respond to special expertise, as well as other types of contributions to the groups's feelings and interactions.

Humanistic Value 2:
People Are Responsible for and to
One Another Because Social Life Is a
Natural and Necessary Human Characteristic.

People are able to take responsibility for each other in a cooperative environment. They are also capable of competing with, exploiting, and ignoring one another, thereby developing utilitarian relationships based on convenience rather than caring. Fulfilling needs at the expense of others precludes taking responsibility and being responsible for oneself and others.

Democratic Norm 1:
Members Interact Through Caring and Mutual Aid
Rather Than Exploitive Relations (Schwartz, 1961)

Efforts to develop and sustain a caring environment confront members' motives to control others, or to turn away from them with rationalized attitudes such as "You do your thing, and I'll do mine"; these signify an avoidance of social responsibility.

Caring for others occurs when members respond to each others' hurts, discomforts, satisfactions, concerns, and fears. Caring means that members do not use what they learn about one another to exploit or idealize each other. This norm is demonstrated through sharing of emotional and practical abilities with the whole group, rather than withholding or hoarding for one's self or a select subgroup. The group that closes one member out from an impromptu group trip to the coffee shop after a meeting subverts the whole group's capacity to give and receive assistance and guidance.

Practitioner role. The practitioner offers perspective to help the group to establish positive relationships. The group worker explicitly presents views about sharing, helping, and learning from each other. The members are encouraged in their development of mutuality to explore their visions of how they would like to participate in the group. The practitioner encourages caring and connecting, affirmations of the unique importance of each member's contributions, and interdependence while fostering the members' collective interdependence and mutual responsibility.

Illustration. Joe, a member in a group for people maintaining their sobriety, has missed the last meeting without calling anyone to explain. This usually means the person is drinking. During the better part of the meeting there is no mention of why Joe might be absent, except when the practitioner asks the group if anyone has heard from him. Members say "no" and quickly go on to other topics.

Further on in the meeting—since Joe has not been mentioned—the practitioner asks what the members are feeling and thinking about his absence. This opens up a discussion focusing on the suspicion that he has been drinking, and whether or not to call him before the next meeting. Several members point to the need to support and confront others, even if they do not like it and get angry. Sally feels that Joe might be ashamed if he is on a binge. Sonny talks about how important it has been for him to call up fellow members between meetings just to let off steam; he feels this helps to keep him sober.

After more discussion, the group members decide that Sonny should be the one to call Joe, because he feels closest to Joe and is comfortable about calling others—including Joe—for support.

Discussion. There are a few probable reasons why members did not mention Joe on their own without the practitioner taking the initiative. One is that the norm for caring and mutual aid is too narrowly defined by an implicit or explicit rule that members can give help only when it is directly asked for. Another dynamic is "the emperor's new clothes": members do not mention another's condition, unless that member or a designee mentions it first. Another probability is "taboo topics" (Shulman, 1984)— subjects that members will not talk about until taboos are challenged by the practitioner. In essence, the group members handle certain problems by avoiding them. Sometimes this comes about because members do not have the abilities to work on the issue. The practitioner is called upon to bring taboos to the surface and air them in order to help members expand their collective abilities to handle all kinds of emotional and social issues.

Had Joe's absence not been made to surface, the members would have felt that this type of situation—and their discomforts with it— were not grist for the mill. They would have believed that issues to be openly dealt with depend on getting one another's formal permission. This state would counter the very nature of mutuality in humanistic group life. In this group, members are learning that they will be cared about and responded to by the group, should they go on a binge or get into other difficulties.

Democratic Norm 2:
The Norm Is for Building Cooperative Rather
Than Competitive Relations in the Group

Evidence shows that cooperative relations among members fosters their creativity in task completion and heightens their sense of self-esteem (Deutsch, 1968; Sherif, 1965a). On the contrary, highly competitive group relations cause one-upmanship and attitudes of superiority, group dynamics that work against mutuality. In competitive situations, members withhold knowledge and abilities from one another for fear of being outdone. Competitiveness in group life shows up through behavior such as inattentiveness, preoccupation with one's own importance and power, interrupting, and ignoring others. Cooperative efforts are presented when members listen and include others' ideas to build on their own experiences, as well as to learn new and different ways of behaving.

Practitioner role. The practitioner points out when and how members are being uncooperative, helping them work with rather than against each other. Members are helped to perceive when they are not listening, and helped to listen. One-upmanship behavior is identified. Members are helped to share resources and capabilities. The group worker encourages members to learn from each other, rather than to covet each others' attributes. When the members are tense or defensive they often form subgroups. The practitioner indicates that by cooperating everyone's needs can be met.

Illustration. A programming committee of the membership at a senior center has been formed recently to take responsibility for composing and distributing a monthly newsletter. The last two meetings have been marked by repeated arguments among three of the nine members, arguments about the kinds of articles to include and about who will author them.

Mike wants to be sure there's something there about the bowling tournament that several of the men are involved in. Tessie wants to write two articles on senior-citizen entitlements, and says, "No one is interested in bowling; it's just a few men who do that." Tessie feels there are many poor senior citizens who are too embarrassed to ask for entitlements information. Faye feels that everyone on the committee should write whatever they want to write; that it wouldn't be a problem to have a longer newsletter. Mike insists that Tessie is stubborn.

While he is the only one to have said this about Tessie in the meeting, Mike has privately told the practitioner that other members see Tessie as a dictator. "She won't listen to anyone; if she isn't controlled the others are going to quit the committee."

At this particular meeting, arguing has erupted just after five minutes. The practitioner had asked members to bring in articles. Before Irene can even read hers, Tessie interrupts her and says, "We all know about people who are sick; we don't need an article on that." The group worker asks the others, "Is that right, are articles on people's illnesses necessary?" Dora quietly says, "Even if we know about it, the sick folks will feel the senior center really cares about them when they see something about themselves in the newsletter." Mike says to Tessie, "You see, I told you." Tessie sputters, whereupon the practitioner explains to Mike that for him to try to prove to Tessie he is right and she is wrong is not going to help the group cooperate in employing everyone's good ideas, "nor is Tessie's trying to prove that she is right and Mike is wrong going to help put together a good newsletter." The practitioner then turns to the group and asks that they try not to interrupt one another, indicating that "it's hard to get points across when people cut in and don't cooperate." Conversation develops about the theme of interrupting. Then the members continue deliberations on how to use several of the ideas people have for the paper.

Quiet for a good part of the discussion, Tessie again begins to cut in abrasively. After stopping her several times with reassurance that she will have a chance to read her piece soon, the practitioner then says, "Tessie, take your turn now and read us your article." Tessie reads a fine piece of work. Members like it and tell her so. With the practitioner's encouragement, the members reassure Tessie that her article will be included.

Discussion. The practitioner is in an uncomfortable situation, because a member has secretly told her that others might leave. (This is not atypical of what happens in community center groups where members have high access to each other through other programs.) Whether departure was imminent or not, it was a message to the practitioner that Tessie's interruptions and competitiveness were not being handled by the group's intrinsic process; it was also a message that the practitioner had to be more direct and engaged in developing the group norm of fostering cooperation. In eliciting their cooperative spirit, the practitioner called upon the superordinate goal (Sherif, 1965b) of writing a quality newsletter as the unifying theme that could motivate members to overcome their personal needs to dominate and compete for attention, affection, and acceptance.

The group is "practicing" a tenuously developing cooperative interaction during the discussion of various ideas for the newsletter. The practitioner purposely subdues Tessie's interruptions, in order to demonstrate that this can be done. Without this action, the group might have retaliated by rejecting Tessie and her work, perpetuating the competitive cycle. Instead the group accepts Tessie's contribution.

Humanistic Value 3:
People Have a Right to
Belong and to Be Included

Belonging provides the most curative experience for group members (Yalom, 1975). It is a pivotal condition in the development of the humanistic milieu that will guide members' behaviors and attitudes. If not built upon humanistic values, some groups might have narrow membership criteria that exclude rather than include people who are perceived as different. They may also move to exclude people who enact antisocial behavior in the group, rather than work on how to change the situation. Working with the group's rejecting and aggressive reactions provides a special challenge to the practitioner and members of the humanistic group. They will strive for inclusion of members who substantially are denotive of the group's raison d'être, regardless of their level of helpfulness or their culturally or physically different characteristics.

Democratic Norm 1:
In a Humanistic Group, the Norm Is for
Inclusion Rather Than for Exclusion

While all groups will establish boundaries that bind them to one another, somewhat closing out others, boundaries should be semipermeable in a humanistic group. The practitioner early on establishes the value of and identifies the means for inclusion. This condition reflects an openness of spirit and a desire to be involved with a broad spectrum of different kinds of people and opinions. The practitioner encourages the group to be wary and to scrutinize carefully its attempts to be overtly and covertly exclusive. This is done to examine and challenge these attitudes and actions.

Practitioner role. The practitioner recognizes that when the members feel insecure about themselves, they are more apt to establish narrow membership criteria. These criteria leave some members feeling tenuous, and exclude others from membership. People feel they are being labeled as "outsiders."

The practitioner sets a tone that inspires the group's confidence in its abilities to collaborate on its objectives and goals. The practitioner airs the members' fears by stating that there should be members with different personalities, perspectives, and experiences. It is stressed that each member's contribution will become part of the group's experiences and outcomes. The practitioner provides perspective and confidence in the group's potential by including others in fact and in spirit. *Illustration.* A senior citizens' reminiscence group is having its fourth meeting. All nine members are attending regularly. The members are talking about what it had been like to go out at night "in the old days" in the inner city—"how friendly everyone was, how unafraid people were, and how inexpensive things were." The practitioner notices that two members are not saying much, and turns to them, asking, "I notice, Sam and Florence, that you've been quiet during this discussion. Do you see things differently?" This opens up a discussion with Florence talking about how she thinks only of having lost her husband, and how they used to do so many things together. She says, "I don't want to talk about it anymore because I don't want to be upset and to upset everybody." Sam says, "I was not yet in this country then. Europe was a difficult place to be before and after World War II." The members are silent.

The practitioner asks the other members how they are reacting to what Florence and Sam are bringing up. One member says that it's possible that when we look at aspects of the past we may find that it's not happy for everyone. Florence wonders, "Should I be in the group?" Elsa says, "Of course you should." There is a silence. The practitioner asks, "Are some saying that we should only talk about happy things?" Dora says, "I don't know if I can bear to hear about World War II." Sam reassures her that he isn't planning to say anything painful. The practitioner asks him, "But what if you change your mind and need to tell us your experiences?" Jerry (who is black) chimes in, "Don't worry Sam, I've got stories about lynch mobs in Alabama that would make your hair stand on end." The practitioner notes, "So the feeling begins to develop that if members agree not to tell each other sad and uncomfortable stories, you would have unauthentic relationships." Conversation continues and intensifies about the members' different backgrounds and experiences.

Discussion. The practitioner easily could have let the discussion end by helping several members, besides Elsa, reassure Florence that she was needed and wanted. This action would have helped them experience acceptance. But Sam obliquely brings up being in Europe during the Second World War. His acceptance into the group, and whatever it brings with it—as well as Florence's and anyone else's—had to be dealt with. Furthermore, had the man from Alabama not been able to refer spontaneously to his frightening life as a black person in a racist environment, the practitioner would have had to address these issues directly.

Under present cultural conditions, interracial memberships are still unusual. If the practitioner did not raise this issue, it would have been unlikely that the group would have easily given Jerry room for full membership. The practitioner must stress the essential need of members to accept and deal with their differences so the group may benefit from them.

Democratic Norm 2:
A Humanistic Group Deals Openly and Rationally With Prospective Members

Criteria governing the inclusion of new members must be made explicit. These criteria must be based on interest, on abilities, and on the person's potential to work toward helping others to meet their needs.

Criteria for inclusion are not to be based on ethnicity, race, class, or other forms of stereotyping and stigmatizing used to throw barriers between people. Membership should be considered in genuinely open and undefensive discussions. There should be no place for overt and covert rejections or hazing procedures. Approach-avoidance issues must be explicitly examined and resolved.

The group's screening criteria have to be readily available and explicitly presented to potential members. And criteria set up for new members that differ from those previously used tend to be exclusive unless these are made explicit and connected to the expansion of the group's milieu.

Practitioner role. It is important to help the members examine different opinions and feelings related to opening membership to others. The practitioner helps the members identify criteria, define procedures, and look at attitudes and feelings. Elitist and other negative criteria that would make the group appear to be sacred and mysterious are pointed out. The practitioner gently and directly attends to prejudice and stigmatizing.

Focus is also drawn to members' needs to exclude some people because of prejudice, or feelings that the person is "too difficult" or won't "fit in." The practitioner, first and foremost, must examine and look into these very same feelings and reactions in himself or herself before helping the members deal with these issues.

Illustration. A group of teens has been meeting for a year with Katie, a school social worker. They are talking about difficulties they are having in school and at home. Recently the group has been trying to figure out if they want to add two more members. One prospective member, Eric, is known to several of them. He wants to be part of the group. Unlike the rest of the members, Eric is into heavy metal music and has a Mohawk hair cut. Janet and Mark know Eric; they feel he is okay, that he has problems at home, and that "he should be given a chance, even if he looks a little weird." Jocelyn says, "Eleven people are enough in the group." Cindi reminds the group that three members are graduating "and won't be around next year." Janet says she thinks that maybe "some of you are prejudiced because of the way Eric looks." Most deny this. The practitioner wonders, "Are some of you afraid to have someone different from you in the group? Sort of like it changes your image of yourselves as a group?" Jocelyn reluctantly says she doesn't want any "heads" in the group. A couple of others nod in agreement. Mark says, "Even if Eric does drugs, he doesn't do it so he's all messed up; anyway, maybe that's what we can help him with. He won't get you to do what he does."

Several members wonder what it would be like for someone to join who hasn't been with them since the beginning. One asks, "Could we get close like this?" The practitioner reacts, saying, "It will take time to get close to a new person. When this group was formed, no one cared what kind of music each of you liked. It was just advertised for kids who wanted to talk about things." Janet joins in, indicating that Eric does have a lot to talk about, and the group might really do him good. The members decide to ask Eric to join them. The practitioner says, "Now that you've agreed to ask Eric, you should deal with the fact that three of you are graduating and leaving the group. Will you want more new members? What criteria will you use? How will you get to others to see if they're interested?"

Discussion. The practitioner, Katie, gently wishes to help the members examine how they feel about the changes the group will undergo when some members leave. She does not directly pursue this. She is able to use the specific issue of the potential new member as a springboard to help them find flexibility so they can accept a new person with different characteristics. The practitioner points out—somewhat tongue-in-cheek—that "in the past, music was not an issue for or against membership; why is it one now?" This helps the members focus on the prospective members' needs and how they might try to be helpful to him.

Reassuring the members that a new person with different values will not seriously disturb their collective values and norms is an important step for the practitioner to take. In this illustration, note that members expressed these concerns in their own process. Had they not, the practitioner would have had to surface the issues. The turning point for this group is when they conclude that the new member cannot make them use drugs. Then they begin to experience their helping potential. As this peaks in the process, the practitioner wonders what they will experience when several members leave and the group considers new membership. The practitioner asks them to consider how new members might be helpful for the group and its meaning in the school and community.

Democratic Norm 3:
A Humanistic Group Develops Ways
of Permitting and Maintaining
Membership to "Difficult" Members

Acceptance of others' rights to belong is fundamental to the strength and fabric of a humanistic group. In it, members are not to attempt, hastily or judgmentally, to exclude the member who offends them, causes anxiety, or brings the group to the angry attention of others.

Members may find themselves challenged by a consistently difficult person or by a particular type of difficulty that evokes their discomfort. Under these circumstances, groups develop the position that the group would be a fine and good one if the difficult person was not a member. This is an exclusionary stance. The stance represents a subliminal collusion with the difficult member and others to replicate earlier emotional and social exclusions from peer and family life.

Taking responsibility for including difficult members acknowledges that all members can derive benefits from dealing with meaningful, although disturbing, issues in group life. Struggling with a difficult member strengthens all of the members' abilities to deal with a range of interpersonal difficulties in their lives.

Practitioner role. The practitioner stimulates and surfaces the members' desire to be helpful, pointing out that anger, fear, and frustration may be causing them to feel like excluding another member. The practitioner helps the group find different capabilities and means for interacting with a member who is having unusual difficulties.

In this process, the practitioner is on the line, having to consider his or her own desires to exclude the person. From this perspective, the practitioner has to carry out a major effort, helping both the difficult member and the rest of the group.

A precipitous exit of the "problem" member brings about a guilt reaction that harms the process. This is because exclusion fulfills a wish to be rejecting, in contradistinction to the wish to be omnipotently helpful. If both motives for the group's guilt are not worked on, these feelings will hamper their future work.

Illustration. A group of people with chronic emotional illness in a continuing treatment program are somewhat aware that one of them, Drew, has AIDS. This, however, has never been discussed. At the very end of a meeting Drew has an angry outburst toward the others. He tells them that he knows they do not want to be with him, and are afraid to touch him because he has AIDS. The other members, stunned by the truth of the accusations, do not know what to say or how to respond. The practitioner responds, "You've been going through feeling extremely rejected and alone here. I'm sorry. Our quietness right now has to feel like more and more rejection." Drew says, "I don't expect anything to change." He gets up and leaves. After several moments of sitting in silence, the other members begin to leave as well. The practitioner, intuiting and empathizing, remains silent and quietly leaves in the midst of everyone else.

At the following meeting, the members seem calm. During the week the incident has reverberated throughout the treatment center. Drew announces, "I am being discharged to a vocational program in one month." He thanks the group for the opportunity to "get things off my chest; I'm sorry for my outburst."

Members begin to tell Drew, and each other, how they feel about Drew's "AIDS illness." Stella says, "I'm phobic when I'm around Drew. This week I realized how unfair I am to Drew when I heard you can't catch it from regular social stuff." Similar talk continues for quite some time. Drew talks a lot more explicitly about his condition. Sal says, "You can blow up anytime, man—get it out." Carlos asks Drew if he can stay on as a member for the next 3 or 4 sessions.

Discussion. During this type of "critical incident" in a group, a practitioner's reflexive reactions include anxiety and urges to instantaneously repair the damage and hurt. In this case, the practitioner contained these reactions, and stayed empathetically connected to the members' processes. The practitioner was responsive to the intense affect without diluting it or trying to smooth it over, acting on the judgment that the strength of positive nonverbal communications after Drew bolted were enough to sustain the group's process into the coming week.

Democratic Norm 4:
The Norm Guiding the Use of Exclusion
From the Group as a Healing Tool

The threat of excluding a person from a group one finds to be a helpful environment may be used to change a member's antisocial or dysfunctional behavior. A member who continues to deviate disruptively from group norms may be reasonably challenged with exclusion unless he or she changes.

The member's due process, however, should not be violated. Warning procedures should be set up and expressed. The member's behavior should be confronted in relationship to its effect on others. His or her behavior should be compared with the values and norms of the group. Should the person be unable to remain in the group, other helpful alternatives must be developed.

Practitioner role. A group can move to exclude a member from meetings—or the group—if that person is not changing destructive ways of interaction. The practitioner has a great deal of power, and the fundamental professional obligation, to influence the development of this situation. The group worker has to exercise empathy, skill, and timing in helping all members use the promise of exclusion and the interactions that result.

The practitioner is obligated to protect the member's due process. The practitioner engages all group members along with the difficult member in negotiation and exploration (by mediating directly), explains needs and feelings, and points out the effects of different kinds of helpful and unhelpful interactions. This is an emotionally charged series of events, with the practitioner maintaining an active and intense affective connection to all of the group members.

Illustration. Daphne takes part in a group for abusing mothers whose children are not in their custody. The group is run out of the local community mental health clinic. Members are referred by the County Special Services for Children Department. All members know that participation is a prerequisite in the process of having their children returned to them. Many members are struggling with their own historical issues concerning their childhood experiences with abusing and neglectful parents. Some admit having turned to drugs to deaden the painful memories that come up when their children make them nervous. Others find themselves in relationships with people who continue to hurt them. All, in varying degrees, have admitted they "took it out on our children."

Daphne has missed the last three sessions. Margaret and Grace have tried to reach her, but Daphne's phone is disconnected. The word is that she had been beaten up by a man with whom she is involved. The group members have been trying to get Daphne to dump him, reminding her that he is part of the reason she has lost custody of her daughter. She has been afraid to get an order of protection. The members have been quite angry and frustrated with Daphne's inability to take this step. They have decided in her absence that if and when she returns, and if she has been beaten up, that they will work with her to press charges of assault.

At this meeting Daphne looks bruised. After reluctantly admitting she has in fact been beaten up, Grace begins to get angry at her, saying to her, "You'd better press charges, girl." Daphne hems and haws. Other members try to impress upon Daphne how she is letting these bad things happen to her, and that she's worth more. In general, Daphne is told, "You have got to learn to help yourself. Each of us goes through bad stuff that is ruining us as parents. But it's never too late."

Daphne, somewhat glibly, thanks the group for their concern. Grace senses her ambivalence and says, "If you don't press charges on this bum, then you just shouldn't come back to the group, because you don't want to make your situation better. You don't want your kid back, either. You want to grovel to this pig who smashed up your face. You are just bullshitting us." Margaret says, "Damn, I'm tired of running around your neighborhood trying to see if you're okay, and finding out that he beat you up." The practitioner asks the group, "How do the rest of you feel about what they've said to Daphne?" Some agree, that she is going around in circles, and express similar frustrations.

Daphne responds angrily, "I'll leave right now if that's how you want it." Margaret continues, "There's no point in you staying unless you make a big effort to change your circumstances." The practitioner says, "To my ear, they're saying that they have been trying to help you in good faith, and that they will continue to help you, but they want you to do your part in good faith, too." Daphne says to the worker, "So you think I've gotta go, too. Okay, fine, I'll go. That's it." The practitioner says, "I don't think you or anyone else should decide anything now, in the heat of the moment. You need to think about that for a while and let people know what you are trying to decide. Bring yourself into the group next week; that's the important thing to do."

Daphne returns to the next meeting. She says, "No one has ever put things to me in that way, that straight, about my self-respect and given me so much support. I have decided to press charges." She begins to cry, saying she doesn't know where to begin to fix up her life. The members, emotional as well, express concern, advice, and hope. They tell her that "things are not easy," and that they will be there for her—in court, and wherever they are needed—as long as she does her part and doesn't leave them shouldering the burden. The practitioner says, "Everyone has burdens they have to shoulder. It's good to get help in shouldering them. This is what the group is all about."

Discussion. It is unlikely that the road ahead for Daphne will be smooth. However, this kind of confrontation presses members to own their goals and self-esteem, and to take personal responsibility for changing their individual patterns and actions. The practitioner's role combines mediation between the group and the member with direct confrontation of the member, his or her situation, and the group's circumstances. The practitioner does not smooth over the member's behavior or the group's reaction to it, for fear of leaving the member in the lurch or losing her and the group. The practitioner helps the group temper its desire to exclude by centering on the mutual desire and effort of the members to pull together to achieve their goals.

The group worker does not protect the member, rather, the practitioner interprets the group's message. By leaving the door open, the practitioner has offered the member a way to reenter the group in future sessions. In this way, the practitioner has provided an alternative—something which might have been difficult for the others to do—while making the members aware of how they have to handle themselves when "she comes through the open door."

The member returns in a frame of mind that lets the other members know she is willing to work, thereby providing them with the willingness to support and be available to her.

Humanistic Value 4:
People, Having Emotional and Intellectual Voices That Are Essential to Their Existence, Have a Right to Take Part and to Be Heard

The opportunity to be heard by others insures the potential to use the group as a sounding board for experimentation and opportunities to contribute to others' growth. Without a chance to have a positive position and space for expression, members do not feel that their ideas and feelings will be significant for others.

Democratic Norm 1:
A Humanistic Group Develops Procedures
That Permit Everyone to Participate

Participation in group life cannot be quantitatively equal. The group's procedures need to include mechanisms that limit the input of members when they are overzealous, overanxious, or overbearing. The group also needs to develop the means for including quiet members.

Ambiguous norms governing the nature and extent of participation cause questions and concerns about participation to remain unstated. This heightens and perpetuates the approach-avoidance reactions (Garland et al., 1973) people have toward others they feel unable to communicate with or influence. In such instances there is risk of generating nonegalitarian norms, with highly talkative participants developing an inflated sense of their roles and contributions at the expense of others. Members need to learn to respond actively to cues that others wish to speak. They also need to recognize that the creation of opportunities for participation is a collective responsibility.

It is very important early in the group's life for the practitioner to assist in the development of a collective experience, one that emphasizes valuing the contributions of each member. Each individual problem should not become the dominant and exclusive focus of attention. Without efforts toward embracing all of the members' needs and interests, cohesion will be an illusion. Highly self-disclosing and assertive members will become grandiose, dominant, and prideful about their special contributions.

Practitioner role. As members talk, the practitioner scans (Shulman, 1981), looking to see how quiet members are reacting. The practitioner addresses the obvious inequalities in participation. Those who have not been heard from recently are asked for comments. The practitioner is also sensitive to the need for the group to create opportunities for each member to participate. Picking up cues that a member has not made or been allowed space, the practitioner encourages the member by interrupting an ongoing interaction for the person. The practitioner notes that the person wishes to speak, modeling the creation of space; then asks the member what is on his or her mind. In this way, the practitioner helps the group take collective responsibility for creating opportunities for everyone. The practitioner asks the group to consider how it will involve those who feel unable to aggressively interrupt the process. Members all too often attribute their silence to the feeling that their opinions have already been expressed by others; they need to know that the group wants to hear from each member because each person is different and has helpful contributions.

The practitioner runs the risk of attending too often to one member's self-disclosures and encouraging only the most vocal participants. If a cohesive group is to emerge, everyone has to be engaged, and no one member's experience can be allowed to overwhelm the group's process. At such junctures the practitioner modulates the expression of an individual's self-disclosures, generalizing them into concerns common to all. This fosters group building and participation.

Without a concerted effort toward valuing all members' contributions, the group's cohesion becomes illusionary rather than actual. The practitioner, often startled by this outcome, feels unsure of what went and is going wrong. False cohesion stimulates the group to dissolve, because members become distanced from the group and one another.

Illustration. In a group where members are dealing with the many issues and complex feelings they have about placing their relatives in nursing homes, several people have been dominating the discussion process. One in particular, Nellie, is expressing a combination of guilt along with contrary beliefs that she has done the right thing by placing her mother. She says, "Mother is angry with me and doesn't talk to me when I visit." Without giving anyone else a chance to participate, Nellie goes right on to say, "I am so terribly upset." The practitioner, Faith, looks around the group and sees that some people are starting to tune Nellie out and to get uncomfortable with her. Bill and his wife Sydelle are throwing glances at each other; Marlene and Vanessa seem to be retreating.

The practitioner cuts into Nellie's now-emotional monologue, saying "I'm sorry to cut you off, Nellie, but you've been saying so many things that are very relevant for you and everyone here." Turning to the rest of the group, the practitioner goes on, "I was wondering, since others of you have been quiet for a while, if you were feeling guilty about or getting rejected by your parents or relatives, too?" Vanessa says, "I do feel guilty; Mom is so nice to me, it makes me feel even guiltier." More talk continues about guilt, with all speaking except for Bill.

Faith turns to Bill, saying, "And you, you've been quiet. I wonder how it's been for you and your father." Bill says, "Well, I agree with my wife. She said it all." Faith smiles and says, "Sydelle did say your father is giving you, but not your brother, a hard time. How do you react to that? Tell us." Bill says, somewhat reluctantly, "This is the way he has always been with my brother and me; I don't take it to heart too much." Several members ask Bill how his brother reacts. He says his brother is usually very helpful, and that's why he doesn't take it to heart. The practitioner says, "And I guess your wife is, too?" Bill replies, "Oh, very much so."

The group goes on. Nellie, who has been comparatively quiet and inactive for the last half hour, listening to the others attentively, joins in and supports the couple. She adds, "I wish I had more support from my family." Marlene says, "Well, at least the group is here for us, Nellie." Nellie says, "Yes, I'm grateful for that. I would be feeling alone without this group."

Discussion. The practitioner interrupts Nellie's "long story," especially after scanning the group and noticing that several members are not listening. To leave a member in a social and emotional vacuum because he or she is talking into the air would sabotage the group's milieu. It would also interfere with the member's chance to become part of the group's mutual aid. The member with this presentation needs support. The overbearing member in this case has the experience of finding out that she can be comforted by attending to others' experiences and needs.

Interrupting the group is very difficult for a beginning practitioner. When a member does not stop to take a breath, the practitioner tends to experience "cutting in" as rude. Actually, the group does not experience the interruption this way; nor does the member, who usually is overventilating. Often the member tacitly appreciates being stopped. The group is grateful because it is rescued from its urge to distance itself from the member. The practitioner shows the member that she has been

Table 1.1

Values, Norms, and Practitioner Role

Value 1: People are inherently worthy.

    1) The *norm for protecting the rights of every member*
        Practitioner role
        –to make explicit that all contributions and members will have value.
        –to acknowledge difference, including worker's difference
        –to slow down process to foster egalitarian sharing

Value 2: People are responsible for and to others.

    1) The *norm for caring & mutual aid vs. exploitive relations*
        Practitioner role
        –models caring
        –reinforces importance of hearing from all
    2) The *norm for cooperative vs. competitive relations*
        Practitioner role
        –points out competition nonjudgmentally
        –enables resource sharing vs. hoarding for self or clique
        –enables use of subgroup needs to establish broader goals

Value 3: People have the right to belong, to be included.

    1) The *norm for inclusive vs. exclusive relations*
        Practitioner role
        –prevents establishing narrow criteria for membership
        –models acceptance of difference
    2) The *norm for dealing openly & rationally with prospective members*
        Practitioner role
        –directly points out implications of hazing and antidemocratic nature
          of two-tiered membership structure
        –shows group that trial periods are for both new and old members
    3) The *norm for permitting membership to "difficult" members*
        Practitioner role
        –enables stretching of resources and capacities to sustain membership
          of dissident
        –examines own needs to exclude member
    4) The *norm guiding use of inclusion vs. exclusion as a healing tool*
        Practitioner role
        –protects member's due process if group moves to exclude
        –helps group confront member
        –maintains affective ties to all sides
        –enables member to find ways to use group

Value 4: People have the right to take part, to be heard.

    1) The *norm developing procedures for the participation of all*
        Practitioner role
        –scans group, creates space
        –reaches for silent members, models for group
        –helps group take responsibility for inclusion of all
        –directly enables fullest participation of all

---

heard; she restates what the member has been saying, and by presenting it to the group creates a general connection between the member's circumstances and those of the other members.

SUMMARY

In this chapter the eight basic humanistic values that underlie the group method have been presented. These emphasize members' rights, along with their mutual responsibilities for one another. These rights revolve around inclusion, free speech, being heard, being different, self-determination, and the right to challenge the practitioner.

Specific democratic norms the group develops that operationalize these values have been discussed. Among them are the following norms: the norm for cooperation, rather than competition; the norm for caring and mutual aid, rather than exploitive relations; the norms governing and guiding the inclusion, rather than the exclusion, of members; the norms guiding inclusion of difficult members; the norm guiding the use of exclusion as a therapeutic tool; and the norm for an open communication system.

The role of the practitioner as a guiding force in the development of each norm was delineated, specific skills were identified, and illustrative examples were described and discussed.

The next chapter will describe norms governing freedom of choice, free speech, the right to be different, and the right to challenge the group practitioner.

NOTE

In modern times—at the turn of the century, and once again during the rise of fascism in Europe—educators and social scientists from John Dewey (1923) to Kurt Lewin (1951) concerned themselves with defining and operationalizing the principles of democracy and humanism along with their leadership forms. These concerns grew out of experiences and convictions that led to the recognition of democratic milieus as positive arenas of change for people. The experiments of social psychologists such as Asch (1965), Milgram (1963), and Sherif (1965a) have taught us that people can be influenced, and have jolted us with the evidence that people are capable of dominance and submission even in the face of what is evident to their own good judgment (Asch, 1965). We have learned that some people will yield to the pressure to obey authority at the expense of other people's physical well-being (Milgram, 1963).

From Deutsch (1968) and Sherif (1965b) we have learned about the conditions that foster cooperation and competition among group members; from White and Lippitt (1968) we have learned that people are affected by leadership styles; and from Clark and Clark (1965) we have learned that racism is a toxic value system that attacks the core of self-esteem in the victim and the persecutors.

Chapter 2

FURTHER HUMANISTIC VALUES
AND DEMOCRATIC NORMS

OVERVIEW

This chapter will continue to identify the democratic norms which are developed in the group to operationalize the humanistic values presented in Chapter 1. The norms specifically related to value 5 (freedom of speech), value 6 (the importance of accepting difference as enriching), value 7 (freedom of choice), and value 8 (the right of members to challenge the authority of the practitioner) will be discussed. The practitioner's role in the development of these norms will be presented, along with practice illustrations.

Humanistic Value 5:
People Have the Right to Freedom
of Speech and Freedom of Expression

To function in a free environment, people have to feel that the expression of ideas and feelings is welcomed by all members. It is vital to feel free from intimidation and the possibility of destructive consequences. The milieu needs to be experienced as a testing ground for the members' feelings, ideas, and actions, rather than a place that supports only a narrow ideology and excludes those with different opinions and attitudes.

Democratic Norm 1:
The Group Develops a Free and
Open Communication System Without
Reliance on a Narrow Ideology

A group where members speak freely and authentically, where they are listened to, and where each member has access to optimal numbers of communication channels is important for supporting and stimulating the human spirit. Positive sanctions that include recognition and praise for expressing new and developing ideas and feelings, in an atmosphere which values experimentation, are important. A group designed for the enhancement of a narrow ideology within a narrow set of opinions will not permit freedom of expression.

Practitioner role. The practitioner encourages members to directly speak their minds to many members, weaving a broad and flexible network of participation and communication. The practitioner actively encourages the expression of different opinions, helping members test out unformulated ideas and feelings in a receptive atmosphere.

Illustration. A group of high school students has been working on developing and running a community service program for economically disadvantaged children. The adult leader of the group is bent on getting the students to understand the effects of poverty on every aspect of life, and to get them to understand the need for redistributive justice. Whenever the students get into developing a plan for taking the children to the zoo or to a movie downtown, the practitioner engages them in a discussion about the meaning of the situation involved and the values they will be conveying to the youngsters. This essentially blocks and impedes their efforts. The students feel a mixture of frustration with their lack of movement and a sense of intellectual inferiority with regard to their understanding of broader social issues. This form of inferiority is a motivation that keeps them engaged in the group process with the practitioner, who often states, "You cannot design a program unless you understand your goals and values."

A minority of members caucus outside the meeting. They decide that they are less interested in goals and values and more interested in doing something productive with the children. They also have a sense that other members are discontent with the group, but that it is not possible for them to buck the leader's authority. With some trepidation, they decide to raise this in their next group meeting.

In the meeting, when they say that "we would rather run a program than talk about our values," the other members are quiet, looking with fear to the leader for approval. The leader interprets the silence as an indication that this subgroup is wrong, and that the other members do not have clarity about their values. He goes on to imply that this confrontation is the reason why the group should continue to discuss its values.

Eventually, after weeks of efforts to convince other group members to change the direction of the group or to disband it altogether and run it without an adult, these four members leave the group.

Discussion. This leadership style represents totalitarianism in a small group. In this meeting, there are several serious problems. Caucusing in the subgroup represents an effort to gain control in a situation where members are feeling intimidated and ineffectual.

For the young people, the caucus provided an extragroup setting where they could test out and clarify unformulated thoughts and feelings. Expression of these ideas in the group without prior caucus would most likely have been frightening and surely squelched by this leader. A practitioner committed to humanistic values would have accepted the feedback and opened up the discussion; this would have benefited the group as well as his or her own leadership style. However, this leader persists in maintaining his prejudicial view of others' opinions and feelings. He does not help others speak their minds; in fact, he interprets the meaning of the silence as tacit agreement for the direction he has set for the group. The leader is more involved in meeting his own needs to have a forum than in helping the students develop ways of raising their social consciousness.

This type of leadership is dangerous for the members and the group. The young people who leave the group will experience guilt because they left their friends behind, even though they tried to influence them. They realize they cannot change the group from within, so by leaving they try to change the group from without.

Democratic Norm 2:
The Norm Guiding the Open Expression of
Feeling and Tempering Premature Self-Disclosure

In new relationships, highly personal self-disclosures are usually dysfunctional for the member, and can result in the member and others leaving the group. Members need to feel free to express important feelings, while at the same time recognizing that these expressions should be shaped by the group's nature at different points in its development. When a strong cohesion and the capacity to work on difficult issues exists, self-disclosures are appropriate and necessary for fulfilling the group's purpose. At this juncture members can experiment with sharing relevant information and feelings in undefensive ways, and seeking others' reactions to them.

Practitioner role. The practitioner directly supports the expression of feelings. However, when highly personal self-disclosures occur too early in the process to be taken in by the group, the practitioner stops the story from unfolding in its fullest form, turning self-disclosures into general themes related to the group's purpose. The practitioner enables the group to examine feelings about the here and now of its experience. The practitioner does not let the group members deflect anxiety by focusing attention on one person's self-disclosures.

Illustration. Members in a bereavement group in a senior center are meeting for the second time. Several members are talking about how lonely they are feeling without their spouses. Maureen is talking about the shock she felt when her husband of 42 years died suddenly of a heart attack. He had been well, and the doctors had told him he was healthy. Vera tells how difficult it was for her during her husband's extended illness, his diabetes, his amputated feet, and his anger with all his circumstances. Frances begins to cry, saying how hard it is for her to have lost two husbands this way. Her husband of many years died eight years ago, and she was remarried to her present husband six years ago. She does not understand how this happened.

After a good deal of discussion about how some of them keep expecting their spouse to appear in the doorway when they return home, and how quiet the house is, Vera starts to say how she is so guilty, but that she felt relief, too. The practitioner says to Vera, "When someone has been so ill for a period of time, there can be a sense of relief when they die." She tells the group "You might find yourselves feeling all kinds of ways you don't want to feel—like angry at the person for dying, or relieved, or even remembering that your relationships were not good. There will be plenty of time to talk about those very difficult things if and when you want to."

Discussion. In the open atmosphere of a bereavement group, a good deal of feeling is usually expressed quickly and spontaneously. However, while the practitioner validates the member's self-disclosure, it is with the awareness that precipitous and intense expression of negative feelings about the spouse may not be helpful to either the member or the group. Thus the practitioner uses the opportunity to validate the feeling, universalizing it and suggesting that these and other feelings will continue to be grist for the mill further along the way in the process.

Humanistic Value 6:
Differences Among Members
Are Enriching to One Another

Difference provides rich opportunities for interaction and learning. The trepidation that people experience about facing differences is connected to their anxiety about conflict, exposure of their prejudices, and their ulterior motives to control or subjugate others.

Differences in experiences, attitudes, physical ability, and appearances are the nature of the human condition, reminding everyone of the variations that exist and the various ways in which people can represent their uniqueness. In a humanistic group, the rights and due processes of different members are protected.

Democratic Norm 1:
In the Humanistic Group, Members
Foster Each Other's Diversity
Rather Than Push for Conformity

It is known that a person in authority can pressure others to conform to expectations despite their better judgments (Milgram, 1963). Peer pressure can also be applied to secure conformity. This may cause conformity in social situations even when the conformity is in direct conflict with their perceptions and feelings (Asch, 1965). For example, more than a decade later, the totalitarian leadership and community conformity of the people in Jonestown are too enormous to grasp and systematically study.

A group that is unable to accept or tolerate one person—or a small cohort that displays differences in ideas, feelings, beliefs, and backgrounds—is usually governed by rigidities and a set of narrow norms that do not allow new ideas or solutions to emerge or to be examined (Shulman, 1984). The ability to tolerate difference and protect the rights and due processes of different members come from exposure to and experience with diversity and its value for people.

Practitioner role. How the practitioner helps bring about the group's acceptance of difference is partly determined by how threatened he or she is by the differences. Unthreatened, a practitioner can ask directly about the difference(s) with an air of curiosity and excitement. This indicates his or her fundamental appreciation of diversity. A practitioner who can accept a member's deviance is able to assist the group to reflect on its own reactions of acceptance and rejection. Protecting the rights of the different person is crucial. The practitioner indicates to the member that the group wants him or her to change, but the member is free to think whatever he or she pleases as long as all are safe. The worker points out to the group its responsibility to accept the person's right to be different, even if the majority does not agree with the belief.

Learning to accept differences of all kinds is supported and expanded by a practitioner's unequivocal statements that show respect for one's fellows and do not sanction prejudice and discrimination. The boundaries defining membership are broadened when the practitioner stretches the perimeter, enabling inclusion of people who are most different in ideas and interactional styles.

Illustration. A group of elementary school teachers meets regularly with a school social worker to discuss some of the problems they are having in class with problem children. At this meeting Jim, a twenty-year veteran in the school system, expresses strong negative feelings about some of the children's upbringings. He tells the group that he feels the parents should be made to work, that welfare is of little help, and that some children come to school unkempt and unfed. Several other teachers react with comments such as "here he goes again, blaming the victim." A fight ensues, with Jim saying, "The children can't learn if they don't have a structured day when they go home." One teacher reminds him sarcastically, "Children can't learn if they don't have good teachers, too."

The social worker finds herself getting angry at Jim. However, she reacts to him by saying, "You seem to be expressing a lot of frustration in the situation. It's hard to teach kids who need so much from you." Jim tells her, "I like the children, but it's the parents I don't like; they are parasitic. I would rather have them forced to work for their welfare benefits." Others in the group react angrily. The practitioner says to the group, "I think Jim has a right to his opinion. And you have a right to yours also." Members talk more about how they do not like teachers who are down on the kids. The practitioner points out that Jim was not "down on the kids, but on the parents." Others reluctantly agree, but call him "conservative" and "redneck." The practitioner asks Jim,

"How do you feel when they react to you this way?" Jim says, "I feel they will only accept me if I believe the way they do." Marylou replies, "Come on Jim, you love to bait us, because you love your different opinion," and laughs. Selma says, "We know he's a good teacher, and he likes the children." The practitioner presses them, "So what bothers you about his unpopular opinion?" More dialogue develops about people with unpopular opinions and about how they have rights to take part without being harassed.

Discussion. In this situation, feeding into closing off Jim's access to the group because of his beliefs would be contrary to the values of a humanistic group and detrimental to all the members. Thus the practitioner modeled a way for members to include Jim in the process while not asking him to change his beliefs. In this case, the deviant member's frustration with the children's circumstances and concern for their well-being was shared by the other group members. The practitioner makes use of a common feeling as a means to help the others link up with Jim and accept an unpopular minority opinion.

Humanistic Value 7:
People Have a Right to Freedom of
Choice, to Determine Their Own Destinies

When people are supported to determine their own destinies, they must have their rights guarded to make free choices in an environment that is not coercive. Self-determination recognizes that people have the right to use their abilities in assertive ways to determine their destinies in the face of oppression. Members join a group to fulfill needs in a collaborative environment. In the humanistic group, power for decision making resides in the hands of the entire group—not the leader, or a small cadre. For this power to be distributed, several norms must become operationalized.

Democratic Norm 1:
The Norm Fostering the Equal
Distribution of Power in the Group

At various times in the life of a group, especially early on, power surfaces as an essential issue. Examination of members' needs for power over others' behaviors establishes an open (rather than a closed) group structure, one where members can assert influence as well as accept the influence of others. Implicit decision-making processes should be examined. Members learn to recognize that leadership should be shared, fluid, and not fixed.

Practitioner role. The practitioner encourages the group to examine implicit decision-making processes in order to make them explicit. He or she asks the group to reflect upon which members, including the practitioner, have influence. The practitioner, by encouraging the taking of leadership and follower roles, helps the members recognize that leadership does not have to be fixed, but can vary with the resources needed in the situation.

Illustration. A singles group of young adults has been meeting regularly for the last two months in a community center. Jake, Claire, and Matt have been trying to get the group to run a big dinner dance at the center and to invite lots of people. They have made plans to hire a disc jockey and have spoken to several caterers. They come to this meeting and present their plans.

The meeting begins with Matt saying that he would like to talk to the members about the plans they've gone ahead with for setting up this dinner dance party. The group is quiet. Matt talks about the disc jockey, the cost, and that he will play a variety of dance music. Claire interjects that she and Jake went to two different caterers. They preferred a buffet, because it is somewhat cheaper. Claire tells the group that one caterer is a friend: "I know this one will do a good job, because I've been to another party they catered." The group is still quiet. Some members are passing darting glances to each other.

The practitioner, Beverly, says, "Wait, let's hold on a minute. I think we need to know how all the other members feel about this idea for a dinner dance." Susan says to the three, "I hope you made no promises to them, because we've never talked about this." Other members begin to mutter and talk to each other. The practitioner asks, "What are you all saying? Let's talk one at a time to each other." Andrew says, "I don't really want to have a dinner dance. It's too much work. I'd rather spend time going to singles parties that other people are giving. Besides, who said we wanted to run this program?" Claire says, "I resent that, after I went out to get all this information." The practitioner says, "I don't think the issue is related to you getting the information. That's always useful to have. The issue has to do with members wanting to be sure that people who do things speak for them." There is a pause. Ben says to Claire, "I don't even know whether or not we should do such an event. The point is, we never talked about it together and decided to do it. You, Matt, and Jake look like you're railroading it. I don't know if you mean to do that, but that is what's happening." Henry says, "Maybe it's our fault they did all the work, because we haven't been doing much in the social area lately." Members nod in agreement.

The practitioner asks, "How can we develop plans and ideas and be sure that things happen in a direction we all want? On the other hand, how do we make certain we don't interfere with people who like to do things?" Derek says, "I don't want to prevent people from taking initiative. It just has to be brought back here for approval." Maureen says, "I think it's a question of whether or not we talk about it. Then whoever goes to investigate something knows they have to bring it back to us. No strings; that has to be the ground rule."

The practitioner says, "It looks like some of you feel things have to come back to the group for discussion first." Sondra agrees, saying, "I have an uncle who is a caterer. But I didn't have a chance to put his name in. I didn't know we were planning to have this event." The practitioner says, "That's a good point, how did we decide to do this? Did we decide?" Maureen says to the three, "You took it upon yourselves." Matt says, defensively, "But you people don't ever want to do anything. Every time I try to get you to do something you back away. So, yes, we're tired of that." Claire adds, "Look, we don't have to do anything. I'm not going to work on this." Fred says, "Come on, don't be a drag." "No, really," Claire says, "Sondra, you handle the catering." The practitioner says, "I don't think that's the point. The point is how people feel when some of us try to make decisions we're not all a part of. How do you feel?" Derek says, "Well, I feel like I have no chance to get my point across." "Even if they have a good idea?" interjects the practitioner. "Right, even when it is a good idea, like this one," Derek responds.

The practitioner asks the group, "What about others, how do you feel?" Members express similar reactions; talk continues about how people take initiative in the group. Matt, Jake, and Claire concede that they were "overzealous in getting things done." Members act to support their initiative and enthusiasm, and mechanisms are established for deciding things in the group. The group makes a great effort to move away from centering their issues on the three members. They then go on to discuss if they should run an event and what it should be.

Discussion. The three members have gone off on their own in an effort to get the group to do something they want to see done. However, they have not used the group's process to air this plan. This can be due to impatience with the democratic process, or a desire for power and control. Much dissension occurs in groups where a small clique—like this one—is permitted to dominate the group.

The practitioner in this illustration was careful to support the initiatives of these members. The group needs members who are willing to take initiative and risk advancing an idea. On the other hand, she helped the members express their feelings of powerlessness and feeling controlled that resulted when others attempted to "railroad" an idea through, bypassing the process. Members were able to express how they felt to the subgroup. With the practitioner's help, they offered support and affirmation of them for their initiatives. Had this not happened naturally, the practitioner would have been called upon to react directly and assertively to help the group recognize the usefulness of the initiators for the process, and their own fears about being controlled.

The subgroup got the point that they would not be permitted to control the process. The group established the ground rule that actions would come back to the group for discussion and approval, and could not rest solely with any one member or subgroup.

Democratic Norm 2:
The Group Develops Open
Decision-Making Processes

Humanistically framed groups work on mastering the decision-making skills needed for optimal democratic functioning. Members learn how to make decisions together. They learn to include the thinking and feeling of members who are in the minority (Lowy, 1973), learning to empathize with minority views. This enables the members to appreciate the value of and move toward compromise and consensus. The group members need to seek interpersonal ways for decision making, rather than simply voting or yielding to aggression, or to opinionated members (Lowy, 1973).

Practitioner role. The practitioner helps members empathize with minority views, moving the group to acts of compromise or consensus (Lowy, 1973). The practitioner models an empathic group member by actively checking out members' feelings as the group moves toward making a decision. Recognizing when a preemptive or implicit decision has been made, the practitioner slows down the process, pointing out the interaction and asking the group if everyone concurs with the decision. This helps the members distinguish rapid consensus from intimidation. The members' views of one another's—and the worker's—authority are of special importance for the connection between decision making and the distribution of power. A group whose members have many fears will require a great deal of help in arriving at a decision.

Illustration. The young adult singles group is still faced with the possibility of running a dinner dance program. The three members who have been proponents of this idea—Jake, Matt, and Claire—have looked into caterers and disc jockeys. The group has not had a chance to discuss these suggestions, or to consider whether or not they want to hold such an event. After resolving their difficulties around the attempt to railroad the decision to hold a dinner dance past the group, members begin talking about having this type of event. Several quickly agree, "Let's have it." Others follow suit. The practitioner says, "Wait a minute, if we are going to agree on this so fast, I think we have to be sure we know what has to be done for the event, and the time involved." Derek says, "I like the idea of doing this dinner dance because if we do a nice job we can eventually become a center for singles." "Yes," agrees Claire, "Maybe we can run small informal events every Friday night." "That's a good idea, but hold it for later," says Maureen, adding, "What would we have to do to prepare for this dance?"

Andrew, who has been quiet for a while, says, "I want to know how much work there is." "So do I," chimes in Matt, "because even though I want to do it, I know we need a lot of people to get involved—mailings, invitations, follow-up phone calls." The practitioner asks, "What about those of you who haven't said anything? Sondra, Loren, Fred, what's your view?" Sondra agrees that she is willing to do the work. Matt asks Sondra for information about her uncle's catering business. Fred says, "I think it is a very good idea to have a big social event, because it can be used by the group to expand the singles' program in the center." Loren expresses her willingness to work by saying, "I have had some experiences before in another organization. It is very hard work. We all have to pitch in, otherwise it won't go right. The last time, people said they would work and didn't." Andrew says, "I am willing to do work, but we need to have some people to coordinate things." The other members agree. Andrew suggests that Claire, Matt, and Jake chair the program. There is more agreement. Jake reminds the group, "But you can't get mad at us for doing things." "No, we won't—we'll be glad," says Maureen, laughing.

Discussion. This group has already gone through a process of establishing that power has to be distributed among the members. Now they have to deal with the decision itself about whether or not to hold an event. Members quickly agree that they want to undertake one. The practitioner is mindful when she asks them to be certain they want the event, that there is work to do, and that making a decision also involves delegating tasks and recognizing the responsibilities that the decision entails.

In doing this, the practitioner reaches for everyone's opinions and support for the decision. In asking for the participation of the quieter members, the practitioner further insures that all opinions about the decision come to the surface. Several members talk about the jobs to be done, and there appears to be a consensus about the program.

As the group considers aspects of the event, it becomes apparent that several members have conceived of the event as the forerunner of an institutionalized singles' program for the community center. These members' views provide innovative direction for the group's purpose. Finally, by inviting the quiet members to offer their opinions, the practitioner helps them to examine further options, including the issues of division of labor and leadership. The members' suggestion that the three originators of the plan chair the event is happily accepted by the group in a spirit of collaboration and mutuality.

Democratic Norm 3:
The Norm Fostering Freedom
to Change Versus Coercion

Implicit in group life is the movement toward change. The process of change is difficult to discern. Trust in one another, risk, self-disclosure, and experimenting with new behavior in a context of support are part and parcel of the change process. Trust, risk, disclosure, and experimentation come about through the freedom to choose when and to what degree to express one's self in the group. While support is needed for a person to change dysfunctional behavior, coercion has no place. The group must protect its members' right to choose what, when, and how to change.

Members need to ask one another directly if they wish to go on with a topic or to stop, recognizing that confrontations can become overzealous and potentially coercive.

Practitioner role. As members feel a desire to change their social interactions they will require help from others. The practitioner informs the members that change involves risk and trust of others, as well as acting differently—all of which may be difficult. The practitioner also insures the members that the what and how of change is up to each one of them. Support and help for the member will come from the group. The practitioner lets the group know that a member can stop the group if he or she is feeling pressured by its members. The practitioner must act directly to interrupt overzealous confrontations, indicating that coercion will not help others change.

Illustration. In a group for 12- to 14-year-old girls in a child guidance clinic who have been sexually abused, some youngsters have been taking time out to tell their stories of molestation to the others. Usually, members listen attentively. One member, Kathy, for whom the abuse went on since she was 5 years old, has great difficulty sitting through the stories. She wanders around the room. The practitioner has alternately asked her to join the group and given her tacit and explicit permission to walk around as long as she is not disruptive.

In this meeting, Tanya begins by asking the practitioner, Anna, "When is Kathy going to tell us her story?" The other girls echo the same desire. As this happens, Kathy starts to fidget and tap her crayon on the table. The practitioner says, "Kathy will tell us her story when she wants to. That's how you all did that." Then she asks the group, "Kathy, Tanya, Meryl, girls; would you like snacks?" While the girls are agreeing Anna is handing out snacks, making sure to get to Kathy and Tanya first. She then asks the group to tell Kathy how they feel now that they have told their stories. They all say they feel better.

Anna continues, "Does everyone feel better?" Lisa says, "Yes, because you can tell your secret to everyone." Kathy—who has already finished her snack—gets up and sits on the floor playing with crayons and markers, alternately fidgeting and coloring. The practitioner says, "But you don't know when you'll feel better, or if you'll feel better, do you? Each person has a different time when you want to tell your story, isn't that right?" The girls agree. "And you, Tanya, you care about Kathy, that's why you want to hear her story." Tanya looks down and quietly says, "Yes." "Kathy?" Anna says in her direction, "Do you know that Tanya wants to know about you because she cares about you?" Kathy, who has stopped fidgeting now, quietly nods. Anna turns to the group and says, "But you know, it isn't fair to try to get someone to do something when they don't want to do it." "No," the girls agree to how unfair it is.

The practitioner goes on to talk about how people respect one another "when we let each other do things at our own pace." Colleen suggests that it is like her bad cousin who molested her, who "didn't care if I said no." "Right," Anna says, but "here we care about each other and we will try to do things that show that." Anna continues, "But I think what you're trying to say to Kathy is that you care and when she's ready to tell her story, you are all ready to hear it." "Yes, yes," was echoed. "Whenever you want, Kathy," Colleen said.

Kathy by now has stopped coloring and returned to be closer to the group. The topic changes as the girls go on to talk about making friends in school.

Discussion. This practitioner is keenly aware of how unproductive and even destructive it will be for members to pressure Kathy to tell her story before she is ready. She quickly lets the group know that Kathy will not be required to tell her story unless she wants to.

The practitioner then intervenes with the snack to provide nurturance for the group and for Kathy, who at this moment is especially vulnerable. Kathy's fidgeting is an indication that she needs outlets for containment of feeling. Eating together while talking about this painful group process gives the girls a chance to sustain the supportive environment they have developed and to go on handling this issue.

Having the girls explain that each told her own story at her own pace is important for Kathy as well as for the others. The practitioner has, of course, noted that Kathy leaves the table when she finishes her snack. She makes an effort to let Kathy know how much the girls care about her, and that they will be receptive to her when she chooses. This reaffirmation of the group's caring for Kathy and their empathy toward her is heard by Kathy. She returns to them at the table as the group moves on to another topic.

Democratic Norm 4:
Members Need Opportunity to Try
Out and Take Different Roles

To enable experimentation and taking risks with new forms of behavior, members must be encouraged to develop many options and outlets for a variety of roles. Members are to be supported in playing various roles in the group, rather than fixed or stereotypic ones. For example, members who play task roles need chances to assume maintenance roles. Initiators and organizers need to try out spontaneity and taking someone else's lead. The member who approaches interaction with bravado should try to be gentle; those that are timid should try assertive roles.

Practitioner role. The practitioner brings role behavior to the members' conscious awareness. They are helped to examine their behaviors and decide whether to modify patterns. The practitioner points out when members are viewing themselves and one another stereotypically. When the group suggests that a member change, but then fails to offer necessary support, the practitioner points out that sabotage of change is occurring. Role plays and other structured exercises are useful tools in helping members practice new forms of expression, and to hear various reactions to them.

Illustration. The boys in a group for children who have been misbehaving in the classroom are talking about the ways in which their teachers are misjudging them even though they have already begun to behave better. Keith tells the group, "The other day two kids near me got into a fight in the lunchroom. My teacher immediately called 'Keith,' as if it was me who was fighting. But it wasn't!" Vincent says, "I thought it was you." Jamar says that he was told by children in the school that it was Keith and "I figured it was you." Keith starts to get angry, exhibiting his earlier behavior: "Hey, you're not fair! This group sucks!"

Paul, the practitioner, says, "Relax, Keith, we know you weren't in any fight." Paul turns to the others and asks, "Why did you think it was Keith?" Vincent says, "Because that's the kind of thing Keith does, he doesn't take anything from anybody." Keith mumbles, "I'm gonna getcha later." Paul says to Keith, "Keep cool," turns back and asks, "Come on, Jamar, why did you think it was him? Was there anything Keith has done lately that made you think that?" Jamar says, "Not lately, but that's what he's known for."

Paul says, "The group is supposed to help you guys not do things like get into fights." "Right!" says Keith, "And I didn't! But teachers and you guys think I did. You were a witness, Richie, did I hit that kid, did I?" "No, man, you didn't," says Richie. The practitioner says, "When we expect that Keith is going to do what he always did to get in trouble, we don't give him a chance to change, and we don't even see when he did change." The group is quiet.

The practitioner goes on, asking, "How do you guys think Keith has been handling things lately?" After a pause, Jamar says, "Keith's been keeping out of trouble lately." "That's interesting," says Paul, "Does anyone remember Keith getting into any trouble or hitting anyone at school recently?" None of them can remember. The practitioner goes on, "Some of us did the same thing to Keith that his teacher did to him. We prejudged him. But he didn't get into the fight." Members agree. Vincent says that his mother expected him to have not cleaned up his room, but he did. She yelled at him as if he hadn't, then she was surprised because when she went into the room, it was all neat. More talk ensues about how hard it is to try to be good when no one acknowledges the effort. The kids laugh and say, "Yeah, we're going straight." The practitioner spends more time helping them think about how to deal with these inevitabilities.

Discussion. The practitioner uses the opportunity that Keith's situation presents to help members connect to how they feel when teachers and other adults expect them to misbehave when they have already incorporated a change. Keith's example is used to help the members understand the ways in which they prejudged Keith, almost forcing him to revert to earlier dysfunctional behavior. The practitioner supports Keith to prevent this from occurring.

The practitioner asks the members if they remember Keith getting into trouble recently. This motivates them to relate to reality, rather than imaginations and stereotypes. By doing this, the practitioner offers support to the boys and their efforts to change in spite of the conflicting messages they receive from others.

Democratic Norm 5:
The Norm Governing How Member
Behavior Outside the Group Is Shaped by the
Standards That Guide Behavior in the Group

Norms governing behavior in the group can modify self-expression in other situations. This is especially true as the group matures, and the internal frame of reference (Garland, Jones, & Kolodny, 1973) developed within the context of the group becomes part of the member's internalized interpersonal repertoire.

Members learn to trust that the newly developing milieu will become a crucial vehicle that enhances autonomy and affects external interpersonal relationships in expansive ways. However, a word of caution is in order. Authoritarian member and practitioner attitudes expecting adherence to internal norms in members' daily lives may become invasive. The group under this condition can no longer offer a chance for experimentation and risk taking. Group cohesion in this case is being used negatively to control and coerce members.

A group that becomes overly authoritarian needs extra support that will carry over between meetings to avoid fears of regression in group behavior. *Practitioner role.* Much as helpers would like to effect change in members' behavior, the use of group process and group cohesion to control and coerce is dangerous because it can turn into authoritarian reactions and controls. This is a practice dilemma for the practitioner and a membership dilemma for the participants. The practitioner must regularly ask in the group: Are the practitioner and the group exerting authoritarian control within and outside of the group? The practitioner helps the group find ways to maintain equilibrium without resorting to aggressive authoritarianism to regain it. This sets the stage for subsequent work with the group in developing a strong support system so that members may use relationships from within the group between sessions.

Illustration. A group of young people take part in a community center program, an important focus of which is drug prevention. These young people are in a constant struggle with their environment; drugs are all around them. They tell of party after party, outside of the auspices of the center, where young people are using drugs and abusing alcohol.

In this meeting, Freddy comes in wound up but not easily willing to talk about what is bothering him; some members seem to know. The practitioner, Yolanda, begins the effort toward doing work by asking the group as a whole, "What's been happening that you'd like to talk about today?" There is silence. People look around at each other. Ellen says she doesn't know what's going on, but that something is. Tom says, "That's for sure." The practitioner responds, "I think you'd better talk about it, because I don't think we're going to be able to get anything else done if you don't." "Go ahead, Freddy, tell her," says Bob, looking at the practitioner.

Freddy begins to tell Yolanda that when he was at a party this past weekend several of the group members were there; some were smoking pot, and several were drinking booze. He is upset: "We have a rule at the center, no drugs, no drinking, and you guys broke it." Tom says, "The rule applies to the center itself, not to what we do outside. We never come into the center smashed and you know it."

Yolanda says to the group, "How do the rest of you feel about all this?" Ellen says that she's afraid of drugs and wishes they didn't use them at parties. She would feel more comfortable if the kids didn't "go sneaking into the other room to smoke a joint. You all look so stupid." Freddy says, "That's why we need a rule that we don't do that stuff out of here." Tom points out that he doesn't want to be told what to do morning, noon, and night: "What I do when I leave here is my business. I won't agree to such a rule, and I'll break it anyway." "So leave the group," Freddy says. Betsy says, "Freddy, every time someone does something you don't like, you either want to make a rule or you ask them to leave. You're worse than my father." Members are quiet.

The practitioner says, "I think the issue here is, how do we help one another without intruding on people's lives?" Ellen says, "I don't know, because I agree with Betsy; but I'm mad at you, Tom, for smoking pot at that party." Yolanda responds, "It's true, but I think we have various issues here. Freddy, you want to make rules. What bothers you about what Tom did besides that it broke your rule?" Freddy considers for a moment, and says, "He left the party, went to the other room, and hung out trying to act cool for the girls." Ellen says to Tom, "I never thought you looked cool, though."

The practitioner looks at Tom and asks, "Well, how are you reacting to this?" Tom says, "I know you're not going to like this, Yolanda, but I only smoke a joint once in a while, and I'm most likely going to keep on doing that, but I will try not to do that at parties where I know my friends will be mad with me." Yolanda asks, "How do others feel about what Tom said?" Sal says, "It's his right. I don't want to tell him what to do. I wouldn't want you people constantly telling me what to do." "I play by the rules in here, but out there it's a different world," Gloria chimes in. "Come on, Yolanda, are you mad at what Tom said?" Freddy asks. "I don't like it that you smoke anything, Tom," Yolanda replies, "and I hope as we continue in this group you and everyone else who uses drugs and booze outside of the center will consider stopping. But I wouldn't want us to set up rules that won't be followed." Ellen asks, "Why not? What if we did have rules like that?" Yolanda answers, "What does your imagination tell you will happen?" Ellen says that no one will follow them, or "we'll have enforcers who snitch." Sal adds. The practitioner says, "Rules provide guidelines for behavior, but they can't be used as a way of controlling people's behavior. Ultimately that's up to the individual to do what he or she thinks is best."

Discussion. In this meeting, one member was anxious about the behavior of another member who violated group rules outside of the group's auspices. To engage a group in deciding not to use drugs or alcohol *ever* is certainly a tempting trap for a practitioner who feels committed to young people. However, the policy of the community center regarding the use of substances on the premises, and in any agency-sponsored activities, provides the necessary guideline and enough leeway for the member who is learning to use the internal group norms as a frame of reference (Garland et al., 1973) outside of the group and the center. With careful discussion and planning, the internal frame of reference developed by the members' process of committing themselves to each other can also become applicable in the social environment.

The practitioner does not agree with Freddy's desire for rules. By letting the issue remain in the group's attention without permitting rigidity, the practitioner enabled all members, the users and the nonusers, to focus on the helping process. Tom is able to reveal in the group what he does outside of it, without worrying about disapproval leading to rigid rules.

When a group attempts to dictate the behavior of its members in all aspects of their lives, it runs the risk of losing the less rigid members; it also usually loses those members who are struggling to use the group as a frame of reference for societal behavior.

The work of this group is not complete; it is in a valuable process. Future efforts will have to focus on male-female relations, sexuality, and when and how the members use substances, so as to develop broader options for social interactions.

Democratic Norm 6:
The Norm for Using Collaborative
Programming To Enhance Members' Needs

A crucial aspect of the humanistic group form is its *externality* (Papell & Rothman, 1980b), its meaningful process outside the time and space of the meeting room. Undertaking of a full-blown program experiment in the group's social environment is necessary to help members enhance self-determination and decision making. The many tasks and endeavors of a group's program develop members' self-determination, mastery, and new experiences. This maximizes the members' opportunities for experimentation and change. Members can work on change in the here and now of the group within external environments that are peopled by significant others.

Practitioner role. The practitioner supports and encourages aspects of the group's externality, including the development of telephone and address lists for members, participation in activities that meet members' needs for role enhancement, support, risk taking, and informal connections and networking options. The practitioner helps the group in the development of programs through exploration and carrying out of the tasks associated with the programming process (see Chapter 6 for a fuller discussion of programming).

Illustration. A group for women who have recently had mastectomies has been meeting for two weeks. At the end of the last meeting, the members expressed an interest in having each other's phone numbers. The practitioner asked if this was something all of them wanted, or if there was anyone who for some personal reason did not want her phone number on a list. Once agreement was received, the practitioner circulated a list, and asked if anyone could easily get it copied for the next meeting. Vivian quickly volunteered.

At this meeting, Vivian distributes the list; members are pleased to have it. In fact, several members have already called one member, Jean, during the past week. Jean was beginning chemotherapy, and Vivian and Dierdre had called her to find out how she was; the practitioner had called her, too. Jean was not present this night because she did not feel well, but said she planned to return the following week.

Sally asks Dierdre if they had been able to give Jean the name of a wig maker. Dierdre says "No; as a matter of fact, she asked me to get the name from you. I'll call her later and give it to her." Members seem pleased to have the list, saying they would call her, too. They remark how quickly they had come to feel close to each other. The practitioner comments on the utility of this kind of roster, and "how important it is to call someone when you need to talk."

As the meeting is drawing to a close, Dierdre asks the members, "Will you all come for coffee tonight? Several of us just kind of spontaneously went out last week after the group, and we'd like to go again with whomever can." The members nod that they would go tonight. Vivian invites the practitioner, who says, "Thanks so much—it's a good idea, but I have to get home."

Discussion. The practitioner early on in this group's process supports the members in circulating a roster, and is careful to respect the privacy of those members who might not want their names on the list.

The practitioner asks a member to circulate the list so as to encourage the networking to occur through the group's channels and auspices rather than through hers. This encourages the group's ownership of its externality and network. The phone calls to the absent member who was in a crisis further strengthen the supportive external structures. The practitioner did not need to explicitly support the phone work; it was already happening in the process. When the practitioner is invited to have coffee with the group, she declines. She supports the group's effort on its own behalf by indicating that she is not a necessary part of the informal process. A practitioner's participation should not and cannot be expected in all of the external events conducted by adult groups. How participation is handled is guided by agency practice and professional judgment.

Humanistic Value 8:
People Have the Right to Question and Challenge Those Professionals Who Have Sanction to Guide and Direct Their Lives

People who recognize the persuasive and symbolic power of the practitioner are able to take these factors into account and challenge the authority of the practitioner. The anxiety about violating a felt taboo (Shulman, 1984) against expressing feelings about the practitioner in the group must be overcome if members' rights to are to be supported. Members are required to develop and maintain ways of directly expressing feelings, opinions, and challenges to the practitioner who should be viewed as an accountable participant with a specialized role in the group.

Democratic Norm 1:
In a Humanistic Group, Members
Develop Direct Ways of Expressing
Reactions to the Practitioner

The direct expression of feelings toward the practitioner is necessary. It prevents the practitioner from developing, feeding, and maintaining an aura of mystique and unapproachability that keeps the members from holding the practitioner accountable. Furthermore, unexpressed concerns about the practitioner's intentions and actions go underground, coloring and masking the group's spontaneity and depth of intimate relations (Levine, 1979).

Practitioner role. It is very important to know that the feelings members express about other helpers or authorities (Shulman, 1984) are likely to be indicative of the group's concern about the practitioner. Helping the members express reactions directly to the practitioner is important in the group's early life. It helps center the practitioner, and lodge the ownership of the group with the members.

When members begin to make indirect comments about the practitioner's authority, he or she takes note of the comments and directly asks the members how they are feeling about the practitioner's power and influence. It is valuable to note that some look to the practitioner for approval when they speak, while others seem consistently to ignore the practitioner's input. Bringing these behaviors to awareness helps further the group's understanding of its reactions to the practitioner's power (Shulman, 1984).

Encouraging members' negative reactions, nondefensively accepting them, and responding with honesty shows members that the practitioner is fallible and values their criticism. It is of considerable help to the group not to preempt the full expression of criticism of the goals set early on by the practitioner by hasty efforts to re-contract with them. This would sidestep further discussion of the practitioner's role.

Establishing a norm that the group may engage in dialogue with the practitioner about the meaning of his or her actions solidifies the egalitarian distribution of power, demystifies the practitioner's role, and sets the condition for trusting the practitioner as a caring professional with a stake in the group.

Illustration. The 9- to 11-year-old children in a group convened to help deal with their parents' divorces has been talking about seeing the parents they don't live with during their Christmas vacations. One child, Alex, excitedly talks about going to a football game with his father and uncle. Teddy is quiet, and looks like he is pouting. Bill, the practitioner, asks Teddy, "How come you look so glum? Is something wrong?" Teddy says that he is confused because he wanted to spend Christmas with his mother and cousins, not his father: "I want to see Daddy, but later on." Bill asks, "Did you tell your mom or your dad this?" He says that he didn't, that "they won't understand."

Bill asks the group, "Have you had this happen?" Gary says yes. Pamela tells Bill that when she told her father she wanted to see him Christmas Eve and then go back to her mother's house he got mad and hurt, but then he was okay, and she is going to see them both: "They can change their plans a little." Teddy asks, "Bill, do you think I should tell my dad?" Bill asks, "Why wouldn't you, Teddy?" "He'll get mad at me," Teddy answers. "But remember what did we say about when someone is angry at you?" asks Bill. Teddy says, "It doesn't mean they don't love you." The practitioner continues, "So you can take a chance and know that if you tell your parents, they'll still love you." Teddy seems comforted by this. After more support and talk, he agrees that he will discuss this with his mom first. The practitioner asks, "Teddy, do you want me to help you tell your mom when she comes to pick you up?" "Would you do that?" Teddy asks. "I would, if that's what you wanted," is Bill's reply. Teddy thinks about it and says "yes."

Gary asks, "Is that what you do, do you tell our parents about us?" Bill says, "Remember, when we started the group I said I wouldn't tell something unless you wanted me to and knew about it, except if there was some special danger I had to tell about." The group goes on to talk about how they could get Bill to intervene with their teachers, too. Eleanor asks, "Like when they don't like what I do, or when I get in trouble, would you talk to my teacher?" Bill asks her if there is "something special that happened with your teacher." "No, not lately," Eleanor replies and giggles. Bill responds, "You just want to be sure that if something does happen you'll have someone on your side?" Eleanor agrees. "We're lucky you're not a teacher, because we can get to call you Bill," she says, "and you will sit on the floor with us and let us say bad words, too!" The children laugh.

The practitioner asks, "How about when I get angry with you in our group?" The children talk about how he's not "mean," adding that "we know you do it for our own good." He says, "Okay, but just remember, you can tell me if I get mean. Getting angry is different than getting mean. So you can say, 'Bill, you're being mean,' okay?" The children agree. Bill asks again, "Or if there is something else I do that you don't like?" The children agree once more.

Discussion. This illustration demonstrates the practitioner's overall accountability to the members. The practitioner responds to the individual members' needs, then reminds them that he will not betray their confidence except when someone is in danger. This seems to assure them, and they focus on the various ways in which the practitioner can and does use himself. Some see him as an advocate, a person who is on their side when they get into trouble. Others experience him as a nurturer who lets them be familial with him—on a first-name basis, and by allowing them to say things they cannot say elsewhere.

Recognizing that early in the meeting the issue was raised about parents' expressions of anger with the children as a sign of possible rejection, the practitioner wonders how the children experience him

Table 2.1

Values, Norms, and Practitioner Role (Continued)

Value 5: People have the right to freedom of speech, and freedom of expression.

1) The *norm for maintaining an open communication system without reliance on narrow ideology*
   Practitioner role
   –encourages members to speak directly to each other
   –helps weave flexible communication network
   –enables expression and acceptance of unformulated thoughts, feelings, ideas

2) The *norm guiding the open expression of feeling and tempering premature self-disclosure*
   Practitioner role
   –cognizant of stage issues, may or may not encourage self-disclosure
   –enables and models sharing about here and now

Value 6: Differences among members are enriching to one another.

1) The *norm fostering members' diversity rather than a push for conformity*
   Practitioner role
   –examines own feelings re: deviance, difference
   –models openness to dissent, unpopular views, feelings
   –protects individual's rights

Value 7: People have the right to freedom of choice, to determine their own destinies.

1) The *norm fostering equal distribution of power*
   Practitioner role
   –encourages group to look at decision-making process
   –enables and teaches flexibility in leadership

2) The *norm for developing open decision-making processes*
   Practitioner role
   –uses decision-making techniques to clarify issues
   –reaches for feelings of intimidation

3) The *norm fostering freedom to change vs. coercion*
   Practitioner role
   –explores risks involved in change
   –interrupts zealous confrontations
   –enables acceptance of change goals as member's choice
   –protects individual's right not to change
   –checks out members' feelings: "Do you want to go on?"

4) The *norm for maintaining an open role system*
   Practitioner role
   –encourages, enables flexible role taking
   –helps group scrutinize its need to lock member(s) into self-fulfilling prophecies and stereotypic behaviors

(Continued)

Table 2.1

Values, Norms, and Practitioner Role (Continued)

---

5) The *norm governing how member behavior outside the group is shaped by the standards that guide behavior in the group*
   Practitioner role
   –does not permit group process to be used coercively
   –helps group develop support outside meeting
6) The *norm for using collaborative programming to enhance members' needs*
   Practitioner role
   –helps group understand use of program to enable ownership and meet needs

Value 8: People have the right to question and challenge those professionals who have sanction to guide and direct their lives.
   1) The *norm for directly expressing reactions to the practitioner*
   Practitioner role
   –enables direct sharing of feelings to worker
   –reaches for indirect cues re: worker authority/power
   –reflects group's overdependence on worker in process
   –shares stake in group

---

when is he is angry with them. They discuss "meanness," a typical concern and reaction children have to people in authority who try to control them. The practitioner shows them respect by telling them he wants to know when they think he is acting mean toward them. Furthermore, he gives them permission to tell him if there are other things they don't like. This will have to be picked up further along in the group's life.

For the time being, however, the members have been given full opportunities to express negative and positive feelings. This has great importance both in their relationships with the practitioner and with their parents, with whom they are struggling to express pent-up and confusing feelings.

SUMMARY

In this chapter the norms that are particularly effective in operationalizing the values of freedom of speech, freedom of expression, the value of difference as enriching, freedom of choice, and the practitioner's accountability to the group were presented.

The following norms were discussed: the norm maintaining an open communication system without reliance on a narrow ideology; the norm for an open role system rather than one built on stereotypes; the norm fostering the expression of feeling and tempering premature self-disclosure; the norm fostering a broad spectrum of deviance rather than conformity; the norm supporting the equal distribution of power; the norm for collaborative programming; the norm guiding the application of group rules to member behavior outside of the group; and the norm for the direct expression of reactions to the authority of the practitioner. Specific skills the practitioner uses to effect these norms were discussed, and practice illustrations demonstrating the development of each norm in a group were presented.

In looking back at the last two chapters, it is safe to assert that the confluence of these values and norms creates a humanistic and egalitarian ethos which gives special form to interpersonal expression within the group milieu as well as out of the group. Participation in such a group can provide a corrective social and emotional experience. As members engage with one another, the practitioner, and significant others, their interactions combine the special features of difference along with cohesion.

The next chapter will show the evolution of group life as patterned and sequenced flows of feeling and work. It will look at the unique feelings the members and practitioner experience during the group's stages of development, highlighting effective practitioner stances and strategies for each stage. How humanistic values and democratic norms are reflected during the group's cycle of development will be evidenced.

Chapter 3

STAGE THEMES IN GROUP DEVELOPMENT

OVERVIEW OF STAGE THEORY

To comprehend more fully members' interactions in the group as they move toward and away from humanistic and democratic forms of relationship and work, the practitioner views the changing patterns of process through the lens of stage theories of group development. Many practice theories organize the members' reactions in the process as a set of behaviors and concomitant themes known as phases, stages, or cycles in the group's development (Bennis & Shepard, 1962; Garland, Jones, & Kolodny, 1973; Sarri & Galinsky, 1985). This model of change proposes that particular reactions emerge among the group members in patterned and sequenced forms. By being distinctive, these reactions offer the practitioner coherence for taking professional action in relation to the salient themes presented in the group's evolution.

The Boston Model and the T-Group Model

The Boston University model delineated by Garland et al. (1973) provides an important anchor for our understanding of life in the social work group. This model systematically examines various group types, looking at interactions in and out of the meeting room, as members participate in varied programs, take on varied group and life roles, and interact with real workers.

The T-group model described by Bennis and Shepard (1962) is being utilized because its distinctive focus on the here-and-now events in the group results in a considerable emphasis on the group's reaction to the authority of the practitioner-trainer, thereby illuminating another dimension for practice.

The Boston model identifies five stages of growth or "problem levels through which members and the group as a whole pass in the course of development" (Garland et al., 1973, p. 29). Through this lens, the authors posit that a significant and fundamental theme in group life is *closeness*. Each of these stages has a salient frame of reference through which the members view the group, and the closeness and distance within it. In Stage 1, Preaffiliation, where members show an approach-avoidance conflict, the frame of reference is societal; in Stage 2, Power and Control, the frame of reference is transitional. This refers to the ambiguity in norms and the normative crisis that occurs as people struggle for power and vie for leadership positions with each other and the practitioner. In Stage 3, Intimacy, the frame of reference is familial, with members referring to each other with reminiscences of significant others in their lives. In Stage 4, Differentiation, the frame of reference is internal with members exhibiting more clarity and connection about group goals. In Stage 5, Separation, the frame of reference now becomes a newly developed societal one as the members use growth gained in the group to guide future actions. It appears that Stages 1 and 2 center most on the development of democratic mutual aid processes, and Stages 3, 4, and 5 focus on the achievement of psychosocial purpose.

In describing the T-group, Bennis and Shepard (1962) posit the two distinct themes of power and love as central themes for group life that run through the stages. They identify two phases in group development: Phase I—Dependence (Authority Relations), and Phase II—Interdependence (Personal Relations).

The first phase has three subphases: Subphase 1, Dependence-Flight; Subphase 2, Counterdependence-Fight; and Subphase 3, Resolution-Catharsis. All these phases in the process come about from members' reactions to the power and authority of the practitioner-trainer. First, members anxiously look to the trainer for direction and approval; then, while overtly ignoring the trainer (although covertly paying attention), they vie amongst themselves for power. Finally, "there is a sudden increase in alertness and tension" (Bennis, 1964, p. 258) as they gather the strength to challenge the actual and illusionary position of the trainer.

Phase II, which concentrates on the quality of relationships among members, includes three additional subphases: Subphase 4, Enchantment-Flight; Subphase 5, Disenchantment-Fight; and Subphase 6, Consensual Validation. The group in this phase moves from seeing itself as a romantic icon to be worshipped (and not challenged) to becoming disgusted with its members' foibles and withdrawals, and to accepting itself finally as a realistic work group whose task it is to provide feedback to its members about their roles in the here and now of group life.

In the T-group model, the reaction of the group to authority is viewed as a basic emotional underpinning of small group life. In the Boston model, though power and control is clearly acknowledged and dealt with as a stage, it is viewed more as an obstacle to closeness than as a separate theoretical entity. Thus power conflicts in the social work group may not be encouraged in full-blown forms to the extent that the authority rebellion may be encouraged in the T-group. This is an important observation to ponder and experiment with, because the substance of the humanistic group involves giving the members all the power and energy they are capable of using, and assisting the members in their efforts toward empowerment (Berman-Rossi, 1987, 1988).

Beginning, Middle, and Ending Phases

The change process in a group is intertwined with the beginning, middle, and ending phases of the helping process described in generic social work practice theories. The beginning phase reflects preaffiliative adjustments having to do with initial trust, authority, responsibility, and leadership. The normative crisis as a turning point leads to a consideration of standards that will be used by the members to guide their interactions.

The middle phase is recognized as the time when the members work in a differentiated form on meeting their objectives. These objectives may be limited ones in a short-term group, and comprehensive in a long-term one. Members learn to accept each other without false illusions of intimacy and power, and without necessarily agreeing with or liking all that happens among them. Members will deal with the failures, avoidances, successes, and elations of the change process.

The ending phase of the group signifies separation and reflecting on accomplishments. Ending reactions should not become debilitating, even though fear and avoidance are noted during this final step in meeting members' goals and moving on to other ones.

Group Process and Group Purpose

Process in a group refers to the changing psychosocial actions and relationships the members and practitioner have with one another (Garvin, 1985). *Purpose* is what is being worked on, the material reasons the members are together. Without a well-developed process rooted in humanistic values and democratic standards, the group's purpose cannot be achieved. Process and purpose are inextricably linked. In the group's beginning phase, it is its process rather than its purpose that is emphasized and developed. During the middle phase, it is purpose that is highlighted and worked on within the context of the processes of democratic mutual aid. Thus as members work on meeting their mutual objectives, the means they have developed for democratic interpersonal relationships are used.

Stage Theory and Member Differences

The change process in the group is also related to members' differing capabilities. During the stages of the group's growth, each member brings different interpersonal abilities to meetings. The members' abilities for interaction in the group are a function of their physical, political, emotional, familial, and group experiences. As a group member, the person will have to develop relationships, find common ground, delineate differences, work on personal issues and goals, and assist others and the group in working on their issues and goals. The time spent on affiliative states, rather than on working on objectives, will vary in relation to the members' interpersonal skills, leadership efforts, and the extent to which domination, shyness, and stereotyping are overcome in the group.

The normal characteristics that go along with the maturational processes of childhood and adolescence, adulthood, and aging—along with physiological disorders—will affect members' capabilities in the group's life (Lang, 1972). Certain longstanding psychosocial factors may inhibit full forms of participation; some are the result of cultural and political stereotyping and stigmatization. These may limit some members' full capacities for interaction and participation because of anticipatory reactions and externally imposed inhibitions. Other factors are internalized by-products of the members' experiences in primary family groupings which now affect self-esteem, and expectations that relationships are ones of domination, victimization, or persecution. Yet whatever course individual development has taken, members are capable of growth or modification of internal and external states through the group process, although timing and pace will vary (Chapter 9 delineates how to assess individual members).

Stage Themes: Practitioners and Members

Stage themes have been defined to shed light on the practitioner and members' transactions as the group develops experiences to meet members' goals. The social work stage theory of Garland et al. (1973) and the T-group theory of Bennis and Shepard (1962) have been used to identify these themes. As the group enacts and tries to cope with stage-related themes, the practitioner also experiences several generalizable theme-centered reactions in and about the group. Stage themes help guide the practitioner by highlighting interpersonal issues and feelings the practitioner will experience while trying to engage with and assist the members. This knowledge should help the group worker examine feelings and other perceptions to learn to use them as a barometer for understanding the group's collective experience as well as his or her own.

The practitioner's personal-life situations can become a useful part of group life, or interfere in members' efforts. The practitioner must work with whatever emotions are stirred up by the different phases of group life. While personal in content, many of these reactions are not merely idiosyncratic countertransferences, but a theme-related and necessary part of the group experience.

In the beginning phase, the practitioner is also concerned with being accepted and heard as a capable worker with a professional stake in the group. The practitioner is part of and contributes to the resolution of the normative crisis by presenting values and norms that yield humanistic and democratic relationships. During the middle phase, the practitioner is concerned with how to be helpful while the members receive, react to, and use feedback, interpretation, and confrontation. Attention also centers on how to react to the different ways in which the members use the practitioner's contributions.

Stage Themes: Humanism and Democracy

This sequence of stage themes also serves as a significant conceptual mechanism for distinguishing the difference between process in response to a humanistic group work method and process in a nonhumanistic one. All group approaches reflect upon the values and techniques of the method used, as well as those of the practitioner. It is the philosophical position of this book that humanistic values are more fully representative of the nature and interpersonal potential of people than other configurations of values. Thus a humanistic approach is better able to achieve fuller forms of democratic and differentiated interaction among members. Approaches with authoritarian or ill-defined values stifle the potential of full group development and do not allow each member to make active use of the group, assume leadership, share power, follow others' leads, and identify with many different people. These groups evolve structures and dynamics that, at best, achieve partial forms of their potential. At worst, groups that are developed along authoritarian lines of relationship may become destructive to members and significant others. A group with an authoritarian character cannot achieve a full form of interpersonal and emotional differentiation, because its cohesion centers on attitudes and acts of domination and submission.

As the practitioner employs the values, norms, and skills of the method, stage theme reactions occur among the members about the expectations of membership in such a group. The resolutions of the members' thematic issues are viewed as evolving in some significant ways from the practitioner's use of the humanistic method. For example, the practitioner's work with the members' perceptions of his or her intentions to control the process in the group is a central issue. By opening up and facilitating discussion of the practitioner's behavior and role, the practitioner chooses to demystify the role, enabling members to assume leadership and share power. While groups of many types—whatever the members' values and norms—go through stages and reaction states, what is distinctive in the humanistic method is that members focus on their abilities to evolve and monitor their own processes in cohesive and differentiated ways. By comparison, utilitarian or authoritarian values stimulate different interactions and present a different picture of the practitioner to the members.

STAGE THEMES

Juxtaposing the stages defined in the Boston model against the phases and subphases of the T-group model yields several newer perceptions. The Boston model does not focus on the ways in which the group deals with and resolves its authority crisis with the practitioner. The phenomena described in the Boston model's power and control stage are delineated into two subphases in the T-group model (Counterdependence-Fight and Resolution-Catharsis). The stage of Intimacy in the Boston model is similar to the Enchantment-Flight in the T-group model. While the Boston model clearly delineates separation processes at the group's end, these are absent completely in the T-group model.

The stage themes developed and described below are an effort to integrate the Boston model and the T-group model, in order to highlight those important processes in the humanistic group that can be used to inform practice. The stage themes are: (1) "We're Not in Charge"; (2) "We Are in Charge"; (3) "We're Taking You On"; (4) Sanctuary; (5) "This Isn't Good Anymore"; (6) "We're Okay and Able"; and (7) "Just a Little Longer." (Table 3.1 clarifies how these themes have emerged from the Boston model and the T-group model.)

The following material is an explication of each theme, listing the relevant stages in the Boston and T-group models as well as the humanistic values and democratic norms for each stage theme. Furthermore, the practitioner's issues and key roles are highlighted along with practice illustrations.

Stage Theme 1: We're Not in Charge

Boston Model Stage	T-Group Stage	*Relevant Values and Norms*
1 (Preaffiliation)	Dependence-Flight	Right to belong, to be heard

As members begin meeting, they approach one another with varying degrees of caution. The members look to the practitioner to provide them with clues and direction about how to respond (Bennis & Shepard, 1962). While there are approach and avoidance feelings and actions (Garland et al., 1973), members' comments are specifically designed to

Table 3.1

Stage Themes: Boston Model and T-Group Model

Stage Themes	Boston Model	T-Group Model
Stage Theme 1 "We're Not in Charge"	Stage 1 Preaffiliation	Phase I Dependence (Authority Relations) Subphase 1 Dependence-Flight
Stage Theme 2 "We Are in Charge"	Stage 2 Power and Control	Subphase 2 Counterdependence-Fight
Stage Theme 3 "We're Taking You On"	Stage 2 Power and Control	Subphase 3 Resolution—Catharsis
Stage Theme 4 Sanctuary	Stage 3 Intimacy	Phase II Interdependence (Personal Relations) Subphase 4 Enchantment-Flight
Stage Theme 5 "This Isn't Good Anymore"	Stage 4 Differentiation	Subphase 5 Disenchantment-Fight
Stage Theme 6 "We're Okay and Able"	Stage 4 Differentiation	Subphase 6 Consensual Validation
Stage Theme 7 "Just a Little Longer"	Stage 5 Separation	Subphase 6 Consensual Validation

gain approval and direction from the practitioner "whose reactions to comments are surreptitiously watched" (Bennis, 1964, p. 257). The members look to the practitioner to understand the meaning of his or her interventions, interactions, feelings, attitudes, and nonverbal signs. Members wish to find out if they will receive approval from the practitioner, given group members' proclivities to imbue the person in the leadership role with power over them. This desire to gain approval from the practitioner symbolically represents the members' desire to gain approval from one another as well.

Practitioner Issues

A committed professional is dedicated to the success of the group as a productive environment and experience for each member. The practitioner tries to figure out a variety of approaches to members and the group that will help sustain investment in the group experience. The practitioner has most likely put in much social and emotional effort in forming the group. Thus it should not be odd that the practitioner becomes professionally and personally invested in the success of the group, measuring success by the members' willingness to return, to try it out, and to make tenuous commitments. The practitioner is at risk of interpreting members' inabilities to develop commitment as professional failure in working with the group rather than as a normal stage reaction.

The practitioner may avoid or resist the members' dependence on him or her and not give the help and support necessary for them to make their initial commitments to the group. In this way, the practitioner defends against experiencing the anxiety of responsibility for the group, replacing it with rationalizations disguised as professional jargon. Feeling the group to be a failure, the practitioner avoids responsibility with phrases like "This group is yours" and offers the members minimal visions of their future together.

The values and norms of the humanistic group method lead the practitioner into interactions that recognize and empathize with the members' needs for attention, involvement, and direction with the practitioner as well as one another.

Practitioner Role

The practitioner helps to identify needs and interests that are held in common, linking individuals' reasons for being in the group to collective ones. The practitioner points out that whether or not needs dovetail, as members of the group they can help one another to be effective, and that mutually supportive efforts of this kind are ubiquitous in all kinds of situations. By inviting trust (Garland et al., 1973), and encouraging the expression of feelings toward and ideas about the practitioner and the group, the practitioner paves the way for helping members achieve eventual autonomy from the perceived and actual authority of the practitioner, and a partnership in mutual aid that can include the practitioner.

The practitioner recognizes the feared "taboo" (Shulman, 1984) about addressing latent interactions (that can be "read between the lines"), and sets the stage for future discussions about latent and manifest aspects of the group's process. This is done within a context of humanistic values and democratic norms, so as not to permit damage to the group, or to a member, that may result from anomic or authoritarian group situations. For example, saying that "I hear some of you have some concern about how much you will be asked to share here" helps members accept their cautious reactions as vital. Recognizing the members' caution and couched reactions to the practitioner's authority as a necessity for the group's development helps all to discern the value of caution for their autonomy, rather than suggesting that these are deviant affects. The practitioner participates in and listens to discussion about people in the teacher and parent roles or experiences with prior helpers (Shulman, 1984). By asking if the members are fearful that the practitioner will do something that will make them uncomfortable, and by not defending other professionals, the practitioner allows the group the opportunity to openly criticize his or her expression in the group.

Illustration

A group of blind, frail elderly persons is getting started in the skilled nursing facility. This is their second meeting. Mike, the worker, went to every room along with one of the nurses and brought the members to the meeting. Sara and Louis put up a battle about coming, saying they were tired or not feeling well, but with some encouragement agreed to come. The practitioner says, "If you start to feel like you want to leave, I'll have one of the aides bring you back to your room, okay?" Ruth, Monica, Wilber, and the others agreed to come willingly. Several of the people are wheelchair bound as well.

After going over introductions to remind everyone where the others are sitting and how they sound, the practitioner notes that last week they said they wanted to talk about how some of them would like to have readers and taped books to help them spend their leisure time. Wilbur raises the fact that some of the residents and the nursing staff are not so considerate of them as blind people: "We don't get included in activities because there isn't always someone to help us get there. And since we can't see, we can't spend the time watching TV like others do." The practitioner acknowledges Wilbur by name, wondering if this is a common problem. Some agree. Then there is a silence. Sara says, "None of these groups work out. Last year we had a group for blind people, and they never came up to take us to the meeting. How did they expect us to get here?" Some laughter ensues. The practitioner says, "Thank you, Sara. Yes, we will come to get you; no matter what time or effort it takes. But are there other things you're afraid I might do that won't help you? What does everyone think?" Louis says that in the last group, "We talked about leisure time and taped books, but it never came to anything." The practitioner asks, "Louis, do you want me to help you carry out your plans and wishes?" He agrees, and Ruth chimes in, "Yes, because we can't always do what we say we want to do." "I understand, Ruth, that it's hard when you have things you want and can't get without help, because you can't see," Mike says. "Right," Wilbur agrees. "And if that wasn't bad enough, we're old too," Sara says with humor.

Discussion

The practitioner carefully arranged for the members to be transported to the meeting room. This represents a commitment to the group, and a recognition that members will be more ambivalent than the practitioner and need to feel expected and welcomed in an atmosphere that considers their limitations and frailties. He also accepts their ambivalence by encouraging them to attend while at the same time promising to return them to their rooms if they do not feel well.

The practitioner takes ample time for the introductions, cognizant of the fact that these members are blind and have to develop voice recognition. This communicates respect and consideration for the unique situations of the members. This also permits the group to talk about feeling left out of activities conducted by other staff who, by implication, are not as considerate. The practitioner affirms his commitment to bring them to the group, "whatever it takes."

Mike focuses the group's attention on the development of future strategies to meet their needs as blind elderly in this nursing facility, using their needs and interests to offer them a vision for the future of the group. Having heard their unhappiness with the previous worker and with the nursing home staff, he uses the opportunity to focus on how this group might feel about and deal with him. He asks them if they are afraid he will do something they do not like.

Stage Theme 2: We Are in Charge

Boston Model Stage	*T-Group Stage*	*Values and Norms*
2 (Power and Control)	Counterdependence-Flight	Open decision making
		Accept differences
		Open role system
		Open communication

Behavior in the group is marked by varying intensities of arguing among members, and assertions of will to set directions and establish agendas. Some may withdraw from the fight, being fearful of taking sides or apparently uninterested in having power. Some will admonish the practitioner to take sides or take control of some members or the group as a whole. Some members experience the open and permissive atmosphere of the humanistic and democratic group as a failure on the part of the practitioner to take charge. Having in their estimations found the practitioner unable to exercise skill or use power properly, some members will move to exclude the practitioner by ignoring his or her interventions or comments. It is through the ensuing normative crisis that the group will develop *norms*—standards and rules about how they will interact together in this group with the practitioner. The standards that ensue come about as the members and the practitioner relate to the practitioner's use of a professional method. In developing group norms, the members will move from relying on a frame of reference that is societal (external to the group experience, with impersonal norms) to an internal frame of reference (with interpersonally oriented group norms) (Garland et al., 1973). The ambiguity of norms—as the group attempts to develop new ones—creates degrees of anxiety for members, contributing to the struggle for stability and control. As the members struggle with leadership, attempting to examine some of the difficult behaviors and emerging norms, they gather strength and develop mutuality.

Practitioner Issues

Being ignored or not responded to when intervening or trying to engage the group may leave the practitioner feeling threatened, tense, and ineffectual. Also, the conflicts for power, control, and leadership can create anxiety when a practitioner has difficulty accepting power struggles, especially those which focus on the practitioner as part of the problem and the resolution. The normative crisis the members experience (and the concomitant anxiety that results, followed by skirmishes and more anxiety) challenges the practitioner's ability to handle and deal with the powerful and stark ambiguity of this portion of the members' experiences with one another. When he or she does not recognize the significance of these dynamics, the practitioner may over control the fighting in the group by asserting authority, or may abdicate too much responsibility in order to placate the group.

Practitioner Role

While not preempting the conflict, the practitioner finds ways to help the members examine the ensuing process. Herein the practitioner is helped by the explicit values and norms of the humanistic group work model, which hold differences and give-and-take in high regard. Pointing out the frustrations inherent in this struggle for control, stability, and standards of behavior facilitates the group's forward movement. The practitioner responds to the members' testiness—brought about by the ambiguity of norms—by nondefensively pointing out to the group that they can work on developing norms about how they will work together along with the practitioner, rather than excluding the practitioner or expecting that the practitioner will regulate their process for them. The prototypic response to the practitioner at this juncture ("you will make the rules anyway") must be met with an invitation to the group to explore the meaning of these opinions. By clarifying observations and pointing out events in the process to the members, the practitioner helps them to move to a more direct challenge of the practitioner's role.

Illustration

A group of young teenage boys, new to a residence, are having difficulty with their young adult female worker, Lois. In this, the fourth meeting, they are misbehaving all over the place, often getting up to go around the room to slap or poke each other; so far, none of it is dangerous.

The practitioner gets them to settle down. They begin to jokingly make sexual innuendos, while making sure not to look to Lois for her reaction. The practitioner notices that when she is looking in one direction a couple of boys on the other side try to steal a glance at her. Several boys—Jimmy, who tries to control people when he gets uptight, and Leon, who is more quiet—try to switch topics, saying that "we're not supposed to say dirty words here." The practitioner asks the group, "I wonder what all this sex talk is all about? Is it that you want to have a chance to talk about sex in this group?" The boys laugh and snort. A couple of them, Frank and Terry, get up and go over to Leon, poking at his backpack. Jimmy indignantly gets up and tells them to "sit down and shut the fuck up." Terry says, "Who the hell made you boss?" "No one," Jimmy says, "but you can't do that here." "Who says I can't?" says Terry.

A verbal battle ensues for a couple of minutes, and then a fight breaks out among several of the boys. This causes Lois to have to get up and physically go over into the midst of three of them and quietly say to "stop fighting, and sit down."

After a few moments, they respond to her and sit down. Lois suggests that "there are other ways to express how you feel here besides fighting; what do you think? Maybe we can talk about things in here that are too scary to talk about outside, even though you're male and I'm female."

Discussion

This group of boys is dealing with the newness of the total residential environment, and being away from their familiar surroundings, whatever their limitations. While an assortment of societal and familial rules have governed their lives, many of their circumstances have been dysfunctional for them, providing at best a confused frame of reference. In this new facility, the boys are testing and trying to make sense out of the rules for the sake of their own survival. They place the practitioner, a woman with all these boys, in the position of having to absorb their challenges and tests; they watch her responses carefully.

Lois appropriately says nothing about the curse words. This is a group whose rules are in flux; they want to know if and how she will tolerate their sense of "boyness." However, when the group begins to fight physically the practitioner intervenes, using her adult authority to limit their behavior. Once they sit down, the boys are controlled. This allows her to approach them nonpunitively, bypassing discussion of their behavior and asking them to figure out if they can talk about "scary" things, even though she is a woman.

Stage Theme 3: We're Taking You On

Boston Model Stage	T-Group Stage	Values and Norms
2 (Power and Control)	Resolution-Catharsis	Worker's accountability to group
		Equalizing power

The task of relating to, challenging, and joining with the position of the practitioner represents the group's foremost collective enterprise to this point in the process. This effort entails gathering the momentum and strength the members have been developing to collectively react to and engage with the practitioner. The members must find out about the practitioner's intentions by posing direct questions such as, "What are you doing here? How much will you share here? In what ways are you like us?" They need to develop the emotional capabilities to hear the practitioner's initial reactions without being overwhelmed by the fears, projections, and screens that have dominated their perception of the practitioner's role up to now.

This type of interaction sets the stage for learning how to include the practitioner and his or her technical skill and expertise in working on the group's purpose. The intense focusing of the group's attention to dealing with the practitioner's authority—in an almost voyeuristic way—offers the fullest arena for the members to observe the group's latent themes and processes as they band together.

Practitioner Issues

The practitioner, in anticipation of the group's challenge to his or her authority, may develop fears of being at the mercy of the group. Underneath doubts about his or her competency and skill is the feeling that another more skilled practitioner would not be found to be at fault. The practitioner might try to get the members to bypass the challenge by asking them to reconsider their goals, rather than to engage with the practitioner about his or her role. Or the practitioner might attempt to direct the members to redefine how they want the practitioner to behave, thereby indirectly causing the members to reconsider their own relationships while in actuality avoiding engagement with the practitioner. Such moves deflect the members from the emotional imperative and social necessity the challenge to authority holds: that of learning about their perceptions of and reactions to the authority role, as well as their own roles in furthering democratic group process and purpose.

Practitioner Role

When the challenge comes, it is helpful to assist members in exploring their feelings about the practitioner. This enables the group to develop its here-and-now awareness of the practitioner role. This process helps remove projections and screens that have prevented two-way communication, and begins to permit the members to use the practitioner's technical expertise, life experience, and feelings. The practitioner, while helping members to look at their reactions, also has to reveal his or her own reactions to the group as a member who takes part in the process—not an outsider. Because the humanistic method is postulated on members' rights and responsibilities to question those in authority, the practitioner is helped in this process by his or her adherence to the method's values and norms of conduct. This involves talking openly about his or her purpose and feelings, and sanctioning the group's feedback to the practitioner.

Illustration

A group of pregnant women in a prison cell block are in their fifth meeting with a male practitioner, Dan. The focus to date has been on developing means for social and emotional survival.

The women are involved in educating the practitioner about what goes on in prison, and suggesting that he change the system. The practitioner responds, "I know how badly you feel about being here and how awful it can be for you, but I can't change the system for you. This leaves me feeling worried. But in this group, you all have work to do, with each other and me, to figure out how to support each other and air your emotions so you are not bottled up." The women blow up, yelling in angry voices, "Who are you? What do you know about this place coming in once a week . . . social worker?!?"

Somewhat anxious and wavering, Dan takes a deep breath and responds, "I don't know all that you know about this place, for sure. But I do feel convinced I'm on the right track about you all needing to deal with what's going on, so that you can use each other in this session and on the cell block for support." He goes on, "You're questioning me, and I'll try to answer. But also let me know more about how you think I have been handling myself in these meetings—what helps, and what doesn't." They continue, at first talking at once: "You're like this . . . you're like that." One member says, "When we talk to each other you listen too hard and make us paranoid." The practitioner says, "I don't intend for you to get paranoid, but I just don't want to miss something that could be useful."

The process of arguing and give-and-take moves more and more toward becoming effective, rather than accusative. The members begin to talk more openly about how much they feel demeaned in the prison by everyone in authority, and how the practitioner shows them respect. More talk develops about the practitioner: "Come on, Dan, why are you here? What are you getting out of this?" The practitioner responds, "We talked about that in the first meeting. You know, it's just that as a social worker I want to come here and contribute. I know something about your situation, I've had friends and family who got into trouble—none of us is immune—and I just want to try to change things this way, to help you get a better chance."

Discussion

The expectation that a prisoners' group might become angry is one of a practitioner's worst fears. That these women have a great deal to complain about in their situations cannot be denied. The practitioner does not deny the validity of their complaints; to do so would damage the relationship. It would show that the practitioner is not truly connected to their current reality.

It is not accidental that at this time in the group's development the issue of authority in the prison becomes a central concern. However, the practitioner holds to his conviction that the members' needs will best be met by staying focused on their work within the group that centers on supporting each other through their pregnancies, and developing future plans upon their release. Issues revolving around their own stigmatizations and those of their children will have to be dealt with as well. The practitioner walks a fine line with these members; he validates their concern about the correctional system, but stays with the work of the group. By asking them to respond to his efforts, the practitioner offers them direction for moving ahead to understand their issues with his authority and his power. As the members react to the practitioner, weaving and developing a collective set of perceptions, they once again ask him what he is doing there. The practitioner responds openly, acknowledging their situation within society as people who need a chance, and offering his desire to be of help in the context of his own history. This kind of authenticity is essential in an environment so full of mistrust, authority, and control.

Stage Theme 4: Sanctuary

Boston Model Stage	T-Group Stage	Values and Norms
3 (Intimacy)	Enchantment-Flight	Right to belong

The feelings of accomplishment and inclusiveness gained from working on power and authority issues bring the members to new feelings of caring, effectiveness, and closeness. These include wishing for comfortable, relaxed, and uncomplicated relationships with one another and the practitioner. Along with the authentic desire to include the practitioner as part of them, the members hope that the practitioner will stop working and collude with them in their safe haven away from the pressures of their real-life relationships, as well as the pressures attendant upon changes they anticipate within themselves and their group relationships.

The members feel that the group and its members, even the ones they had intense differences with before, are wonderful. In this "love" reaction, the group is held up as an icon (Bion, 1959). While serving the purpose of providing a breathing spell and setting the stage for work to come by motivating strong affective bonds among the members, this state may also be used counterproductively, to avoid further difficult tasks by pressuring conformity from those members who attempt to alter the comfort and uniformity it provides.

In this stage there are many familial-type transferential issues (Garland et al., 1973). These paradoxically serve both to enhance cohesiveness and to resist moving on to a more inclusive and differentiated process.

Practitioner Issues

The practitioner is vulnerable to feeding the group's desire for closeness by overengaging and wishing to connect with it. On the other hand the practitioner may feel threatened by the closeness, and by the fear that his or her authority and the demand for work may be disregarded. This heightens the risk that the practitioner will emotionally withdraw from the group so as not to be seen as part of the closeness.

The practitioner may not understand the meaning of family talk as a symbol of the members' desire for closeness, thereby stopping it by interpreting it as an immature dependency reaction. This would deflect the members from their needs to strengthen their affective bonds so they may proceed to work on purpose with a concerted emotional effort.

Practitioner Role

It is important that the practitioner experience a feeling of membership, inclusion, and warmth in the group. This strengthens the ability to cue into and motivate nuances of affect that are necessary for the members if they are to function at deeper emotional and intellectual levels. At the same time, the practitioner tunes into members' strivings to assert their wants and differences, and to get beyond the glow of the "happy family." The practitioner, recognizing and respecting the group's desire to maintain its sanctuary, taps into its latent urge to begin productive work on its purpose by exploring how the members might wish to put their cohesive feelings and interactions to use. Raising questions about future goals and actions, while supporting the cohesion and affective tone of the group, helps it use the cohesion to proceed to more difficult tasks.

Illustration

A group of spouse-abusing males has been having a lot of difficulty defining their behavior as abusive. They have argued a great deal with the practitioner and one another. After much conflict and many power struggles, including threats of violence, they have had to swallow feelings of entitlement and personal hurt derived from their own abusive family experiences. They have had to face up to their view of the practitioner as a more perfect and less impulse-ridden fathering male. They have come to a point where they see themselves in a more positive light, and feel they can overcome their problems through each other's support.

At this meeting, they are talking about how they feel they can suppress the anger they've turned on their wives. Al says, "All I have to do is remember that you guys are here supporting me and I won't strike out at her." Mel agrees. Rick says, "My wife left me, and has an order of protection against me; she'll never take me back."

The discussion continues with members talking about how nice the group of guys is, and how if they had this as kids maybe things wouldn't have turned out like they did. The practitioner is quiet for a while. Then he says, "It's true, it would have been nice if you guys had a warm group like this when you were younger. But what about now, how can you use this atmosphere to help better your difficult situations?" There are some angry reactions at first, then Mel yells out, "We gotta cut the crap, and stop bemoaning our fate, and stop crying over spilled milk!" The group is quiet. Then Al says, "Mel is right. We can't go back. We have to try to get it right this time. I've got children. I've got to get it right for them before I lose them too."

Discussion

The members in this group are experiencing the hurts and letdowns of their family situations, and their current feelings of loss of their wives and children. They have been able to acknowledge the group as a nurturing milieu—one which they currently need and would have needed in their own childhoods. The closeness they feel in this sanctuary can provide a second chance for them to extract a newer set of behaviors from this sustaining environment.

With the practitioner as part of their process, they have had to acknowledge his less impulsive behavior. With this in mind, the practitioner has affirmed the group's caring and support and permitted himself to be part of that process. His silence during their idealization of the group permits the members the time they need to feel good about themselves and their accomplishments, and to experience the wish for this sustenance in their childhoods. The practitioner directly affirms their need for the group as a nurturing milieu, agreeing with their perception that this atmosphere was necessary but lacking in their childhoods. He gently takes the opportunity to direct them toward thinking about how they will use the group to improve their current situations. Although reluctant to move ahead, the group is sparked by the quick response of one member to the practitioner's intervention. Another member follows suit. If he hadn't, the practitioner would have had to support the dissident member in pushing the group to newer arenas, and given affirmation to the other members as well.

Stage Theme 5: This Isn't Good Anymore

Boston Model Stage	T-Group Stage	Values and Norms
4 (Differentiation)	Disenchantment-Fight	Accept differences
		Accept deviance
		Right to self-determination

When group members find themselves unable to take the risks necessary to change, some become angry—disenchanted with the group, and disparaging of one another. While some members may continue to work trying to stem the tide of group dissolution, others distrust the attempts and risks members are taking, at times denying their sincerity altogether. Eventually, the negativity of some members prevents others from moving forward, because purposeful movement requires everyone's involvement and cooperation. This results in a loss of faith in the capacity of the group to work together toward reaching its goals. When the members are in an extreme form of this conflictual mode, they may move to disband the group—saying that "this isn't good anymore." While it is uncharacteristic for the members to blame the practitioner for their dysfunctioning, they do compare their activities and attitudes to the practitioner's—and, as is the risk of comparisons, their efforts often appear futile. If the group ends at this time, members are bound to be left with lack of resolution that results in feelings of anger, frustration, and disappointment with the group and group life in general. (It is less frustrating and more positive, however illusionary, to end at the point of sanctuary than at this juncture.)

Practitioner Issues

A practitioner experiences the blame the group places on its members as a sign of his or her own ineffectiveness. Feeling unnoticed or peripheral to the struggle results in a sense of helplessness rather than helpfulness. Afraid of addressing the negative reaction in the group—and of interpreting the latent fears and avoidance—the practitioner may become overanxious jumping in to rescue the members by a frantic affirmation of their accomplishments. The practitioner might also become angry and punitive toward them because of their lack of productivity. All in all, when the practitioner fails to recognize the imperative of this theme, he or she inadvertently stimulates the group to disband rather than assisting it in actively developing interpersonal and practical means for working with the practitioner.

Practitioner Role

An attitude of confidence in the group's capacity to continue with its work is required. To accomplish this, the practitioner must address the members' negative reactions by identifying them and exploring them rather than through direct confrontation (the latter might be experienced as punitive). Refocusing the members on their objectives, while actively affirming the reality and normalcy of the difficulties, is necessary. The practitioner helps the members restore their visions about the future and their abilities to continue effective work.

Illustration

A group of Vietnam veterans has been meeting for nearly a year. They have dealt with many issues regarding the war itself, relationships to people in the war, things they did that they hated, drugs, and what happened when they returned home. One of the recent issues has been the mixed feelings of wanting to let go of the bitterness of the past, yet at the same time not wanting to violate either the memory of people who died or the truth of their own anger.

At this meeting Jim begins by saying, "I don't think there is anything more that can be said in this group about being vets. The truth is, the war ruined our lives, and we couldn't even come back to a heroes' welcome, and that is that!" Felix says that Joe, right now, is still letting it ruin his life: "You never go through with anything you start—like getting an education so you can put it behind." Joe angrily responds, "There's no point just to be in a two-bit state job sucking up to some asshole like some other black folks do, and keeping our people behind bars." Members argue back and forth about how some black people made it out of Vietnam gritting their teeth and into education and a job. "Yeah, and others made it into drugs, just like they learned there," comments Ron.

Fred (who is black and has a good construction job) says, "I do not want to talk about this anymore. Each of us has to do what we have to do. I can't tell you how to run your lives and you can't tell me how to run mine." The group falls silent. The practitioner wonders, "Does this mean some of you have given up, that there is no point in trying to go for it, or trying not to see everything as 'the war' even though it was horrible? It feels like you're moving forward and backward."

Members begin to talk about how hard it is to go forward, and that while they were in Vietnam other young people were going to school, getting on with their lives. Ron says "I was foolish, I should have protested the war, stayed in college; I would be in a better place now." Several members agree and talk continues. The practitioner acknowledges how hard it must feel to go forward "when you have so many angry and hurt feelings. . . . I don't blame you for being stuck; I don't know where I would be if I were in your shoes. Angry and stuck, too, I guess."

Discussion

The practitioner here is not afraid to react to the negative and fearful feelings. Rather, he points them out empathically in the hope that members will start to reconsider their own obstacles to getting on with their lives. The acknowledgment about how difficult it is to go forward when one harbors so many hurt feelings might provide support and impetus for members to accept their feelings and turn them into constructive action rather than having them remain latent, causing feelings of refusal. By identifying and empathizing with these feelings, the practitioner does not become caught in self-blame or in distancing himself from the realities of the members' past and present experiences.

Stage Theme 6: We're Okay and Able

Boston Model Stage	T-Group Stage	Values and Norms
4 (Differentiation)	Consensual Validation	Open communication Difference is enriching

In the process of working through ambivalence toward the group experience, members develop a deepening confidence in their abilities to attempt more difficult work. A range of difference among the members is valued as important for enriching the experience. As they assume more responsibility for sharing their perceptions and conflicts, these feelings are more readily accepted as essential for the problem-solving process. The members learn to choose from among options and reactions that reflect the different styles and capacities of each person in the group. A fuller ability to present their feelings, perceptions, questions, and views of one another's contributions in reaching their goals is evidenced. The members feel capable of encouraging and assuming collective and individual leadership in caring about one another. They are better able to assist one another in meeting their objectives.

The practitioner is implicitly expected, and explicitly requested, to explore and clarify members' interactions and emotional efforts. The members are able to be spontaneous in asking the practitioner for feedback, advice, and assistance in defining alternative roles, forms of expression, and options. The members also readily ask the practitioner to share feelings, opinions, and real-life experiences.

Practitioner Issues

The practitioner is affected in positive ways by the group's open ambiance and productivity. The group worker's opportunities to fully use skill and empathy without meeting resistance and fear, along with the members' activity in looking back on their own and the group's change processes, yields a feeling of professionalism and competence. One risk the practitioner faces at this time comes from feeling lulled into a sense—albeit a positive one—of not being needed anymore; this may result in relaxing involvement and directiveness. The practitioner is also at risk of not being able to admit to a lack of resources, and to professional and personal limitations.

Practitioner Role

At this time the practitioner is in a position to confront the members and their processes to motivate action. The group is strong enough in values, norms, and structure to work on itself while being aware of the changes everyone is going through. The practitioner assists the members in enhancing their abilities to explore and clarify issues that will help them to focus their efforts in more productive directions; helping the group explore and resolve its conflicts is also needed at this juncture. Sharing feelings of vulnerability and frailties, as well as capabilities and successes, that relate directly to the members' needs is necessary. This heightens mutuality and closeness in order to enable even more detailed and complex processes to unfold.

Illustration

As the men in a male support group are coming into the meeting, they are talking animatedly. Ralph, the practitioner, enters the group and finds a seat. Greetings are exchanged. Bart, looking to Ralph, says, "We've been talking about the shit that goes down at work where we don't sit with the white guys or the Hispanics." Maurice chimes in, "It's the way of the world; it's dumb, forget it. It won't change." Andy says, "Absolutely. In here we talk about making contact with other men at lunch and break times, and then we group off, just like when we go home to our neighborhoods. I met Raphael on the bus the other morning; he was talking Spanish with some guy. He said, 'Good morning,' then went back to talking. I could have punched him. But I also realized I'm into my own stuff too with you guys."

Jerry says that he and his wife went to a jazz club with Red and Bertha, a white couple: "It was a real good time . . . and we joked about racial barriers that are here, Ralph." Ralph says, "Racial barriers are definitely part of the need people have to band together, like in this group. People make friends and they're also forced to congregate in neighborhoods with their own kind. Your motives are mixed, too. You partly come here so you can 'integrate' the scene, and advance on your jobs, right, huh?"

Rick says that Ralph is damn right, that "this is the way the business world turns in America, and I'm getting on the carousel with the white horses." Ralph comments, "There's that theme of bitterness that comes up." Maurice says, "Come on, Ralph, you told us about how you were going back and forth with your colleagues, the white ones you work with." (Ralph is with the union's Employee Assistance Program.) Ralph says, "Ooooshhh. You caught me. What the hell, I am as real and fake as each of you, and as the scenes out there. This is the point, cutting through it to be with others; it's a tough dream."

The discussion goes on, with the men—including the practitioner—talking about whether it's worth it to try to cut through barriers, with some of the bitterness surfacing, and more discussion about how to try for the dream.

Discussion

The practitioner is easily a part of this process. At the beginning, the members spontaneously tell him about their perceptions concerning how they separate themselves from the white men during lunch. They express a comfort with his role as practitioner, and an ease in talking with him openly about what they are feeling. The practitioner is able to actively listen to their issues, and to confront their ambivalent feelings about overcoming racial barriers. In addition, he is able to point out the theme of bitterness that seems to recur in the group without incurring defensiveness on the part of the members.

When a member points out that the practitioner, too, bounces back and forth between his white colleagues and his black ones, he does not become defensive. Rather, the practitioner reacts honestly to the observation and uses his own feelings to nudge the group into further work. As the work continues, the practitioner remains part of the process.

Stage Theme 7: Just a Little Longer

Boston Model Stage	*T-Group Stage*	*Values and Norms*
5 (Separation)	Consensual Validation	Self-determination
		Difference is enriching.

As time approaches for the group to end its experiences together—to disband—the members may spend difficult amounts of time in interpersonal forms and themes that appear to be like those of earlier stages. The latent objective of this particular process is to convince the practitioner that they need the group "just a little longer," that there is yet more work to be completed and that things are not as good as they seem. As anger and disappointment mount, both members and the practitioner become targets. Members directly and indirectly act as though their interpersonal skills, problem-solving capacities, and abilities to be close are not as well-integrated as they appeared to have been.

On the other hand, when the members connect to the processes and the fact of ending, facing the disappointments and anger, they also come to terms with their accomplishments. They take pride in their experiences and relationships. The practitioner is asked to provide support and to reinforce their capabilities to use what they have learned in order to move ahead into enhanced interactions and new experiences.

Practitioner Issues

In this period, a practitioner with a strong attachment to the group and its members is vulnerable to difficulty in separating from them, colluding with the members' doubts about their accomplishments and competencies. The practitioner may also regress to using earlier types of interventions to deal with the group's reaction out of the fear that the group really is regressing and/or unaccomplished, that it really has had a fragile learning experience. The practitioner may not recognize the members' doubts as their symbolic expressions of not wanting to end. The practitioner also may not recognize his or her own desire to remain within this group setting as a reflection of anxiety about other challenging and unpredictable professional experiences. An additional dimension is brought about by fears regarding unfinished issues—have members been sufficiently helped to do well?—as well as the concomitant vanity that the process has not had a perfect ending.

Practitioner Role

The practitioner's reaction during the ending phase should be governed—as with all practitioner reactions at any point in time—by the values and norms of the humanistic group work method. Its values and standards of interaction continually lead to a recognition that people are interdependent in mutually supportive ways, and that each is as purposefully motivated as the other. Furthermore, people remember one another after the group experience because it is human nature to be social rather than asocial. The humanistic method enhances these characteristics.

The practitioner acknowledges how all participants—practitioner and members alike—are approaching and avoiding, and how all are having difficulty going on to other situations. The practitioner also helps members accept the imperfections of endings. The importance of valuing the memories of the experience is stressed as well; the practitioner shares his or her own feelings about the meaning of the experience, about ending with these particular people, and about plans for future professional projects.

Illustration

The discharge planning group is in its ninth (and next to last) session on the inpatient adolescent psychiatric unit. Marsha, the practitioner, has spent the last two hours contacting schools, workshops, residences, and families to help develop plans for each girl when she leaves. The girls, too, had been asked to find out information from staff about places where they would be going. Marsha walks in, clipboard and lists in hand, greeting the girls. She begins the meeting by telling them she's got more information to add to what they already know.

As the practitioner is about to continue, Hilda falls to the floor, with head between her legs and sobbing. Marsha and a couple of the other girls crouch to hold her. Hilda sobs, "It's there again. My brother and his wife won't let me come to live with them in their house. I have to go to the group residence in Queens. I hate that place. I will be back here again in two months, mark my words!"

Amy and Rose help Hilda get up, hug her and say (almost simultaneously), "Look, Hildie, you and I and Rosie here, and Toni too, we will see each other weekly in the aftercare group, and at Gregory's where the cutest 'bods' hang out." "Come on, Hilda, don't get sucked into your brother saving you and giving up his wife for his younger sister; please don't!"

Silence falls on the sound of this poignant and defensive issue that Hilda has been on for years. Hilda remains silent. Marsha does not focus on this painful issue; she lets the silence continue, then says, "Rose, what have you found about the aftercare program?" Rose talks about the chance to live in supportive apartments when she gets stronger. More members share information; Hilda is paying attention.

Near the end of the session, the girls sit in dyads, identifying chores to carry out for next week's information-gathering assignments. Marsha asks the dyads to report back to the whole group as to their individual assignments, whereupon she writes a note for each member with her assignment on it.

After the session, Marsha somewhat anxiously runs to her office to call the residence that Hilda is going to. She leaves a message that she will call back, "but Judy can try to call me too. I'm here all day." Marsha goes on to supervision.

Discussion

In this meeting, the practitioner is very much a part of the group's ending process. She has helped them maintain their autonomy in spite of the possibility that they may regress at the group's end and upon discharge from the hospital, by structuring assignments for each girl that involve partial planning for her own aftercare.

The practitioner chooses to allow Hilda to remain silent after her outburst, and not focus on her sad feelings of abandonment and rejection by her brother that have been triggered off by the discharge from the hospital. Her threat to return validates her special vulnerability when she is faced with endings. The practitioner recognizes this vulnerability when, at the close of the meeting, she puts in the call to the aftercare worker. The group members, recognizing Hilda's recurring issue, help her face her present reality and offer their support to her in the aftercare program. Thus it is not necessary for the practitioner to intervene. In fact, during the "just a little longer" period, it is most necessary for members to experience their abilities to take responsibility for one another so as to foster confidence in their autonomy and capability in their future enterprise. (For clarification of stage themes, practitioner issues, and practitioner roles, see Table 3.2.)

Table 3.2
Stage Themes and the Practitioner

Stage Themes	*Practitioner Issues*	*Practitioner Role*
Stage Theme 1 "We're Not in Charge" Members look to worker for cues; size up worker and members	Invests in group's success, in own success. May relinquish own responsibility to avoid anxiety	Sanctions expression of feeling toward worker & group; connects talk about past group & worker to present group. Invites trust; identifies common needs
Stage Theme 2 "We Are in Charge" Looking to each other for cues; ignore worker; vie for leadership; pecking orders	Feels tense, ineffectual; anxious in reaction to group battle for control over controls to assert authority, or abdicates to placate	Helps group own its needs & conflicts; helps group see frustration of struggle to control group
Stage Theme 3 "We're Taking You On" Develop strength to ask worker, "What are you doing here?"	Doubts skill; fears group; sidesteps by recontracting or redefinition of worker's role	Encourages exploration of feelings toward worker; presents stake and role in group
Stage Theme 4 Sanctuary Members feel good about group: "This group is wonderful."	May avoid intimacy by withdrawing; may over engage in feelings of cohesion and intimacy	Encourages exploration of direction of intimacy; reflects good feelings; recognizes differences
Stage Theme 5 "This Isn't Good Anymore" Members feel disappointed in group; move to disband	Rescues group; sidesteps negatives; blames self or is angry at group	Encourages exploration of negatives; exhibits confidence in group capacity
Stage Theme 6 "We're Okay and Able" Members feel hope; work to achieve goals	May relax direction in face of positive; May fear sharing positive and negative options & feelings	Focuses, guides group desire to work; encourages ownership of experience; shares in effort
Stage Theme 7 "Just a Little Longer" Members try to stay; doubt accomplishments; consider future options	Joins in doubts about accomplishments; joins regression to earlier worker forms of behavior; prolongs the end; fears separation	Encourages exploration of regressive trends; shares feelings about leaving; identifies future options

SUMMARY

This chapter has established and identified seven stage themes as patterned and sequenced changes in group life. These are (1) "We're Not in Charge"; (2) "We Are in Charge"; (3) "We're Taking You On"; (4) Sanctuary, (5) "This Isn't Good Anymore"; (6) "We're Okay and Able"; and (7) "Just a Little Longer."

The chapter has delineated practice principles associated with each of the themes. These include taking responsibility for helping members affiliate at the start, helping the group challenge the practitioner's authority, supporting and taking part in closeness with the members, prodding the work effort, accepting negative feelings, and helping members end the group.

The special vulnerabilities the practitioner may expect to experience during each have been identified. These include the desire to avoid responsibility for his or her own membership in the group, subverting the group's challenge to authority, denying professional limitations, and avoiding endings.

The humanistic values and democratic norms as enriching forces in the process were shown during each of the stage themes.

Part II

DUAL OBJECTIVES AND TECHNIQUES OF HUMANISTIC GROUP WORK

Chapter 4

THE DUAL OBJECTIVES

In the description of the humanistic method of group work, emphasis has been placed on the importance of the practitioner comprehending, owning, and expressing humanistic values through attitudes and interactions. Given this state of affairs—the relation of values and norms to degrees of interpersonal expression—it is important to recognize that it is by design and practice skill that the group work practitioner helps members attain experiences and resources that are meaningful for them and others in their lives.

THE DUAL OBJECTIVES:
DEVELOPING THE DEMOCRATIC MUTUAL
AID SYSTEM AND ACTUALIZING PURPOSE

The practitioner of humanistic group work attempts to effect two complementary objectives (Glassman & Kates, 1986a). The first is the *development of the democratic mutual aid system*; the second is the *actualization of purpose*. These objectives are addressed, worked on, and worked through during the entirety of the group's life. Their interactions occur with different intensities in the different stages in the group's evolution.

Developing the Democratic Mutual Aid System

The first objective, developing the democratic mutual aid system, addresses the domain of process and the multiplicity of transactions that evolve (Garvin, 1985). To aid in the development of a democratic mutual aid system, the practitioner assists the members according to their capabilities and needs in developing genuine and productive ways of interacting. It is important from the first contacts with the members for the practitioner to express humanistic values and to exemplify democratic forms of interaction as powerful means for the change process.

It is not a fait accompli that people will employ values and norms that are expansive, inclusive, and considerate of one another's differences. This will depend on their prior social experiences, and current social skills and limitations. This is a crucial fact to comprehend and incorporate. The practitioner must work with the members, taking their social skills into account, filling in with professional, institutional, and technical support when necessary. The members' attentions are drawn to the effects their interactions are having in providing one another with opportunities to gain from experiences, while making certain that the nature of their interactions is not at any one member's or the group's expense.

The evolution of a democratic mutual aid system as a series of helping experiences occurs earlier in group life than the actualization of purpose. This milieu provides the medium within which purpose is elaborated. Lang (1981) supports this view. She suggests that the guiding, building, and owning of a democratic group occurs in the early stages of group development, during which members and the worker are concerned with affiliation issues including those of power, authority, and trust. Lang further proposes that the practitioner must pay careful and sensitive attention to helping the members develop norms that foster democratic values and egalitarian sharing so that a democratic group can form, rather than one where the most powerful dominate.

Lang (1981) further suggests that—lest a group form with norms destructive to the human spirit—the practitioner must not rush the process or it will be affected by anxiety and arbitrariness. The early formation stages should be prolonged. The practitioner should directly point out when the group is speeding the process, and empathically subdue the group's pressure to move too quickly and deeply into working on the members' needs without attending to the effect of values that are extant in the group's interpersonal process. The practitioner helps members to consider how they are valuing one another, directing them to open up their modes of interaction for the scrutiny and participation of all members. In helping the group to be patient with its process, the practitioner recommends, exemplifies, and supports the use of humanistic values and democratic norms. The practitioner may also help members face interactional limitations that inhibit social cooperation. Time is very rarely of such an essence that the group's decision-making processes should be rushed forward. Should there be a real need for speed, it will be met by the members.

When members move too quickly to meet their needs without having developed different mediums for the experience, the group may meet the needs of some members—to certain degrees—without truly challenging all of the members to real efforts and changes. The group may begin to disband after the first few sessions, because the members can neither protect themselves from one anothers' demands, handle their anxieties, nor meet their needs.

Important in developing the democratic mutual aid system are the members' abilities to gain understanding of themselves as a group and their relation to the authority of the practitioner. In a humanistic group the members develop and enhance their abilities to view, question, and challenge the professional role, position, and functions of the practitioner in an open manner within the group's process. This subsequently enables a distribution of power between the practitioner and the members (Glassman & Kates, 1983).

Other group forms addressing themes familiar to social group work omit or pay little attention in their design to the specific and purposeful development of a democratic mutual aid system. For instance, the structured group—where agendas are made entirely by the "leader"—is not built upon the group's ability to develop its own power and participation dynamics, design its own agendas, question the leader's authority, and extend its life outside the auspices of the group's meeting time (Papell & Rothman, 1980b). While these groups may utilize discussion methods with a high level of member participation, they do not address the issue of the distribution of power in, and ownership of, the group experience in its complete form (see Chapter 10 for discussion of humanistic group work approaches in open-ended groups [Galinsky & Schopler, 1987] and collectivities [Lang, 1986]). Some of these groups are for parent effectiveness, assertiveness training, and psycho-education. Groups designed primarily as politicized social-change agents also do not systematically establish democratic processes that express the members' humanistic values. Quality-circle groups in industry (Middleman, 1981b), while capitalizing on members' high commitments to each other and the work at hand, run the risk of exploiting members through autocratic leadership structures. While some mutual aid is felt in these several group types, the active examination of power and authority relationships is not explicitly built into their designs.

After the resolution of power and authority issues that revolve around the practitioner's role, as well as some members' needs to control, members in a humanistic group experience stronger processes of cohesion. Leadership issues among the members of how they will allow and encourage each other to take initiative—and when they will follow, yield, and lead—will become more resolved. This becomes a turning point for the members and practitioner. Establishment of patterns of working together then permits the group to move on to purposeful change.

Actualizing Purpose

Actualizing group purpose, the second objective, centers on the individual and collective goals to be worked on in the process. From the start of the process, the members try in different ways to pursue the issues that have brought them together. After the practitioner's efforts have focused on establishing a democratic arena for caring, mutual aid, decision making, and participating, the practitioner's efforts turn to helping the members meet their needs for personal and environmental change. Now group and member goals are more explicitly examined by the practitioner and the members.

As the practitioner pursues the actualization of purpose, he or she draws the members into dealing with issues related to purpose and process in order to work on their goals in interactional terms. Groups lacking a clear sense of how they are pursuing their purpose use the supportive environment they have constructed as a sanctuary, shielding them from the role responsibilities of life. If the group is composed of abusing parents, then the safe haven of mutual aid without a focus on inhibiting acts of abuse will be what Shulman (1984) calls an "illusion of work" (p. 71). The safe haven must be used purposefully and productively to help members take steps (and risks) to more effective role performance. By the same token, a support group for alcoholics will not meet its objectives if the norms and actions that are necessary to help maintain sobriety are not part of the process.

The practitioner helps the members further their purpose by helping them experience meaningful types of interactions in a variety of ways and situations. The humanistic group is constituted to examine and enhance members' psychosocial functioning and qualities of life, in relation to selected psychosocial phenomena such as aging, parenting, employee relations, community relations, mental or physical illness, and life-cycle socialization issues. The commonality of theme and interest brings each group together and motivates its work. Members experience an enhancement of role abilities in the middle-phase processes when purposes are actualized. Prior establishment of democratic ways of interacting now assists the members in working on and through purposeful and focused change. Members gain clarity through examining each other's life-space issues and behaviors. This helps them to take risks and experiment with changing unhelpful patterns and actions. Members are able to accept their own and each other's weaknesses and strengths in the group, and to transfer these attitudes and abilities into their life-space situations.

The more traditional psychoanalytic-therapy groups, wherein psychosocial issues are secondary to personality change, are aimed at heightening and working out transferential reactions to others, rather that working on adaptations in effective social life. These groups rely less on the group as a social and democratic entity to promote participants' changes, and more on the group as a vehicle for fostering and heightening the idiosyncratic transferential distortions that come up among the participants and therapists. As a rule, members are discouraged from seeing one another outside of the psychotherapy group in the "real social environment" (except perhaps in a structured "alternate session" without the therapist). This is done so that the transference is not diluted.

In humanistic social group work, the "real" milieus are the central foci of the group's experience within, as well as external to, its formal sessions. The group's ability to plan and produce programmatic events that enhance social functioning and quality of life is a special feature of group work method. This feature is the group's "externality" (Papell & Rothman, 1980b), that is, its ability to exist outside of the meeting time.

Practitioners in other group approaches also make efforts to develop groups grounded in values that are humanistic and democratic. Groups such as T-groups, leadership training groups, and education groups are quite concerned with members' rights, due process, decision-making abilities, abilities to cope with group pressure to conform, and diversity as a positive value (House Plan Association, 1965; National Training Laboratory, 1966/1967). Other group approaches—more oriented toward treatment, rehabilitation, or remediation—use processes of acceptance, belonging, and inclusion as means for helping members grow and change, but do not systematically propose these processes as central to the organization of group experiences. What is unique in humanistic group work is the explicit development of a democratic group form *in conjunction with* the actualization of group purpose.

This unique combination of process and purpose has significant practical implications. For the social action group, it places negative sanctions on overly rigid and dictatorial attempts to develop change tactics that are at the expense of members' feelings, due process, collective decision making, and rights. Rather, both democratic process and purpose-related outcomes go hand in hand in a means-ends relationship. In the social work clinical treatment group, members examine what is dysfunctional in their self-expressions to actualize purpose and simultaneously review, own, and modify relationships with each other and the practitioner as an experiential opportunity and as a responsibility of group membership. This effort is immediately brought into relationships with significant others in the members' own lives.

DUAL OBJECTIVES AND STAGE THEMES

There is also a relationship between the dual objectives and themes in the group's stages of development. Members in the processes of Themes 1, 2, and 3 ("We're Not in Charge," "We Are in Charge," and "We're Taking You On") in effect end up evolving and strengthening their interactions for developing and sustaining their mutual aid systems.

Throughout this process the members essentially focus on building cohesion, with less concentration on the more difficult issues of personal change in the group and the environment. Once the group basks in the intensely felt safety of Theme 4 (Sanctuary) there is a turning point, and members' efforts shift from group process to purpose-related efforts. The myth of the group as deity (Bion, 1959) is relinquished as members move on to the current realities of the work at hand. The dynamics of Themes 5 and 6 ("This Isn't Good Anymore" and "We're Okay and Able") are related to the frustrations and accomplishments of undertaking personal and collective efforts to change the dysfunctional behaviors and interpersonal arrangements that comprise the members' collective purpose. In the ending phase, as the issues of prolonging the end become manifest through Theme 7 ("Just a Little Longer"), the members struggle with solidifying and owning what they have learned so they feel confident and better able to function without the group.

DUAL OBJECTIVES AND THE CHANGE PROCESS

The change process involves a continuum of trust, risk, and experimentation. This continuum encompasses the helpful dynamics of the members' working-on and working-through efforts. It results in successes and failures in the members' attempts to change, and to master change. It is repeated any number of times as different aspects of interaction are worked on and through. In the development of the democratic mutual aid system, the continuum occurs as the members build and sustain milieus of cooperation and caring. In actualizing group purpose, the continuum occurs as the members, trusting one another, risk changing ineffective actions and patterns.

In long-term groups the change effort is a complex of events and experiences, usually dealing with personal and group issues that revolve around a panoply of role-enhancing experiences and interactions. In time-limited groups, agendas are less complex, usually relating to one or two specific behaviors for experimentation. The change process nonetheless involves trust, risk, and experimentation, albeit in a more clearly delineated process within a narrow frame of reference.

In the change process, members are held accountable to one another, experience doubts and disappointments, regressions and hurts, and joys and successes, all in an atmosphere of cooperation, effort, and mutual aid. Conflict and confrontation mark the members as participants in a group strong enough to take on difficult issues that are not to be avoided or denied because of fears and anxieties about retributions and rejections.

INTERACTIONS OF THE DUAL OBJECTIVES

As the group is woven with threads of humanistic values and democratic norms, its members develop interactions that are characteristic of the achievement of the dual objectives. The practitioner may use his or her awareness of these interactions as a barometer to evaluate the ups and downs in the process and members, and identify strengths as well as difficulties that occur in meeting these objectives. Members may be directly acquainted with these interactions in order to widen their spectrum of choices and enhance their autonomy. While each of the following interactions occurs throughout the entirety of group life, the two typologies of group member interactions are distinct to each of the dual objectives, having salience to addressing different dilemmas associated with each one of them. Table 4.1 below lists the interactions of the dual objectives.

Forms of Interaction That Foster
the Democratic Mutual Aid System

The interactions expressed as a product of the mutual aid system are reflective of the members' efforts and are consonant with the theme-centered issues of "We're Not in Charge," "We Are in Charge," and "We're Taking You On."

Developing and appreciating democratic norms, which include rights to belong and to be heard. A humanistic group needs to develop conscious understanding and ability to enact democratic norms as the reflection of the explicit values of the method (see Chapters 1 and 2). These values become the property of all, the members as well as the practitioner. The more conscious the members are of the necessity for establishing and safeguarding democratic principles, the more they enhance each member's autonomous functioning. Being heard is reflected when members feel "We're Not in Charge," as well as when they feel "We Are in Charge." Their appreciation of democratic norms as the culmination of accepting that all members have rights to belong in an egalitarian and cooperative system become more intensely highlighted as the members put some of their internal power struggles to rest, adopt standards during their normative crisis, and gather strength to confront the practitioner ("We're Taking You On").

Making decisions and developing rules. Whether implicit or explicit, the members' abilities to make decisions and play by rules govern how

Table 4.1

Interactions of the Dual Objectives

Forms of Interaction That Foster the Democratic Mutual Aid System

The members are:

–Developing and appreciating democratic norms, which include rights to belong and to be heard, to freedom of speech and expression.

–Making decisions and developing rules.

–Developing the leadership and followership skills of cooperation, yielding, listening, flexibility.

–Respecting differences among members.

–Expressing feelings about the practitioner with particular attention to power and authority issues.

–Collectively developing and setting goals that enable the group to move toward purpose.

–Developing a beginning expression of feelings toward members, laying groundwork for future expressions.

–Developing affective bonds and furthering cohesion.

Forms of Interaction That Foster the Actualization of Purpose

The members are:

–Identifying themes to be worked on, e.g., making agendas, prioritizing efforts, dealing flexibly with new issues.

–Taking risks in expressing and experimenting with role-enhancing behaviors.

–Expressing and identifying feelings that help the group and members work on change.

–Sharing perceptions and feelings about each others' behaviors.

–Creating activities in the milieu and external environment to actualize group's externality.

–Identifying group process issues and structures to heighten the group's self-awareness.

–Identifying projections and self-fulfilling prophecies as they interfere with collaboration and role enhancement.

–Reflecting on and reinforcing member and group change in order to motivate change in life space situation.

they deal with one another as the group goes on to actualizing purpose. Members come to terms with issues of cooperation and compromise to enable them to meet all—rather than just some—members' needs. As democratic norms are established that center on equality and participation, decision making requires the members' abilities to stay focused, to draw together, to integrate implicit and explicit demands, and to choose helpful experiences. Effective decision-making processes guard against the surfacing of unbridled interpersonal conflicts during the middle phase, when purpose is being worked on.

Developing leadership and followership skills. At the onset of the normative crisis, the members are faced with the problem of developing a flexible leadership structure, rather than solidifying a rigid and inflexible one in which leadership consistently resides in the hands of a powerful member or clique. In a humanistic group, leadership and followership skills become reciprocal and flexible; they are collectively used. Members take initiative. All can respond according to their needs and the requirements of situations. A preordained, rigidly fixed pecking order (Garland, Jones, & Kolodny, 1973) becomes antithetical to the values and interpersonal objectives of a humanistic group.

Respecting differences among members. This interaction is reflected in the members' abilities to listen to, to respond to, and to incorporate different opinions, values, cultures, and personalities without requiring adherence to a narrow ideology or to a narrow spectrum of permissible behaviors. Veiled reactions or avoidance of differences are brought to the members' attentions.

Expressing feelings about the practitioner with particular attention to authority issues. In all groups, members will have a multiplicity and range of feelings about the practitioner. In many types of groups these feelings will rarely surface, thereby remaining underground and affecting the level of intimacy among the members (Levine, 1979). In the humanistic group this "taboo area" (Shulman, 1984), which includes the feelings about the real and imagined power of the practitioner as well as the practitioner's expectations of the members, is surfaced and aired. Exposure and examination bring about deepened work and feelings of integrity and autonomy from the point of first confrontation (with "We're Taking You On") and thereafter.

Collectively developing and setting goals. The ability to move toward defining and carrying out group purpose is reflected in the humanistic group when the group members are able to work on their relationships to the practitioner. The newfound integrity, autonomy, and strength are then used by the members to focus their collective attention on establishing goals related to the needs of each member. Members engage with the practitioner and one another in sharing leadership, which enables goals to develop.

Expressing feelings toward the members. This newly developing ability is also a direct result of the members' efforts to engage with the practitioner regarding issues of power and authority (Bennis & Shepard, 1962; Garland et al., 1973). Basic acceptance of one another and support of each person's membership and contributions insure future support among members. These dynamics set the stage for future relationships and experiences.

Developing affective bonds and furthering cohesion. For the group to work on difficult tasks related to purpose, cohesive effort and affective bonds have to be substantially in place in the process. With collective well-being, members take the necessary risks to further their activities in the group and in their role relationships outside of the group.

FORMS OF INTERACTION THAT FOSTER
THE ACTUALIZATION OF PURPOSE

These interactions occur more noticeably throughout the middle and ending phases of the group's life, after the members have developed the interactions of the mutual aid system. Herein the themes of Sanctuary, "This Isn't Good Anymore," and "We're Okay and Able" are reflections of the intense desire and frustrations of working and changing. "Just a Little Longer" is a reaction to the members' concerns about moving on in new ways into future experiences, without the actual external social supports provided by the other members and the group milieu.

The following interactions help the members actualize purpose.

Identifying themes to be worked on. Group agendas that meld and distinguish individual interests are identified and refined through the collective participation of all members. Without harnessing productive problem-solving efforts, members will "muck around in the work phase"—finding comfort in relating and belonging, but lacking motivation to change themselves and their situations. Members begin to accomplish more results than the internal time they are in the group would suggest.

Expressing role-enhancing behaviors. It is especially crucial for members to give and to be motivated to carry out different and effective ways of interacting with significant others. Anticipatory planning, role playing, and the programming of in vivo experiences should occur. These offer the members cognitive, emotional, and interactional opportunities for experimentation, observation, and changes of forms of expression that have inhibited as well as have enhanced their abilities.

Expressing and identifying feelings that help the group and members work on change. The change process for members is significantly enhanced by their abilities to identify feelings and actions that are obstacles in situations and in the group experience. At this point, a significant level of trust has developed along with feelings of autonomy and initiative. This condition is sustained into the work stage. This helps members to express their difficult and threatening feelings, motivated and supported by a group norm for change and independence.

Sharing perceptions and feelings about each others behavior. The feedback process is a unique opportunity of group membership. Focusing on the here and now, members learn how their behaviors affect others, and how they in turn are affected by others. This helps them to deal with how they really come across outside of the group. The immediacy of feedback does not support avoidance of face-to-face engagements; it fosters opportunities for concerted change efforts.

Creating activities in the environment. One of the distinguishing features of the social work group is its externality (Papell & Rothman, 1980b). Its members design group life and their relationships within the group to be a part of their actual lives beyond the group meetings. To fulfill the group's objectives the members develop programs in their actual social environments for the group, subgroups, and for significant others. Programming is an important part of the group's expanded effort to enhance and transform social functioning. In planning, members work on anticipatory anxiety and misperception. The program activity itself is an opportunity for role rehearsal, experimentation with different behaviors, and the creation of new environments for experiencing different types of interactions.

Identifying group process issues and structures to heighten the group's self-awareness. Interpersonal learning and enhanced role functioning occur when the members examine and clarify the meaning of the process and social structures that result from and affect change within their interactions. Looking at ongoing processes provides the members with opportunities for clarification of their perceptions, heightening of empathy, and the development of skills in resolving differences. The members' collective abilities to reflect on their history and themes, as well as their content and their allegiances, contribute to their growth. Members can see how allegiances are made for behavioral enhancement or for stagnation and inflexibility, which often is disguised as subgroup agreement that subgroup members are doing well when in fact they are not.

Identifying projections and self-fulfilling prophecies as they interfere with collaboration and role enhancement. Projections and self-fulfilling prophecies are more frequently identified and confronted in interactions, so they do not fester as distortions that interfere with the group's efforts. The ability to sustain meaningful, purposeful relationships will be impeded by a member's projections and self-fulfilling prophesies. The members' negative experiences and unmet needs now become central to interpersonal and inner conflict in group life.

Reflecting on and reinforcing individual and group change in order to replicate change. Much of the work related to the group's purpose involves members' experiments with new behaviors in and out of the group. The change process involves personal struggles to alter dysfunctional or uncomfortable behaviors in the interest of role enhancement and the development of abilities; members give one another mutual support for these undertakings. Members review change processes in order to identify progress and agendas, and to consider the various forms of thinking, feeling, and behaving that have gone into the change and its process.

SUMMARY

The dual objectives of humanistic group work have been identified as *developing the democratic mutual aid system* and *actualizing purpose.* It has been emphasized that the development of democratic processes of mutual aid has to occur before the group works deeply on achieving its purpose.

The relation of the dual objectives to stage themes was delineated. The development of the democratic mutual aid system is related to Stage Themes 1, 2, and 3: "We're Not in Charge," "We Are in Charge," and "We're Taking You On." The actualization of purpose is related to stage themes 4, 5, 6, and 7: Sanctuary, "This Isn't Good Anymore," "We're Okay and Able," and "Just a Little Longer."

Interactions among members that reflect the group's achievement of each of the objectives were identified. Forms of interaction that foster the democratic mutual aid system are: developing democratic norms; making decisions; developing leadership and following skills; respecting differences; expressing feelings about the practitioner; setting goals; beginning to express feelings toward members; and developing cohesion.

Forms of interaction that foster the actualization of purpose are: identifying themes to be worked on; taking risks and experimenting with role enhancement; expressing feelings that help the group work on change; sharing perceptions and feelings about each other's behavior; creating activities; identifying group process issues for group self-awareness; identifying self-fulfilling prophecies that interfere with growth; and reflecting on change in order to replicate it.

Chapter 5

TECHNIQUES FOR THE DEMOCRATIC MUTUAL AID SYSTEM

INTRODUCTION TO TECHNIQUES

Group work techniques are patterned versions of professional self-expression the practitioner uses within the guidelines of the values and norms of humanistic group work to achieve the dual objectives. These techniques represent the collective experiences of group work practitioners who have shared in their development.

Although techniques provide important means of practice, serious concerns have been raised about developing and using them in codified forms. Klein (1970) cautioned that a mechanistic practice would result. Schwartz (1961) addressed this concern, stating that the development of skillful use of technique comes about in the interplay between intuitiveness and technical skill:

> There is nothing in the conception of a professional methodology which denies or subordinates the uniquely personal and artistic component which each worker brings to . . . the helping function. On the contrary, the concept of a disciplined uniqueness is inherent in the definition of art itself. In a broad sense, we may view artistic activity as an attempt . . . to express strong personal feelings and aspirations through a disciplined use of . . . materials. (p. 29)

While these points of view primarily focus on whether or not the practitioner will be inhibited by using predetermined technical patterns and technologies, they also reflect concern for the effect of techniques on the well-being and performance of the group members. Both the members and the practitioner are in the same milieu, trying to assist one another in maintaining and achieving effective interpersonal relations and situations for the members. Concern that members will be manipulated, coerced, and controlled by the practitioner's use of technique is important. Schwartz (1961), by focusing on the artistry of the practitioner, indirectly addresses this concern. Within this frame of reference, the practitioner can be both disciplined and creative, unique and individual. By extension, members also can share these characteristics.

The concern that techniques can be used incorrectly and dangerously is important to consider. The expression of ingratiating attitudes or aggressive emotions by a practitioner can stimulate threat, anxiety, awe, and submission. The expression of technique within an attitude of neutrality and scientific curiosity can also elicit anxiety and concern. The combination of technical patterns and procedures, along with certain attitudes and emotions, can have a powerful numbing or controlling effect on group members. Safeguards are important. They must be built into the practitioner's methodology, ideology, and use of techniques.

Techniques in the humanistic method of group work have safeguards. These are the feelings, ideas, and interactions that result from humanistic values and democratic norms. These govern the practitioner's self-expression and view of the members. The application of techniques requires cognitive, affective, and purposeful use of self within the values and norms of the method. In humanistic group work, the explicit and sanctioned values and norms are humanistic and democratic. One reason for this is because the social work profession adheres to these values and norms. In addition, group work has built on and developed these values and norms throughout its history. Within the heritages of the social goals, remedial, reciprocal, and mainstream models, the social group work method explicates these humanistic values and democratic norms (Papell & Rothman, 1980a, 1980b).

Techniques for practice are the product of views about people, what they are like, how they can handle themselves, what they will become, and how they should treat (and be treated) by one another. Authoritarian or utilitarian values will yield techniques and their expression that may limit people's potentials and, even worse, denigrate and control them.

The process and outcome in group work are reflections of both the practitioner and the setting. Technique, then, is one among a number of significant features of the whole of the method of humanistic social group work. The values, norms, unique dual objectives of the method, and stances of the practitioner are fundamentally significant features, as well.

USE OF TECHNIQUE

A practice theory of technique is also related to professional and methodological imperatives. First, professionals practicing a humanistic group form need to attend to the quality of their work: to be responsible for it, to monitor it, to criticize it, and to convey it to others. Developing and conveying techniques creates a medium for criticism, refinement, and accountability. Second, the use of technique creates a self-awareness on the practitioner's part about the various and multiple effects that his or her behavior is having on group members. This ensures that the practitioner's uses of technique are neither mechanistic, impersonal, nor unempathic.

With a constellation of techniques that is transmittable and refinable follows the ability to discern the details of members' responses to them. Techniques are responded to by the members, who contribute to and propel additional aspects of the process as well as the use of different techniques. Because techniques are a creative blend of acts, ideas, and feelings, they can be flexibly and creatively expressed and applied. Techniques are used to assist in shaping the group members' processes of interaction and self-expression.

In the humanistic group method, techniques are both the means and ends of interpersonal processes that assist the group members in becoming effective. Techniques are not mechanical devices to manipulate, control, or condition behavior. They are guidelines, exemplars, and directions for how people can interact with one another in cooperative and differentiated ways within the group and in other social environments. Techniques are meant to be used in ways that are empathically sensitive to and actively responsive to the expectations and needs of the members. They can be expressed in full or partial forms, as well as in combination with one another. How techniques are expressed is a function of the needs of the members as felt and perceived by the practitioner through his or her spontaneous, conscious, intuitive, and empathic interaction with the members.

CATEGORIZING TECHNIQUES

A practice theory of technique that is directly related to the goals of helping members attain flexible and satisfying forms of interpersonal expression is related to social scientific and practical observations. Therefore, techniques have been identified and categorized according to their use in achieving each of the dual objectives (Glassman & Kates, 1986a).

The first set are the techniques for developing the democratic mutual aid system. These techniques assist the members in being attentive to and developing the process of mutual aid, which will be discussed in this chapter. The second set, techniques for actualizing purpose, consists of those which are used to assist members in focusing on and changing the characteristic patterns of interactions and environmental circumstances that have brought them to the group. These techniques will be discussed in Chapters 6 and 7. While each of these sets of techniques is primarily related to developing the specific interactions of the dual objectives, they occur in interrelated ways throughout. Those techniques related to developing the democratic mutual aid system will be used more frequently earlier on, and those related to purpose later on.

A third set of techniques serves to develop the democratic mutual aid system *and* actualize purpose. This set refers to techniques interwoven throughout the entire process, and will be discussed in Chapter 8.

Twenty-nine techniques that practitioners use to achieve the dual objectives of the humanistic group have been identified; these are shown in Table 5.1.

TECHNIQUES FOR DEVELOPING THE
DEMOCRATIC MUTUAL AID SYSTEM

The earlier discussion of the dual objectives of the humanistic method pointed out that the practitioner's primary activity at the start is to help the members develop a democratic mutual aid system. Among the 29 identified group work techniques used by practitioners, nine have been developed and are used to assist the members in achieving

Table 5.1

Techniques in Relationship to the Dual Objectives

Techniques related to Mutual Aid System	Techniques Related to Actualizing Purpose	Techniques Woven in Both Objectives
Facilitating Collective Participation	Role Rehearsal	Demand for Work
Scanning	Programming	Directing
Engaging Group as a Whole	Group Reflective Consideration	Lending a Vision
		Staying with Feelings
Modulating Expression of Feeling	Interpretation	Silence
Facilitating Decision-Making Processes	Feedback	Support
	Data and Facts	Exploration
	Self Disclosure	Identification
Processing the Here and Now	Conflict Resolution	
Expressing Feelings about Practitioner Role	Group Mending	
	Confrontation	
Goal Setting	Dealing with Unknown	
Good and Welfare	Taking Stock	

this objective. These are *facilitating collective participation, scanning, engaging the group as a whole, modulating the expression of feelings, facilitating decision-making processes, processing the here and now, expressing feelings about the practitioner role, goal setting,* and *good and welfare.*

Each of these techniques also has a relationship to the interactions of the democratic mutual aid system. For clarification, see Table 5.2.

Facilitating Collective Participation

This technique is used to foster the acceptance and right of all members to belong, as well as to acknowledge their special importance because of their unique qualities.

The practitioner openly invites members to participate by encouraging opinions from all, with careful attention to those who have not yet offered them. By pointing out to the group when someone is trying to interact, the practitioner creates emotional space for all, while at the same time helping the group see that responsibility for making space for each other is in the group's—not just the practitioner's—domain. By redirecting members to speak *to* one another, not about each other,

Table 5.2

Techniques in Relationship to the Interactions of the
Democratic Mutual Aid System

Technique	Interaction
Facilitating Collective Participation	Develop cohesion and affective bonds
Scanning	Develop cohesion and affective bonds
Engaging the Group as a Whole	Develop cohesion and affective bonds
Modulating the Expression of Feeling	Express feelings Respect differences Develop rules Develop cohesion and affective bonds
Facilitating Decision-Making Processes	Enhance decision making and development of rules Develop leadership & followership skills Collectively develop & set goals Respect differences
Processing the Here and Now	Foster expression of feelings Develop cohesion and affective bonds Develop democratic norms—belonging, inclusion, being heard
Expressing Feelings About the Practitioner Role	Foster expression of feelings Develop affective bonds and cohesion Develop democratic norms—belonging, inclusion, being heard
Goal Setting	Collectively set goals Develop cohesion and affective bonds
Good and Welfare	Respecting differences Develop cohesion and affective bonds Develop democratic norms—belonging, inclusion, being heard, owning the group

the practitioner places further emphasis on the group's responsibility for including each other and in valuing each member's expression. The practitioner also points out when members are inattentive, thereby avoiding risks of misinterpretations and misunderstandings. The practitioner fosters participation by asking the members to build on what is being expressed and systematically inviting members to take part in relation to things that have been expressed by others.

Illustration

In a socialization group of nine- to ten-year-old boys at the child guidance clinic, Freddie is telling everyone how bugged he gets when the teacher yells at him to stop talking, when it's usually his neighbor who gets him into trouble. Dave, the practitioner, notices that the boys want to participate, but they don't know whether or not to interrupt Freddie. He says, "Freddie, stop a minute, I think there might be others who have similar problems." Several boys give Freddie support and share similar experiences about their relationships to their teachers.

The practitioner notes that Joey, who is Hispanic and usually rather shy but attentive to the process, is exhibiting his usual quietness during this time. He turns to Joey, saying, "I noticed you've been listening quietly; do you have something about this topic that you could tell us? How is it with you and your teachers?" Joey tells the group that he didn't like his teacher at first because she was strict, but now she has been nice. And she's not that bad, she just has to be strict because of some of the children's behavior. The practitioner asks the group, "How do you react to what Joey said; is this similar for any of you? Can any of you see yourselves changing your minds about your teachers?" The members talk more about how they have gotten to like a couple of teachers better, and what they could do to improve their relations with them, such as "being quiet, doing homework, listening in class, and not fighting." One member, Ivan, the child of Russian immigrants, makes a comment which is bypassed: "My teacher is mean to me, even when I am good." The practitioner says, "Wait, you guys didn't respond to what Ivan has just said. How do you react to that?" The children talk about how hard it is when they are judged unfairly. The practitioner asks the group to "tell Ivan, because you sound like you're talking about him, not to him, although he's here."

Discussion

This use of the technique sets the stage for the group to learn to include each of the members, by responding directly to them through exploratory questions, affirmation, or just acknowledgments. The practitioner stops Freddie from talking too much and possibly losing the group, which might make it more difficult for him to feel commonality with others. Upon hearing the members' experiences, he elicits more responses directed toward Freddie and among the others.

In this group, Joey is more representative of the black and Hispanic boys in the group; Ivan is the child of Russian refugees, the only one in the group. It is possible that he was feeling distinctly different, as well as being perceived as different, by the other members. These feelings and perceptions may make it harder for a member to feel included and to be included. Thus the practitioner makes a special effort to foster the inclusion of Ivan by not permitting his concern to be bypassed. Inclusion of Ivan may turn out to be complex, due to his unique ethnic difference; by using this technique to involve Ivan, the practitioner sets the stage for helping members respond to him.

Scanning (Shulman, 1981)

Scanning is used to help the group practitioner focus on and become more sensitive to the entire group, beyond any one person who happens to be the center of focus at the moment. It is also used to strengthen cohesion and affective bonds. Perceptions gained from scanning may be shared with the group either at that moment or at a later time.

To enact this technique the practitioner looks from person to person, sometimes to the person being addressed by the speaker, and then around the room to observe, acknowledge, and incorporate the group's full nonverbal expression. Leaning forward, listening attentively, responding to outside distractions, being tuned out, and talking to each other are some of the behaviors the practitioner makes sure to note. By looking around, the practitioner tries to take in the dominant affect of the group at that moment, as well as the possibility that several affects may be concurrent. This technique enables the practitioner to be in touch with the person who is talking, and to be with the group as well (Shulman, 1981). It is used in all forms of group life—during discussion, silences, and activities. The practitioner may be selective about when to make or not make eye contact with members. Eye contact may stimulate the member to respond to the practitioner, when that was not the intention. The practitioner may also test out to see who is willing or not willing to make eye contact with him or her, but usually does not hold the eye contact.

If the practitioner feels vague or confused about the process, scanning can often provide the stimulus for a new empathic awareness. Eventually, members learn to imitate the practitioner's scanning, and therefore to tune in more sensitively to each other as they conduct their work into later stages of the process.

Illustration

A community planning group, made up of a cross section of residents and professionals in one particular neighborhood of a large urban setting, was developed recently to explore the housing crisis in the neighborhood. The group convener, Annette, is the director of the local voluntary agency serving the homeless. Three members are talking busily about trying to get one of the local churches to develop a day program for the homeless. This would not only keep people off the street, but would also give the small-but-dedicated staff a chance to try to get some entitlements for people and do some long-range planning for them.

While slowly looking from person to person, Annette notices another two members looking at each other and still another one silently withdrawing, projecting opposite feelings from the tenor of the three-way discussion. She becomes sensitive to their anxiety about being able to take part, and draws in those members by saying, "I notice some of you are more involved, others are less involved. Any sense of what this means to you and our process?"

Discussion

The idea of a day program for the homeless was an action that the group convener favored. However, for it to happen, the full support of this group would be necessary. Thus as a group convener with an executive leadership role as well, Annette had to bring everyone aboard, make room for their doubts and concerns to be expressed, and (if the idea was to materialize) to enable everyone to own the results by participating in the process. On the other hand—even after full discussion—the withdrawing silent members might never have come around to liking the program idea, thus forcing it to be dropped. While this might be a disappointment to the group convener, it is better to drop the idea now than to ignore the disapproval, push it through the process only to have it aborted later on, and be embarrassed by a public display by disapproving factions.

Scanning the group is necessary, whether or not the group convener or practitioner is positively oriented toward the topic being discussed. Scanning holds the practitioner to the purpose of strengthening the development of a democratic mutual aid process. Had Annette been swept away by the threesome's agreement with her own goals, she would have lost her potential to be with everyone in the group, rather than just those who represented what she wanted to accomplish. In the long run, her leadership capability and credibility may be strengthened by her show of commitment to including everyone's ideas and participation in the process. With this kind of leadership, members in this task force may more easily become aware of her demonstration of respect for their perceptions.

Engaging the Group as a Whole

In many instances, beginning practitioners with groups experience great difficulty in engaging with and addressing the group as a whole. They address only individuals, leaving out a spectrum of connections that may be used and processed by the entire group. As a result, members imitate the practitioner's behaviors, hardly ever addressing the group in its entirety. An intent of the technique that follows is to establish and strengthen the identity and cohesion of the group in order to draw on its energy as a collective.

The practitioner uses pronouns that serve as metaphors for the humanistic social work group. Sometimes the practitioner uses "we" and "ours"; at other times, the practitioner uses "you" and "yours." Through the use of this technique the members are helped to differentiate between the domain of the group including the practitioner, and the domain of the group excluding the practitioner. The use of "we" and "our" refers to and strengthens the human feeling of the group including the practitioner, and connotes a common stake in the process and life of the group. By using "you" and "yours," the group practitioner acknowledges the reality of the uniqueness of the members' experiences, and their separateness from his or her own experiences.

It is not uncommon for group work practitioners to use only "we" and "ours," avoiding the use of "you" and "yours." While many do this from an egalitarian or humanistic perspective, rather than from a manipulative one, it appears that this strategy represents a failure to differentiate the uniqueness of the practitioner's role within the domain of membership in the group. When the practitioner conceives of himself or herself only as part of the collective, then "we" is used manipulatively—disguising the practitioner's power in the group and diverting the members from dealing with the different status, power, and authority issues the practitioner's activities yield. On the other hand, some group practitioners use only "you" and "yours," as if they are not members or have no stake in the group's outcomes. This represents an inauthentic differentiation that does not account for the intersubjective nature of the group's experience for both the practitioner and the members. Falck (1988) has noted that all are members in the group, sharing a stake in the process. Simultaneously, though, each person's membership is unique. Not only does the practitioner have a special role and unique stake in the process, but in that role the practitioner also carries more power and authority than any single member.

The group practitioner consciously uses the humanistic group work method toward fulfilling members' collective needs, not the practitioner's needs. Therefore, the practitioner is sometimes part of the "we" of the group, and sometimes part of the "I" and "you" of the group.

Illustration

The members of a teen group in a community center are talking about how they want to run a fund-raising program so they can collect money to go on a day trip to a large amusement park in the next state. Many ideas are bandied about—a cake sale, a dance at the center, a talent show, or a combination of these. The practitioner, Tim, says, "You've got lots of good ideas for raising money so we can get to Paradise Park." The kids then begin to talk about trying to include another teen group. The practitioner says, "One of us needs to talk to them about it. Shall I talk to their worker, or do you want to talk to their worker, or to the group? If it's really going to happen, then I guess we'd need a joint meeting."

Discussion

The first statement made by Tim acknowledges the group's collective investment in going to the amusement park, while at the same time noting that the practitioner plans to go with the group in his role as group worker. In this case, the practitioner does not offer the ideas for the fundraiser—rather, the teens did. It is not the practitioner who needs funding for the event (the agency covers his fees); rather it is the teens. On the other hand, for the practitioner to have said that, "you can get to Paradise Park" would have been unreal and inappropriate, because the person from the agency who usually accompanies the teens on outings is the group worker. Here a "you" statement would have stranded the teens, because it could be seen as an abdication of role responsibility. At least, it would have required an explanation.

Not only does the use of "we" and "you" differentiate the teens from the worker within the group meeting, but it also accounts for the agency's participation in the life and activities of the group. Since this group exists in a community center where many aspects of the life of one group may be intertwined with the life of another group, the domain of the agency will invariably be a factor for the teens' consideration. Thus the practitioner takes note that he is part of this group in entertaining a cooperative venture with another group at the center. He does not deny membership in the group; at the same time, he does note a difference because of his professional role.

Modulating the Expression of Feeling

Practice wisdom, as well as research (Yalom, 1975), points to the need to temper the premature self-disclosure and exposure of members in the formative sessions of the group's development. By and large, people who prematurely self-disclose very personal information and emotions are more apt than others not to return to the group. Anxiety and embarrassment tend to result, rather than the desired feelings of well-being and catharsis. Therefore, caution needs to be exercised, especially by the beginning practitioner who might be relieved by self-disclosure (feeling that self-disclosure might be a means for rescuing the group from ambiguity and anxiety about how to work together). In other words, the vulnerable beginning worker should take, and not avoid, responsibility for tempering the amount and nature of members' self-disclosures in the early stages of group life.

The practitioner sets up a nonthreatening atmosphere for collective emotional expression. When a member presents personalized material, the practitioner should not probe or encourage the member to go on. The practitioner stops the disclosure from unfolding and becoming a purely affective and personalized presentation. He or she identifies its meaning, and then generalizes it to the feelings and perceptions of other members as well as to the collective significance for the group as a whole.

Illustration

A group of abused women meets in the hospital clinic on a weekly basis. It is a newly formed group, meeting for the third time. The practitioner has been concentrating her efforts in helping them build mutual support; she hopes to get them thinking about alternatives for themselves and their children. Some of the women have moved out of their homes; others have not.

In this meeting one member, Barbara, begins to tell how her husband has violated her sexually. She seems to want to share many of the details of her sex life. The practitioner notices several members looking away; one sighs, and another frowns. Before Barbara starts to discuss some more of the details, the practitioner interrupts her and says, "I have a feeling you're not the only one here that's felt sexually violated. It's positive that you want to share, but I'm not sure people here are ready yet to look at some of the details of these painful experiences. There will be so many feelings and reactions you will want to share as the group progresses and we get to know each other better." After a brief silence the practitioner says to the group, "I noticed some of you were having a hard time thinking about Barbara's experience and some of the material it gives us to work on. If you take each part slowly, you probably will be able to cope with it better and relate it to your own and one another's situations."

Discussion

It is tempting to have and help a member talk about personal issues in detail. After all, one might say that it would be cathartic to talk about the pain one has experienced; others are also in the same boat. But at this time, allowing this level of intensity to be aired is more apt to overwhelm all the members than to help them. For a group to be truly helpful there has to be a collective feeling that the members are ready to listen to, and help one another share, intimate details that will trigger some of their own negative experiences and painful feelings.

The practitioner responds to the subtle feedback of the members— the sigh, the seeming movement away from the member. The practitioner does not avoid or deny the validity of this member's experiences; rather, she takes note of the effect this topic has on the others. She responds to it directly, showing them that it is possible to deal with difficult and potentially overwhelming feelings if they are revealed slowly and in a manageable fashion.

Facilitating Decision-Making
Processes (Lowy, 1973)

The intent of this technique is to help the members arrive at junctures that move them to newer and different productive courses of action and expression, in order to develop their sense of mastery. Learning decision-making processes enables members to meet needs in ways that do not result in rejection and censure. This essential technique is built upon several interrelated activities. Though complex, its parts make up one unique and important technique in helping make use of democratic processes to increase collective, as well as autonomous, experiences (Klein, 1953; Trecker, 1972).

The technique includes three aspects:

Checking for interest, feelings, and opinions. This is used to air the alternatives and the majority and minority views about directions the group can take. In the course of exploratory discussion, the practitioner periodically asks the members to state their feelings and opinions regarding the issue. The practitioner discourages them from arriving at premature closure by directly inhibiting fixed conclusions. Maintaining the fluidity and flow of opinions and ideas is necessary; therefore, voting and silent, head-nodding agreement methods of decision making are not supported.

Weaving collective perceptions/consensus. Herein the effort is to bring the members beyond fixed and narrow sets of alternatives. The practitioner identifies, summarizes and clarifies the different sources of the threads and themes being expressed. The members are encouraged to do the same. The practitioner asks them to select common themes prevalent in their opinions in order to focus the group on its new commonality. Consensus is reached if and when the reweaving of collective perceptions brings forth a newly composed approach that is acceptable to all of the members.

Compromise. Compromise can be used to help members give up vested interests on behalf of collective interests and experiences. The crucial behaviors for the practitioner include asking members to accept necessities of the moment and requesting—as well as eliciting—members' willingness to give up what appear to be their vested interests. Compromise is used after the members have discussed options and felt that consensus is impossible. Voting is an appropriate mode of compromise; it must come only after discussion, however, and only if everyone's needs have been directly considered. The opinions of the minority must be regarded and respected, and members must discuss willingness to abide by the forthcoming decision. The practitioner asks these members how they would feel about going along with the outcome. This is done so that the members do not remain or become more split after different views are expressed and a compromise is agreed upon.

Illustration

The student programming committee of a college residence hall is discussing how to go about supporting a strike of clerical workers on the campus. The residence director runs these meetings. The group is meeting to talk about what to do about a forthcoming party they have scheduled for the weekend with a live band and a disc jockey. Many faculty are supporting the strike by trying to hold classes off campus; In this atmosphere, some students do not want to hold the event on the campus. Mark feels that "the students need something, and programs should not be taken away from them." Several vocal members state their views, and one member suggests they vote on it. The residence director says, "I don't think voting will help us understand the group's needs; let's hear from more people regarding feelings about what to do next."

The feeling about supporting the strikers is clearly positive. The group members talk more about not wanting to cancel an event. Some are strongly in favor of moving the event off campus, while recognizing the difficulty in securing space. For others, there is a strong desire not to cross the picket lines to come into the dorms or to eat in the cafeteria, let alone have a frivolous party on campus. Denise talks about her mother's membership in a union and how important it has been in getting her good health benefits. The salary scale of the clerical staff is also mentioned; students become upset.

The residence director says, "Some of you want to have the event off campus, and some of you feel okay about having it on campus. It seems that no one wants to cancel the party; is that right?" Much vocal agreement is expressed. Denise suggests that the community center or nearby church might support the event. She asks her roommate, Daisy, to "help me call these places to see if the group can hold the party off campus." The residence director wonders what they will do if they cannot find an off-campus place. Several members say they don't want to have the party on campus. The residence director wonders if anyone has spoken to the band or the DJ, reminding them that union musicians will not cross a picket line "and the decision might be made for you." Sharon says she will call her friends in the band right away to see how they would feel about coming on campus. Mark says he has already put out publicity on campus and invited the local colleges; quick actions and corrections are needed.

The residence director says, "It sounds like most of you want to go off campus. How would you feel, Mark, if we did that? And are you prepared to handle notifications to other schools?" He shares his reluctance, but also a willingness to accept the solution. The residence director asks the others, "Denise and Daisy, how would you feel if there is no place off campus to have the event? Will you want to have it on campus?" Denise is adamant: "I will not be involved in the event. I will also not be part of the committee until the strike is settled." Daisy is not sure; more talk ensues. Some people feel it's a mistake to hold it on campus and let students from nearby schools be faced with a picket line. The group eventually agrees to make every effort to hold the party off campus. They decide that if there is no off-campus site, they will hold a small event (without the band or DJ) just for students who will be around on the weekend, but not to invite other schools to attend. Denise says, "I feel better about this decision. I still will not attend if it is on campus, but I will understand."

Discussion

The practitioner here faces a difficult and emotionally charged situation. First, the idea of a strike can bring about many intensified feelings among group members. There is obviously much to be learned in this situation, as well as a great potential for conflict. This group consists of one member, whose mother is a committed union member, who will not cross a picket line. The group has many responsibilities to consider: to fellow students, to the college community, and to the strikers.

First, the practitioner does not permit the group to come to a premature decision. This is a very complex issue that needs to be sensitively and carefully considered to include the opinions of all the members. Not voting allows the members to go forward in expressing various views and feelings. They are also able to examine consequences and begin to develop some strategies for action. When the practitioner discusses contacting the band, the members see themselves as action oriented and begin to mobilize an effort to go off campus. A more or less implicit decision is made that going off campus is the preferred plan. Without efforts at the inclusion of the spectrum of feelings and opinions, the group might have fragmented and the members would have come away feeling badly, disoriented, and alienated.

Processing the Here and Now
(Bradford, Gibb, & Benne, 1964;
Schwartz, 1976; Yalom, 1975)

This technique is used to engage the group in an immediate and active examination of members' self-expressions and group interactions in order to raise conscious awareness of the collective process. It is also used when the practitioner wishes to focus the members' attention on covert events and processes that are occurring simultaneously with overt ones. When the members are able to turn attention on themselves, the group heightens its autonomous functioning. In the course of group interactions, the practitioner points out particularly significant events and reaction patterns, describing them and asking for the members' collective efforts at observation and consideration of the feelings and dynamics that are occurring.

Illustration

In a group of separating and divorced women there is considerable talk about the emotional harassment many have felt and feared from their husbands. Several of the men are already out of the homes, while others continue to remain in the same domicile. This results in a stressful situation for all concerned—including any children. Regardless of the living arrangements, the women are experiencing financial pressures as well; one having no money for groceries, and another finding herself constantly having to figure out ways to get her former husband to give her some money to buy clothing for their child. The women are talking about the hurts they are experiencing, and how some of the children are reacting as well.

Several of the women—Dora, Rhoda, Gertrude, and Audrey—continue talking about the difficulty they feel with their husbands in the house. Rhoda's husband has a lover in another state, but still will not move out; Gertrude's husband won't move out because he "wants to have his cake and eat it, too. We have nothing to say to one another. I wish he'd just go to his mother's house."

Eventually the practitioner says, "I've been noticing how those of you who are talking still have your husbands in the house, and the rest of you who are living separately are being quiet. What's been going on here today?" Several of the women who have been talking say they haven't noticed this. Then some begin to talk about how hard it is to speak to those who have already "gone through with it." The practitioner says, "Is this what's been going on for you today?" Dora responds that it has, and says, "I don't understand how you were able to separate so easily, while some of us seem to be having such a difficult time." Mary says that she had a hard time, too, but having no children made it much easier: "I don't want to sit in judgment of you. I've just been listening today trying to figure it out with you." Vera agrees and reminds the group that she ran away with her son to a shelter: "If you think that was easy to do, you are wrong! I was so scared, but I had to get my baby out of there." Loren talks about how having a job made it easier for her to split up with her husband. Her children were so miserable with the fighting that divorce had to be a better alternative.

Audrey tells the group, "My children think I'm a wimp for not being able to throw my husband out. He makes a fool out of me." She then asks Mary and Loren, "Do you think I'm a wimp for still being with him?" They offer her support, saying how hard it is to leave. Then Mary continues, "But you really seem to want to take the next step; you took the first step in joining this group." There is more talk about the difficulties in splitting up, and the need to have good legal help.

The practitioner points out, "Right now more of you are participating. I had a sense there's been a pattern to the sharing here, perhaps subgroups forming of those who have left or whose husbands have left, and those who haven't." Linda says, "Maybe that's true; I do find myself talking to Rhoda more because I know she's still in the same situation of not leaving. Maybe I should also talk to Loren." Gertrude says, "Vera, I never realized you were so scared until now." Vera acknowledges what has just been said. There is more discussion on the different views of the meaning of separating or not separating from their husbands. Discussion moves to comparisons about which women are stronger or more independent than others. The women start laughing and crying together.

Discussion

In this meeting, the practitioner uses the "here and now" technique to help the members establish a broader level of commonality to enable a wider use of support. The practitioner has focused the group's attention to the process as it is unfolding in the meeting. Certainly the content being discussed is important, too. But without the practitioner's intervention, the equally important process itself would not be considered and made part of the content. Here is a group of women who need help and support in expanding their abilities to deal with and examine various aspects of interpersonal relations with each other as well as with other women, men, and children. Yet they show signs of falling back on the safety of sameness, which for them would undermine necessary interaction and independence.

In this interaction the practitioner does not respond to the individual members' concerns. Rather she takes note that there is a subgroup of people not participating, and that this may indicate the formation of a status hierarchy of two different subgroups. If they become fixed, the subgroupings will serve no useful purpose in meeting the members' goals. Focusing attention to the here and now helps the members appreciate the significance of their own behavior and to recognize the meta messages of their interactions. This results in an expanded ability to ask for help from others who are perceived as stronger.

Expressing Feelings About
the Practitioner's Role

The intent of this technique is to help the members directly express the latent and manifest feelings they have toward the practitioner. These usually would remain or go underground, and not be a significant part of the process. The practitioner is a member with a special position and a professional role and stake in the group; as such, he or she is perceived by the members to be different than they are. Directly discussing their feelings about the practitioner strengthens the group's capacity to take direction and to disagree with the practitioner. Expressing these feelings and perceptions alters distortions that occur when members' projections and idiosyncratic frames of references remain unexpressed. While expression of these types of feelings may be felt to be taboo (Shulman, 1984), not expressing them colors and masks the group's spontaneity and depth of intimate relationships (Levine, 1979).

The practitioner directly encourages the group to express feelings and opinions about him or her. The practitioner asks the group how its members are responding to his or her efforts and interactions. The practitioner may point out when members are avoiding responding to direction from him or her; or when the members seem to want to hear, talk to, or look only at the practitioner rather than the other members, seeming to overvalue the professional and devalue one another.

This technique also requires addressing and interpreting the members' expression of feelings about other helpers (Shulman, 1984) as a reflection of their feelings and perceptions about the present practitioner. Additionally, by owning up to errors and encouraging the group to react to these, the practitioner further demystifies the aura of power and potency unrealistically attached to the person carrying out the professional role.

Illustration

A group of moderate to high functioning retarded young adults is talking about their experiences in the sheltered workshop. Martha, Hubie, and Earline are part of an assembly line that makes desk items. Pandit, Chuckie, and Lorinda are in a print shop. Zoe and Terry are on a housekeeping crew in a nearby office building. The print crew begins talking about the foreman of the print shop and how he "blew his stack today" because they didn't get a job out to one of the schools on time. Talk continues about the different bosses they have. Some tell them exactly what to do, and other bosses "overdo it because we are retarded." Chuckie, Lorinda, and Hubie are quite active in this discussion.

After some time Larry, the practitioner, turns to the others and asks, "How about your bosses, how do you feel about them? I'd like to hear from Earline, Zoe, Terry, and Pandit." After some encouragement, these members also talk a bit about those who are in charge of them on their work sites. Larry then says to the group, "I was wondering how you were feeling about me as a worker in this group? Do you think I boss you too much, or too little, or do things you don't like?" Some laughter ensues, with Larry laughing also, and then encouraging their response: "Come on, I'd like to know what you think. There's no point in you not telling me." Finally, Lorinda says, "You're okay Larry. You don't make us feel dumb and stupid at all." Chuckie says, "At first I didn't like you asking us to say what was on our minds. In the other group I was in, we did exercises, we didn't talk or sit in a circle. You make us talk a lot and it scares me." Larry asks, "Is anyone else scared?" Earline snaps at Chuckie, "You're always scared. You always want your mother around. You're such a pain. You love to play retarded." Larry says to Earline, "You don't like it when other people are scared." She says that she doesn't, "especially when they don't keep quiet about it, and try to get everyone else worried." The practitioner asks Earline, "Were you scared here? Did I ever scare you?" Earline admits that she has been afraid in the group "when you said we would talk about our feelings in here, and about how to have a better relationships on the job and with friends." Zoe chimes in, "You treat me like a person even though I'm retarded. You should see how they treat us when we clean—like we don't exist!" The practitioner says, "I'm sorry about that, Zoe. Please let me know if I ever insult you, okay?" More talk continues about the practitioner, and the group's experiences with one another.

Discussion

In this group the practitioner moves slowly toward helping the group look at his self-expression and interactions in his role. When several of the members are talking about their bosses, he does not immediately ask them to talk about their reactions to him as practitioner. This is because they need special assistance to make certain that all are included in the conversation and that everyone understands the theme that is being discussed. With three members talking, the practitioner had to make certain all were involved in talking about their bosses, so that all could become involved in talking about how the practitioner was acting in his role.

Many professionals would not broach the subject of the practitioner role with people who are retarded. This is an error; a result of the practitioner's stereotyping and stigmatizing the members. Talking about the practitioner offers the members' opportunities for autonomy. It furthers their ability to deal with the many people in authority roles they always have to interact with and to whom they have to answer. It helps the members deal with the hurt about their handicaps that is ubiquitous in social situations.

Goal Setting

This technique is used to capitalize and build upon the emerging collective ownership of the group experience. It is also used to crystallize a sense of cohesion and identity. Use of goal setting marks the beginning of the group's transition from working on developing a democratic mutual aid system to working on actualizing purpose.

When the members question the group's format and objectives, the practitioner focuses their attention on identifying and setting their goals. The practitioner points out different ways in which individual and collective needs are emerging and merging, and how these are a reflection of newer and deeper characterizations of the group as a mutual aid system. This provides motivation and support for the members as a collective in terms of their objectives. The practitioner asks the members to begin to explore the different types of needs and interests the group might work on, given the group's psychosocial raison d'être.

Illustration

The 11- to 14-year-old children of divorced and separating parents have been meeting for six weeks with the junior high school social worker. They have been talking about which parent they are going to spend the weekend with, and about not liking to have to leave their house and friends to go to a different house that's not in the neighborhood. The practitioner says, "I guess whichever way you look at your situations, they're not smooth and easy, right? And there's lots of things not to like about them." Davey says that he doesn't like to visit his father, because "he won't let me watch what show I want to watch. He keeps trying to take me to museums and places like that." Mara says that she has more fun when her father lets her bring a friend for the weekend. The practitioner asks, "What about you, Jimmy? Your dad is far away. When do you see him?" Jimmy says he flies out for long weekends and vacations. "I have a new set of friends there, so it's okay. But it costs a lot to go there, so I don't get to go too often."

The practitioner says, "Some of you are complaining about going, but you know your father or mother wants you to come. How would you feel if you didn't go?" Several say they'd miss and want to be with the parent they don't live with. Some members begin to show some anger at one or both of their parents. Susan, who lives with her father, announces that "I'm going to move in with my mother soon. My little brother is driving me crazy, and my father can only handle one of us at a time." The practitioner asks, "How do you feel about that, Susan?" Susan says it's okay because she prefers her mother's house, and she's mad at her father. Laura says she'd rather live with her father and can't imagine why Susan would leave hers. "My mother is getting a bigger house," Susan replies.

The practitioner says, "You've all got lots of feelings, some of them happy and sad and angry all together, and it's hard, for sure; but as you've been talking it seems there's a lot we can deal with together. Like for one, how do you help each other have it work out well when you visit with your parents? And how do you handle being angry at them? What else do you think you can do here?" "I want my father to get my little brother to behave," says Susan. The practitioner says, to Susan and the group, "It sounds like your brothers and sisters are having a hard time, too. Do you talk with them about the divorce?" Some say that they do, and some that they don't. The practitioner says, "Maybe we can also talk about that, too—how and when you can talk to your brothers and sisters." Many of the children agree.

The practitioner asks, "What about other family members? Who do you talk to? And who do you see? Or who don't you see that you miss?" Davey says, "I like to see my aunt and cousins, and ever since the divorce I don't see them. They don't come to visit my mother." The practitioner remarks, "So your family experiences are a good part of what we can talk about in this group. Aunts, cousins . . . how about grandparents?" Talk about families ensues. Then Marisa, who has been quiet most of the time, says, "I want to know how to get them back together." Everyone becomes quiet. The practitioner says, "I guess that's one of the hardest topics, talking about your hopes that they can get back together again. Most kids in your shoes have that hope; we must talk about it here. We should put that on our list of topics to discuss, don't you think?" Some members nod in agreement, and sorrowful looks are seen on those who don't.

Discussion

The practitioner begins by pointing out to the members that their situations are not easy; that whichever way things happen, they have mixed feelings. The practitioner also relates to the many difficulties they are experiencing in going to different homes, with different friends and social lives to spend time with another parent. For some, new siblings are an issue. For others, getting parents to hear their needs more clearly is potent. For still others, learning how to have a good time will be essential. The practitioner is careful to include the member whose father is living in a different state.

As talk continues, one sees that the members feel angry, and displaced this anger onto their situations. Playing parents against each other is a latent issue in this group. It has to do with the real reactions the members are having about leaving one parent to be with the other part of the time. The practitioner raises their themes and issues as possible future topics. The subject of missing other family members is pointedly asked about to heighten feelings and test reality. Learning to speak directly with siblings is offered as an option for members to consider; the practitioner is focusing the members' attention on their future work in the process.

Good and Welfare

This technique is used to help the group members gain closure of a meeting whether or not there is unfinished business. By providing the members with this structure and approach for expressing their reactions to a meeting at its conclusion, the practitioner's intention is to prevent dissatisfactions and interpersonal tensions from festering between meetings and into the next one. Good and welfare sets the stage for future decisions about issues to deal with through the members' collective efforts. By hearing how others have just experienced the meeting, members can more constructively respond to one another after the meeting time and consider issues for forthcoming meetings. The assumption is that members will carry reactions out of the meeting, and may deal directly with one another. Furthermore, whether members meet one another or not, the current meeting and the next one come to mind as they leave and prepare themselves for future interactions.

The practitioner introduces good and welfare right before the close of the first session. In a go-around structure, each member states what he or she liked or disliked about the session. The practitioner explains the purpose of good and welfare and asks that members succinctly share reactions to "how the meeting went today," telling them not to respond to what is being said, but to just listen to one another. This structure is maintained to because the good and welfare process, which takes place near the close of the meeting as time is running out, should not rekindle issues that cannot be handled. To further enable the group, the practitioner also shares reactions to the session and process. The practitioner offers encouragement to the members to begin the good and welfare process. If no one does, the practitioner can start by modeling positive and negative reactions. As each person finishes, the practitioner looks to another member to stimulate movement and sharing. After several meetings, the group may well initiate this process without the group worker's recommendation.

Illustration

The members in a cancer support group are in the midst of their first meeting. They have been talking about the effects of treatment on them and their families. They have also spoken about the need to discuss treatment procedures with their doctors and about aftereffects of these as well.

Near the end of the session, the practitioner, Gloria, introduces the idea of the good and welfare process. "It's usually helpful," she says, "to take sometime before leaving to just go around, briefly saying how you've reacted to the meeting." There is a pause, and then encouragement by the practitioner: "Does someone want to start?" Murray starts, saying, "It's often hard to talk to your family about having cancer. But here, it's been much easier to talk." The practitioner looks to the next person, Frances, who begins, "My daughter doesn't understand that I don't want to talk with her about my cancer. It just depresses me, but today I started to see other ways, especially from what Sally said." Sally moves her head in acknowledgment. The practitioner looks to the next person, Eva, who was quiet during the meeting. Eva says, "I don't want you to think that I wasn't listening even though I was quiet. I learn a lot just from listening. I feel I would like to say more next time. I am seeing how some of our families won't bring up the subject unless we do."

After everyone has shared reactions, the practitioner summarizes and ends the meeting by offering her view of themes that seemed prevalent: "I guess people are saying we can get together here and be helpful. Some of you feel you didn't say all that you wanted to, but that's often how people in groups feel at the beginning. For myself, I'm feeling positively about this meeting; you've already mentioned ways you might provide help and support to one another, family issues, talking versus remaining silent, and how to deal with doctors."

Discussion

There are several times in this illustration when the worker could have been drawn into beginning or encouraging exploration of issues and themes presented by members during the good and welfare process. First, when one member (Frances) specifically identifies the contribution of another member (Sally) the practitioner—rather than turning to Sally—holds to the structure of the technique and provides for the process of the group by looking to the next person (Eva) and encouraging her to go on. Otherwise the group, never having done this before, could have been drawn into trying to find out what specifically had been said by Sally that was helpful to Frances. Eva, who was quiet today, would have been likely to yield the floor to a discussion between Sally and Frances. In this case, Eva takes the opportunity to indicate to the group that she knows she has been quiet. This helps the other members consider her specific feelings and thoughts, and also keeps them from viewing her as mysterious, withdrawn, or secretive.

The practitioner does not respond specifically to Eva's concern about her quietness. Rather, during her time to sum up, the practitioner takes the opportunity to universalize the concerns about members not having said all that they might have wanted to say. She also gives the group food for thought for the next few meetings. In addition, by letting them know how she feels as a practitioner, she motivates their interest in developing a positive commitment to the group effort.

SUMMARY

In this chapter, the stage was set for the practitioner's use of techniques that would achieve the dual objectives of the humanistic group. It was established that techniques without values would be mechanistic.

Techniques were defined as behaviors the worker uses to achieve particular intents. Twenty-nine techniques were identified and categorized according to the objective to which they were connected.

The nine techniques that were used specifically to establish the democratic mutual aid system were discussed. Four of these assist the members in being a collective: these are the techniques of *collective participation, decision making, engaging the group as a whole,* and *processing the here and now.* They are called in to play to help members develop a "we" feeling and identity; they can also be used when the members are overreliant on the practitioner for an identity and controls.

Modulating the expression of feeling helps all members stay focused on what is possible (and not possible) to do within the context of the group's current identity, cohesion, and implicit decision-making processes.

Expressing feelings about the practitioner role is distinguishable from the others for several reasons. One is the assumption that the members are able to function cohesively and effectively as a whole at the same time as they deal with the practitioner's participation. From these points of view the practitioner anticipates a sense of purposeful unity and integrity.

Goal setting and *good and welfare* are techniques that relate to particular aspects of the process: the members collectively develop goals, and that they react to the group's unfolding process. *Scanning* (Shulman, 1981) is essentially a sensory means used by the practitioner to perceive the group and its manifest and latent processes.

The following two chapters will discuss techniques for actualizing purpose.

Chapter 6

TECHNIQUES FOR ACTUALIZING PURPOSE

Actualizing purpose is the second of the dual objectives of humanistic group work. Techniques the practitioner uses to actualize purpose are aimed at assisting members in focusing on the issues, situations, and interpersonal patterns that have brought them to the group.

Relationships that have been built on humanistic values and democratic norms provide the basic frame of reference for self-expression in the group and in important external situations. Purpose is achieved in an experiential context, governed by the principle of externality (Papell & Rothman, 1980b). Members and significant others carry out needs and interactions in and out of the group's actual meetings. By helping to build a group in relation to its members' needs and interests, the practitioner assists them in creating, owning, and modifying the means for working on and through their needs.

The practitioner recognizes that effective processes related to purpose will vary in their intensity, duration, and frequency. These differ in relation to how comfortable the members are in working together, and their ability to use democratic norms productively. Purpose-related processes vary in relation to prevalent stage themes and external events.

While some beginning behaviors do erupt in the middle phase, especially in instances when group members lose their bearings while working on new forms of self-expression, they usually do not alter or divert the members' focus on purpose. The members are able to maintain useful and helpful forms of cohesion, motivation, and energy. When the members recognize the practitioner's knowledge and skill, strengths, and weaknesses, they do not revert to subjective authority issues concerning him or her.

During a group's later themes of Sanctuary, "This Isn't Good Anymore," and especially during "We're Okay and Able," members will turn attention to deepening and more intently working on their purpose. The practitioner is now more often involved in using techniques to help members actualize their purpose. As they increase their interpersonal work the members incorporate and use these techniques, too. When this happens, the practitioner joins in the group's process.

Shulman (1984) and Yalom (1975), focusing on the middle phase of the group, speak to the members' increased interpersonal intensity and productivity, as well as the members' increased and more intense demands on the practitioner. The practitioner has to be aware that when the group feels "okay and able," he or she may express rigid helping styles, or pull back rather than admit to vulnerabilities and stay engaged in the work. The practitioner must actively help the members steer their own course. At the same time, the worker may experience discomfort at the loss of control, as well as feelings of envy or exclusion when realizing that intimacy and mutuality are developing among the members. Levine (1979) writes as follows:

> The [practitioner] can no longer gain political control of the group or offer professional opinions that will not be questioned and countered by the group members. . . . While the [practitioner] may continue providing insight and opinion as well as empathy, the danger of [the practitioner's] competition with the members is high. . . . The [practitioner] who is reasonably secure in his [or her] professional identity will be able to value the mutual helping of the group members while still providing professional input into the discussions. A here-and-now focus during the mutuality phase provides the major source of growth and change for the members. (p. 200)

Participation through helping to actualize purpose demands that the group worker consistently examine his or her interactions and emotional self-expression. When actualizing purpose, not only are the members' behaviors more consistently connected and apparent to one another, but so, too, are the group worker's. The practitioner has to be emotionally mature, possessing the ability to be unguarded and undefensive, thereby serving as a model (for the members) for participation and change. The practitioner qua member is accepting of the discomforts and misperceptions that make empathic communication what it is—difficult and satisfying. Attitudes and stances such as these help to prevent social defenses such as stereotyping, scapegoating, and stigmatizing—which are connected to inferiority and superiority feelings—from becoming a part of the group's milieu.

There are 12 techniques specific to the actualization of purpose. Of these, the following—*role rehearsal, programming, group reflective consideration, interpretation*, and *feedback*—will be discussed in this chapter.

Each of these techniques is related to the interactions of actualizing purpose. For clarification, see Table 6.1 below.

Role Rehearsal

Some role enactments may be members' habituated responses to and in their situations. Other enactments may be fraught with conflict and anxiety, causing the individual to have unstable and unhappy relationships. Change requires acquiring and learning new patterns of interaction and emotional expression, whether undoing old responses or developing new ones. Fear of the unknown is often related to the inhibition of repertoires of interaction and self-expression to meet expectations.

The intent of role rehearsal is to help members in changing dysfunctional behaviors, and in developing new means during the group as well as in other significant relationships. Role rehearsal may be carried out by the practitioner in a few ways. In one of these, the practitioner engages the group or member in imagining and talking about feelings and actions they are anticipating in a forthcoming situation. The group's collective imagination is focused on detail in order to develop strategies and emotional reactions that widen the options available to members. As members consider consequences of emotions and interactions, the practitioner further prods their efforts.

In another approach, the practitioner identifies plots that may occur between group meetings to help them try new role behaviors. Members are assigned to try out parts they usually do not play in significant relationships or situations.

Still another approach involves a more formalized role rehearsal— role playing. From the situations discussed and collectively (or individ-

Table 6.1

Relationship of Techniques to Interactions that Actualize Purpose

Technique	Interactions
Role Rehearsal	Express role-enhancing behaviors
Programming	Create activities in the milieu Express role-enhancing behaviors
Group Reflective Consideration	Identify themes to be worked on Identify feelings that help work on change Identify projections and self-fulfilling prophecies
Interpretation	Identify group process issues and structures to heighten group's self-awareness Identify projections and self-fulfilling prophecies
Feedback	Foster sharing perceptions and feelings about each other's behavior

ually) worried about in meetings, the practitioner asks the group to develop a role-play situation based on the anticipated events. Role players are selected, characters are assigned, and the practitioner has the players make a circle inside the group—a fishbowl structure. The players are encouraged to begin quickly, despite the expected embarrassment and reluctance they are feeling. A nonevaluative experimental tone is set, within a five- to fifteen-minute time limit. The practitioner stops the players, and involves those not actively role playing in a discussion of observations and feelings in the sharing of reactions. There is opportunity to reflect back upon the important behaviors and feelings that surfaced during the action.

Illustration

A group of substance abusers in a residential treatment program is talking about the rules in the program that prevent them from maintaining certain contacts with people from the outside unless given formal permission. Delia complains, "I want to call my husband who is in a different program now; I have been told I can't until I am ready for my discharge plan, which will include couple and family therapy." Fred tells her he knows she and her husband did dope together and that it makes no sense for her to talk to him now. He also says he doesn't trust her to do things differently: "You'll talk to him and immediately figure out how to bullshit us. I know, I've been there." Lila concurs, but doesn't see the harm of Delia calling her husband just to talk about their kids. Geoff reminds everyone that "since Delia's mother is taking care of her kids, there are no decisions to be made from in here." Delia tells the group that her mother wants her to end the marriage: "She says neither of us has the will to stop doing cocaine when we are together."

The practitioner, Faith, asks, "Is there truth to that?" Delia says, "We got rich in the music business; drugs are a lifestyle there." Larry and Geoff talk about how they did time for dealing drugs, and how "drugs sure are a lifestyle of people weaving a web around each other." Larry says to Delia, "Being in jail—it's worse than a humiliation. I saw it was my life I was ruining. You've got a big problem, because you and your husband earn your living in an environment that is full of temptation to go back to coke. But when I did coke, no one could count on me."

The practitioner asks, "Larry, is there someone you want to have count on you now?" Larry responds, "My fiancé who helped me come to the program; I don't want to lose her because she is my future." The practitioner says, "What Larry just said really relates back to you, Delia, how you get to work on the things that need to be worked on so you can be counted on again—that's the big question." Delia talks a bit about her children not counting on her, although she made believe she was available to them. Fred reminds her, "No, your mother always bailed you out with the kids!" There is more discussion about how their important relationships get sacrificed.

The practitioner then asks Delia, "Would you think about which are the hardest couple of steps you have to take next to help your recovery?" After some silence she says, "I have to start to talk to Richard honestly about what was happening between us as a couple, and as parents. I have to tell him how I let myself be lured into the glamour, the glitz, and the hype." Fred asks, "Can you tell Richie that?" Delia says she is afraid to tell him, afraid that he won't accept it. The practitioner asks Delia, "Any other difficult steps?" Delia answers, "Yes, my kids. I fear for them. My mother is right. Richard and I don't help each other. We don't help those kids." The practitioner wonders, "Can you change that? How would you and Richard change that?" Delia says that they'd have to talk about it. The practitioner invites other members to contribute: "What do you think would help Delia, once she told Richard how she felt?" Larry says that she'd have to stick to it: "You couldn't be a coward, and just do whatever he says, or tell him what you think he wants to hear." Fred chimes in, "That's why they don't want you to call Richard; you are still a sucker."

The practitioner says, "Perhaps you, Delia—and you, Fred—could role-play out how Delia might react even if Richard didn't want to listen at first. Sometimes it helps to play-act it first. We can all look at what happens. Certainly Fred has his view of what goes on between Delia and Richie. Then you might learn something about when you're vulnerable to Richard and when you aren't. The rest of the group could give you their reactions and opinions, too. Do you want to try it?" Everyone agrees. The practitioner says to Fred, "Remember, Richard is also in a treatment program. They're probably getting on his case, too, so don't play him too rigidly." The practitioner instructs the rest of the group to look at times when Delia hears Richie and times when she doesn't, and to look for times when Delia doesn't tell him what she feels.

During the role play Delia tells her "husband" how she knows it will be hard but they have to resolve to work on their relationship to be good parents. She tells him, "My mother has been too generous; we have used her to avoid responsibility, to go out all the time, to party and act like we have no kids."

After 10 minutes or so, the practitioner says to the players, "You can stop now," praising their effort. He asks the members to share their reactions. Different members note when Delia had responded in a straightforward manner to "Richie" that he seemed taken aback, but attentive. One member points out that Delia rushed in too quickly to yell at him for not being available to his children, which closed him off, placing parental responsibility on her. Generally, members felt that when she took time out to explain how she felt, she was better understood.

The practitioner asks Delia how and when she felt in charge of herself. She discusses more about the need to be honest, that she had not been, how she has never told him how important it is for her to be a mature parent. More discussion follows. The practitioner finally says, "It looks like when you do get to talk with Richie there's a lot you're both going to have to start to work on. What do you think?"

Discussion

There are several important events that the practitioner notes. First, with the help of the group, the member is put on the spot regarding her collusion with her husband to continue to take drugs. Her reluctance to accept the observation of collusion needs work. By providing a chance for her to consider future directions and practice new behaviors, the practitioner helps her see the pitfalls of meeting with her husband now. The future directions their work together can take is also identified. When offering the member a chance to experiment in the role play, the practitioner does not let the group get too confrontational, thereby enabling the members to develop an empathic (as well as sympathetic) interactional way of helping Delia. Not dwelling on the need to call her husband propels Delia to think about her role as parent. This is done when the practitioner, focusing on Larry's need to be counted on, brings her attention gently back to her role as a parent, and as an adult daughter.

It is then, and through the subsequent role play, that Delia begins to see how she avoids parental responsibility by using her mother to get her off the hook. As the role play unfolds it becomes apparent that Delia wants to take on her parental obligations and wishes for the strength to get her husband to do that with her. Rehearsing in the group further experientially solidifies for Delia the observation that there is much that she needs to do about her interaction and emotional expression in her marriage. Whether to end the marriage or not is a premature consideration, and is not dealt with directly. The issue is her adulthood, regardless of whether she is mature in this marriage or in another intimate relationship.

Role rehearsal, here, is drawn around the group's functional purpose. It remains separate from the usual drug culture in order to discover new ways of functioning drug free in the community and in one's significant relationships.

Programming (Middleman, 1968/1981a, 1983; Vinter, 1985; Whittaker, 1985)

Programming is the most completely active, interactive, and experiential technique of all. It can take place among the members themselves or with significant others, both in and out of the meeting environment. Programming is the technique that epitomizes the humanistic group's externality (Papell & Rothman, 1980b) because it brings the members to the external environment. While some groups get into programming before resolution of their normative crisis—children's groups because they are experiential from the outset, and groups whose basic purpose is to be action or activity oriented—programming usually occurs following some significant resolution of the normative crisis. At this point, the practitioner and members become more focused on the members' needs in the actual group experience.

Through planning and participating in a program, members experience and learn how to actualize themselves, further their goals, and enhance their potentials with significant as well as unanticipated others in their natural and formal milieus. The psychosocial program is a proving and improving ground. The total programming process focuses on and reflects the actual experiences that bring the members together. The program reveals and brings to life the group's objectives and goals, as well as the members' actual forms of interaction and self-expression.

The program event the members undertake is a central way in which the group as a whole can meet members' needs to be proactive within the social environment. Group programs are some of the most significant statements of what makes this type of professionally guided group a unit of social work. Through the program, members experience the gamut of opportunities for experimenting with new behaviors more than would be possible within the confines of a meeting's usual process (Seitz, 1985). Members can experience mastery and enhanced role responses and repertoires.

The practitioner uses five interrelated acts in carrying out programming technique. These are: (1) initiation, (2) discussing options, (3) tasks and tools, (4) program experience, and (5) evaluation.

1. Initiation. The practitioner introduces one or several program ideas, or responds to program initiatives from the group. The members' abilities to explore these are encouraged. The practitioner also informs the members that conducting a program enhances group pride and mastery through the collective group experience, while providing a unique arena for specialized change and experimentation for any one member.

2. Discussing options. The practitioner motivates members to consider several program options, offering his or her own ideas when necessary. The practitioner helps members consider the range of complexity of a program event—the effort that each undertaking will take. Some programs might be simple, requiring little prior preparation; others, more complex, will require a high level of group organization and preparation. Some programs will be only for the members themselves; others will be for specific significant others, and still others will include a wider spectrum of participants. The members' attention and decision making (see Chapter 5) is directed to ways in which potential program efforts will meet particular group needs. The practitioner helps the members choose a program and develop a commitment to assume responsibility for program tasks and participation.

3. Tasks and tools. When the members have selected a program event, the practitioner directs his or her efforts toward the nitty-gritty of the tasks of planning and implementation. The practitioner may have to be the first to make lists, turning tasks over to members: Program tools may require collection and storage. Collection points and times will have to be identified. Permissions will have to be secured. All phone numbers will again be confirmed. The practitioner insures that the network for extra-meeting communication is in place. The practitioner encourages members to volunteer and accept responsibility for carrying out the tasks. Through the process of assigning and volunteering to undertake tasks, the practitioner also helps the members identify outlets for sharing strengths and developing newer abilities.

Members will want to know if the practitioner will be present at the program itself; this will have to be directly dealt with in the group. The practitioner's participation will be determined by the practitioner and members in the context of agency policy, group need, and professional role constraints. While in some settings it may not be normative to attend events the group undertakes, participation in an event certainly should not be ruled out pro forma. The practitioner relinquishes varying degrees of control by participating in the program.

Whether or not the practitioner is present during the program, the result of his or her efforts and disciplined approaches will be in evidence during the members' experience.

4. Program experience. Once the program experience is upon the members, there will be anxieties and hesitancies. It may be necessary for the practitioner to actively initiate the start of the program. In some groups, because of their feelings and abilities, the practitioner will be required to take a very active part in the start-up, lending support to the members' efforts until things get well underway.

During the program, the practitioner encourages and sustains members' efforts, taking special note of peripheral or floundering participants. The effort is to appropriately move to the background; during the experience, this practitioner is not the primary social and emotional connection for the members. The practitioner circulates throughout the program, modeling for the members an active and engaged participant. There may also be times when the practitioner fills in to help complete tasks, and keeps track of timing of the beginnings and endings of events within the program.

5. *Evaluation.* Once the program event is over, usually at a forth-coming session, the practitioner engages the group in rehashing the experience. Discussion includes a focus on how the program met the members' and other participants' needs. The practitioner may also initiate discussion about how the tasks were or were not achieved, and whether different resources would have improved the event. The prac-titioner helps the group take appropriate pride in accomplishments and accept its failures. The future is considered at that time, with the practitioner helping the group move toward entertaining new ideas about future options and plans.

Illustration

At this group meeting, Sally, Dan, Josh, Harriet, Bernadette, Claudia, Fred, Lee, and George are in the process of planning a party. They have been meeting for almost a year with the practitioner, Tom. Several of the members have discussed the difficult personal and social experiences of their adolescence, including drugs, and dropping out of school. Others are looking for a wider range of friendships and social relationships. Many have admitted that their social events had been characterized by pot smoking, too much alcohol, and an ambiance of wild parties where people did not really get to know each other. Several express concern about being able to mingle comfortably with people they do not know. The practitioner, Tom, sensitive to their fears and aware of their proclivity to intellectualize and avoid experiences, sees a program option. Tom has encouraged them to have a party that will characterize them as the young adults they now are becoming; they have grabbed onto the idea.

The members want this to be a party with a relaxed atmosphere, where people really talk to and get to know each other. They have decided to pick a theme for the party—it is being planned to commem-orate the beginning of the summer. Some members and their friends have been taking high school equivalency, vocational training, and college classes, and the end of the semester seems like a good time to celebrate. The group has decided on a menu. Everyone is bringing food. The written invitations have been beautifully designed by Josh through a computer graphics class, and each member has been asked to invite five friends. Fred, and his roommate, Alex, have volunteered their house for the party. Claudia, Sally, and Dan have helped Fred set up his house. Furniture has been moved, tables have been set up, and music is on hand.

When the practitioner arrives at the party, it is well under way. There are many new people, and several members greet him with food and drink, taking him around to meet some of their friends, girlfriends, cousins, and colleagues. Several of the names are of people talked about in the group, and the practitioner notes this. Claudia wants Tom to meet her fiancé, whom she had described as skeptical about her belonging to the group; Tom finds her fiancé to be somewhat formal with him.

Sally can be seen in one corner talking very seriously with a young man. Dave comments to the practitioner that "it looks like Sally and my friend Pete are hitting it off." Then Dave continues, "This is a great party. The chemistry is great. I've been talking to some very nice people. Did you see that gorgeous woman over there? She is Fred's sister. I have to be careful with a group member's sister, right? I can't hit on her like I used to." Tom laughs and asks, "Did you talk to her, Dave?" Dave says that he discovered she was going to law school and "that made her too much of a brain for me." The practitioner comments, "Come on, Dave, don't be so chicken."

The group has made a small dance floor in one corner of the basement. Bernadette walks over to Tom and asks him to dance with her. He does. While they are dancing, Tom notices several of the members taking note of this. Members are laughing and joking about how "you dance almost as a good as we do."

After more time passes, Tom tells Claudia, Fred, and Dave, "I really have to be going. I have some plans for later." Claudia catches the eye of George, who quickly comes up to Tom and says, "Wait five minutes, we just want to bring out a cake, okay" Tom agrees, "Just five minutes, sure."

While Fred brings out the cake, Claudia asks for the group's attention. People call out, "Speech, speech!" Claudia says, "We are happy to bring all our friends together to celebrate our wonderful group, and the end of a rough year of classes and homework, and the beginning of summer." Lots of "hoorays" are heard. Then George begins to talk about how much the group has appreciated Tom's efforts and "for putting up with us, and encouraging us." Tom affirms his pleasure with the members and acknowledges the opportunity to bring friends together, saying, "I'm going to take my leave now, "before" you people get busted!" Everyone laughs; Tom leaves to calls of "see you Thursday night."

Everyone is present at Thursday night's meeting. The practitioner begins, "Let's go over the events and experiences at the party." Everyone talks animatedly, expressing enthusiasm about the party, the food, the music, and the fact that Tom was able to attend. Fred, noticing that Claudia is quiet, reaches out to her. She tells the members that her fiancé put down her friends, and she was so upset and hurt "at his lack of understanding, that I broke off our engagement!" The members express shock at his lack of support. "He just wants me to be dependent on him, not on anyone else. This is not a new issue, as you know." Bernadette tells her, "I saw it coming." Claudia admits that she also saw it coming, but was hoping they could work it out. She expresses disappointment in herself. After a lengthy supportive discussion with Claudia, the members and the practitioner turn their attention back to the party.

The practitioner asks the members to consider what it felt like for them to be at this party. Several talk about meeting new people, and the ease with which they did it. The practitioner reminds them "you planned it that way." Dave jokes with Sally about her interest in his friend Pete. She smiles and says, "Oh! He is really nice. But I'm not going to say anything else, because I don't want to now." Tom wonders, "How do we handle the issue in the group if Sally wants to talk about herself and Pete, with Dave being his friend?" Sally agrees that she is feeling uncomfortable. Dave says, "Whatever you say won't go back to Pete. And I won't talk with him about you, either." Sally says, "Thanks, that's hard to do; I appreciate it."

After some silence Sally continues, "What was so good was being able to be myself with someone in a warm and healthy atmosphere. That's all I have to say now. That's the best part." More talk ensues about the opportunity the party gave them to feel comfort. George admits that it was the first time he didn't get drunk at a party. The practitioner asks, "How was that?" George admits it was "new and different, but I'm getting used to it—pretty good."

The practitioner asks, "Any other feelings?" Dave cuts in, "Okay man, I got nervous about talking to Fred's sister. Not only is she beautiful, but she's a brain, too." Members talk about how they want to be careful about entering into relationships with each other's family and friends. The practitioner wonders, "Isn't that true about entering into all relationships?"

Discussion

The young adult group's party illustrates a program execution. It was partially the result of the practitioner's use of initiation, discussion of options, and tasks and tools in a partly directed, off the cuff, yet professionally guided process. It had started several weeks earlier, when members talked about their desire to celebrate the end of the year differently than they previously might have celebrated an event.

One key aspect of programming is its flow with the organic psychosocial needs and interactions of group members. While the technique appears clearly ordered to remind the practitioner of necessary business, it is not designed to lock the members into a fixed agenda and process. In fact, programming can start spontaneously. It has to be encouraged by the practitioner, who in this situation helps the members seize the moment.

The breakup of the member's engagement is precipitated by the learning that takes place through the experiential avenue created by the program. This severing of an important relationship will need further consideration by the member in the group. Another member discovers a newer ability to be herself with the opposite sex in the ambiance created by the program. One member attends the party without getting drunk. Another member raises the question of how people will relate to others they meet. Finally, learning to be expansive in the member role tests the group's maturity. Through future events, members will be provided with still further opportunities for social and personal enhancement. The practitioner is supportive in this process, focusing on particular issues of the experience for the members and significant others.

The practitioner chooses to attend this event for part of the time, and to conduct himself in the professional role in a relaxed fashion throughout. He meets the members' friends and accepts one member's request for a dance. To accept the dance is part of the ambiance; not to dance might be taken as a sign of rejection. He does establish and protect the professional boundary between himself and the members by leaving the party early, indicating that he has other social plans that do not include the group members. This is accepted by the members, who easily adjust the schedule in order to include him in the presentation of the cake.

Group Reflective Consideration
(Hollis, 1972)

The intent of this technique is to assist members in considering recent experiences that relate to their purpose. This technique (described as valuable in case work by Hollis, 1972) is used in group work as a refocusing and reframing device to help in the formation of new ideas, attitudes, and perceptions.

The practitioner asks members to recall the aspects, contexts, and effects of particular experiences. Attention is paid to the sequencing of events, and to feelings, interactions and moments of choice. This serves to assist members in reconstructing actions, feelings, and thoughts. Effort is made to keep the discussion focused on details, rather than muddied generalities. The members are able to distinguish helpful and unhelpful patterns. The practitioner wonders how the moment-to-moment awarenesses are affecting the members as they reflect on and bring to the surface insights, intuitions, and facts.

Illustration

A group of women who are lesbians has been talking about how some members have experienced fallout from letting coworkers know about their sexual preference. The pros and cons of keeping this information hidden are also considered. Lola starts to talk about her job in a bank, and her friendship with another woman there who is a manager. She says that when she told about her life and her current relationship with her lover the woman stopped having lunch with her. Other group members echo feelings that these kinds of snubs happen to them, too.

The practitioner, Eunice, says to Lola, "Hold on, let's go back over the events at lunch. Where were you, how did it all start?" Lola says, "We had gone to the coffee shop, and then were going to take a quick look in some of the nearby boutiques." The practitioner asks her how the topic of her sexual preference came up. Lola tells the group that she was preoccupied and anxious about letting this woman know about herself. She wanted to feel less guarded and more friendly toward her, and thought telling would help. Some members interrupt, "No, people don't want to hear." The practitioner says, "Go on Lola, tell us how you started to talk." Lola describes how she just told her, "you know, I am a lesbian," going on at length to talk about her current relationship: "I didn't want her to get the wrong idea, that I was interested in her. But

I think she did, anyway." "Wait a minute," the practitioner cuts in, "How do you know?" "I don't know for sure," Lola replies.

Diane then asks what the woman's response was. Lola can't recall, saying, "She didn't say much." The practitioner asks her, "What do you think was going on for her?" Lola says she doesn't know. The practitioner asks, "What did you do then?" Lola says, "I started to talk about my lover." The practitioner asks, "So what do you think is going on for her now?" Lola says, "I must have scared her." The practitioner asks the group, "How are you reacting to what Lola has been telling us?" Vivian's response is that Lola is anxious and tells too much too quickly. Peggy thinks she wanted to go shopping, not hear about Lola's love life—whether with a woman or with a man—just then. "I don't think you checked out with her what her reaction is," Diane says.

The practitioner asks Lola, "How do you react to what was just said to you?" She responds, "I see their point. I didn't ask her to react or give her a chance to. I just talked a lot." Eunice asks "How are you feeling now?" Lola admits that she is anxious, and had been eager to get this off her chest. The practitioner wonders if these feelings were similar to what she was feeling at lunch. Lola says "yes," they are similar. Diane says, "And you had a hard time listening to us, too, but we interrupted you. Everyone can't do that to you."

The practitioner points out that what happened to Lola seems common in this group: "Sometimes you're just not sure if you're being rejected because you are lesbians, or because of other reasons." Members begin to talk about how to clarify this issue.

Discussion

This technique is used to deal with actual situations the members have been in. The practitioner knows that the member is moving head long into a rush of ventilation and feeling that will not be productive for her. In addition, all members' survival will be intertwined with their abilities to develop vantage points from which to appraise situations while they are in them. The practitioner, by cutting into the venting of the member, slows the process down and turns it into one of reflection. By doing this, other members are given impetus to also cut in, slowing down the story and giving themselves and the member a chance to think about it. A chance to think about the interaction anew is provided.

The practitioner stops the members, redirecting them several times. By asking Lola what she thought was going on for the other woman, the practitioner redirects her toward developing empathic awareness of others. Her response—"I am not sure"—points further to her own self-preoccupation, which gives impetus to others in the group to focus Lola's attention on this trait. Eventually, with everyone's help, the member does begin to think that she might have overwhelmed her colleague in this situation, and that she has the tendency to steamroller in the group as well.

Interpretation

Interpretation is used to expand awareness of the latent content and hidden agendas that play out between members and their significant others in and out of the group.

The practitioner reaches beyond what is presented on a manifest level by "reading between the lines" to bring aspects of latent levels to awareness. The practitioner goes below surface presentations to the point where a new sense or perception can be experienced by the members. The practitioner does not go too far beyond the group's conscious awareness; this is done to avoid defensiveness that may result from overstepping members' comprehension, feelings, and defensive boundaries.

An interpretation is offered when the practitioner judges that the member is ready to benefit from looking at particular behaviors with more complete insight. This may be done when the member continuously repeats dysfunctional or unsatisfying behavior, creating a stumbling block to his or her efforts to change, or when the member is seriously examining his or her motivations.

The practitioner offers an interpretation about the underlying meanings of the behavior with an empathic affect, speaking about feelings regarding hidden intentions, fears and expectations. These perceptions are related to stereotyping, self-fulfilling prophecies, and members' family-symbol representations of others.

The practitioner may use interpretation in conjunction with role rehearsal, aspects of programming—especially during the evaluation time—or along with group reflective consideration. While the practitioner is not intent on having interpretation immediately change the member's form of expression, it often begins the process of change because of the support and discussion members provide for one another. Interpretation occurs most often, and most valuably, when the members are reflecting on their differentiated (Garland, Jones, & Kolodny, 1973) patterns of interaction and emotional expression.

Illustration

At a weekly meeting in the cottage at the group residence for 15- to 18-year-old girls who are unable to live with their families, the practitioner immediately brings to the fore a serious situation. The agency that cares for them is very upset because they have been sleeping with one another. The agency is considering breaking up the membership to different residences because this behavior is viewed as improper, and as the precursor of homosexual behavior. The practitioner, Keith, indicates that he is not an agency emissary, that the "people downtown" know he is bringing this up, and that they have given him assurances that he can work with the group without impediments from "downtown." They have also made it clear that no matter what happens the agency probably will move the girls.

The impact is emotionally devastating. The silence is deafening. The girls look around at one another; the practitioner sees that a good number have anger and hatred in their eyes. He says, "This must be infuriating to you. It must really piss you off and make you want to kill Mrs. Tanner." Boom! Yelling and screaming ensue. This goes on a while, with tears and table pounding. As it subsides, the practitioner asks, "How will you go about stopping this from happening?" Anger and tears begin again. The practitioner says, "You're not talking about what is happening, what you think about it, and how you feel. The only way you can stop it from happening, if you can, is to understand what's going on. Understand means to stand under, to look at all aspects, at what people are into, what they might not even be aware of themselves. Maybe then you can be effective. Joleen . . . ?"

Joleen responds, "I hate Mrs. Tanner. She is a big fuck, always coming in and snooping and telling the house parents we can't have this and that." Consuelo chimes in, "She will make me leave this place; she won't listen to the truth. There is nothing I can do." The practitioner says, "So, she is bopping you and you are her victims. This is just how you set me up when we began to meet months ago. I would control this, you would be dependent, remember?" There is some head shaking, and then Alice starts weeping. Yvette holds and hugs her. Alice whispers, "Another residence . . . from two foster homes to here and another. And when I ask momma to see me she says she has no time. No one has time." The practitioner is aware of the connection between Mrs. Tanner's rejecting behavior and the girls' mothers. He chooses to let it lie because he feels it would be too disabling to explore at this time.

Someone says, "The old bitch! We read an article in a psychology magazine about therapy with adolescents where some social worker and a psychiatrist give baby bottles to messed-up people so they can have nurturance and love. So we decided to give them to each other. That's the God's honest truth, Keith." "How can you explain this to the agency is the question," retorts the practitioner. The immediate answer is, "We can bring Mrs. Tanner right here, show her the magazine and baby bottles." Some run to get the stuff, saying, "This is the truth. This is our home away from home, and we want to be good to each other."

The practitioner says, "Your assertive tone sounds good to me. Alice, I bet from your weak one that you don't confront your mother." Alice sits up and looks with anger at the practitioner. He continues, "Maybe you can figure out ways of explaining yourselves and the reactions Mrs. Tanner has caused so she can hear you girls. I will help; I'll be there in the room if you want. " Alice says, "I'll tell her she is just like my mother." Others agree. The practitioner says, "So the agency isn't helping you by shifting you around. It isn't hearing you and, like with your parents, you have to find ways to say this with strength but without sounding persecuted. I like the idea of having Mrs. Tanner and the others come to hear you out."

Discussion

In this poignant example, the practitioner is very careful to highlight certain latent issues without surfacing others. He does not explicitly link Mrs. Tanner with a rejecting mother at the start. It didn't matter if it ever came out, although when it did it was helpful. He showed concern that their tenuous and fragile identities might become mortified in the face of the mother metaphor. He stayed, however, with the latent (but close to the surface) theme about their positions as victims, rather than rejected daughters. What emerges is their clear explanation for "sleeping together" as a real, age appropriate and caring phenomenon that promises to be a powerful force changing the direction the agency is taking with them.

As a male, the practitioner appeared cautious in allowing himself to be pitted against Mrs. Tanner, although he let the girls keep certain illusions about him as a good father and friend. The practitioner used the interpretation of the victim role to empower the girls to act on their own behalf. He chose not to move the process into slow motion and reflection, or to engage the girls in interacting with one another to address their hidden agendas.

Feedback (National Training Laboratory, 1966/1967)

Feedback is a technique designed to assist members in maintaining their boundaries, eliminating assumptions, and expressing their reactions to one another's behaviors. For the receiver, feedback offers understanding of how one is perceived and reacted to in the group process. For the giver, feedback provides a chance to clarify and express one's feelings and reactions to others' behaviors. Through the feedback process the group as a whole learns that no two members will perceive or feel exactly the same way—a most humanistic observation.

The practitioner slows down the interaction when members are reacting directly to one another to clarify the "I perceive and I feel" perspective. Or the practitioner may decide to introduce feedback more formally by teaching it to the group. In clarifying, the practitioner notes frequent uses of semiaccusatory statements such as "you are acting hostile" by questioning, "What did she do that gave you that perception?" Another question is "How did you feel when you thought she was hostile?" The practitioner may ask members to share perceptions and reactions to interactions, or encourage two members to demonstrate the process by asking one to begin by sharing a self-contained feeling about another's behavior ("When you do x, I feel y.") If the members are reluctant or unclear, the practitioner demonstrates his or her own perceptions and feelings in feedback form.

Illustration

A group in a county-sponsored drug rehabilitation program, made up of members with HIV-positive diagnoses, is involved in expressing angry feelings toward drug-addicted lovers who gave them the disease. Some of the members, who were substance abusers themselves and contacted the disease, are quiet. Justine says, deliberately looking away from some of the quiet people, "Damn them, they're quiet." The practitioner, Laura, asks, "What are you trying to say?" Justine answers, "I hate the quiet. I know it's drug users like them that gave it to me." Lee responds, "I'm quiet because I feel like you won't let me be angry that I have this disease. I gave this to myself. Do you think I knew I was getting it? I have no one to blame. At least you do. You can blame me."

After some angry outbursts, then more calm, the conversation shifts to talk about how there is no use blaming anyone. Darryl begins to cry silently. Justine reaches out to him, saying, "I'm sorry if I hurt your feelings and got you upset. Is that why you are crying?" "No," he says, "It's because I don't want to die. But it's no use. I might as well go back to drugs. What irony. I give up drugs only to find out it's too late anyway." Lee says, "I know, but when you say that I start to feel hopeless also. But then I say that it's better not to be hopeless. I don't want you to feel hopeless either." Todd chimes in, "Hell, no. This group is supposed to help us get support." Justine says, "But what if it's just an abyss and there is no hope?" Todd says, "Come on Justine, you have to find hope."

Others chime in, offering support, and the talk turns toward wanting to continue living. After some time, the practitioner says, "There've been some really heavy things said. It might help if you could look at how you have been responding to what each other is saying." After some silence, Felicia begins, "Well, I feel Justine laid a trip on some people here, and I don't like it." "Tell Justine," the practitioner urges. Felicia continues, looking at Justine: "Like you are so angry, you just have to lash out." Justine is quiet. The practitioner says, "Justine, how do you react to what Felicia just said?" "I know you have a point," Justine answers, "No one likes to be told they laid a trip on someone else. Do others feel I did that?" Marion says she feels that Justine is less tolerant of the drug users than the gays. The practitioner says, "Marion, it would help if you could pinpoint how she shows that." Marion says, "It was just in this meeting that I became aware of this." The practitioner says, "When you saw her do that, how did that make you feel?" Marion says that she felt upset because everyone in the group is trying to cope with terrible luck, and she tells Justine, "You undermine that and get sneaky. I know it hurts. It hurts me too, for myself and for all of us." Darryl points out that he feels "glad you said it hurts you too, Marion, because I was feeling we were just picking on Justine, because we couldn't look at our own stuff." Heads nod, followed by quiet for a few moments.

The practitioner wonders, "What other reactions have you all been having to what's being said tonight?" Todd tells Lee that he appreciates what he said about feeling he could blame no one but himself: "I didn't realize until then how you felt." "Sort of made you feel closer to him?" the practitioner asks. "Yes," Todd answers, "and I see how much I am like you, Lee, because whether you did drugs, or are gay like me, you end up blaming yourself for getting it. I hadn't quite realized that before."

The practitioner says, "I've been feeling particularly connected to all of you today. You've said so many things that hit me. I value your courage to find hope, Todd, Felicia, and Marion. I value also your strength, Justine, Darryl, and Lee, in sharing the despair."

Discussion

The group begins by moving quickly toward a high degree of intensity. At this time, with many feelings being expressed, it is not appropriate for the practitioner to ask members to pause and reflect directly on how they are feeling about what members are saying. Too much is being said; rather, the practitioner merely asks for clarification early on. After it becomes apparent that the members have expressed what they needed to, the practitioner begins to try to help the group look at the meaning of the interactions, trying to make sense of the impact of one another's contributions and intense affects. The initial expressions of anger and despair are not typical of this usually supportive group; this is another reason why the practitioner does not intervene in it. When members seem to have finished venting, the feedback instruction and focusing begins.

When Felicia attempts to offer feedback to Justine but does not address her directly, the practitioner intervenes with "tell Justine." Thereon, members speak directly to each other. The next intervention the practitioner makes is to ask Marion to be specific regarding what Justine has said. It is at this time that Marion, too, realizes that Justine has presented this negative affect toward drug users only at this meeting. This intervention prevents the group from globalizing from one incident. Asking Marion to tell how she felt about what Justine said enables her to accept responsibility for her own hurting reactions. By asking the group for other reactions to each others' behaviors, the practitioner takes the focus away from Justine, opening up channels for others to give and receive feedback.

Finally, as the process seems to move toward a natural conclusion, the practitioner offers her own perspective and feelings about the members' behaviors.

SUMMARY

The practitioner's judgment and emphasis in using the twelve techniques for actualizing purpose was discussed. Specific attention was centered on five techniques: *Role rehearsal* and *programming* are two techniques that are directly experiential in their aim. Through these, members and significant others can interact completely in the framework of meetings, as well as in contrived and actual situations, to meet their needs. These more experientially oriented techniques lead to the examination of members' interactive patterns. *Group reflective consideration, interpretation,* and *feedback* come into play in relation to role rehearsal and programming. They are used to focus attention and efforts on group and member scenarios and idiosyncratic reaction patterns that are interfering with the change process.

The next chapter discusses seven more techniques that are used by the practitioner to help the group actualize its purpose.

Chapter 7

FURTHER TECHNIQUES
FOR ACTUALIZING PURPOSE

Seven techniques used by the practitioner to help the group actualize its purpose will be discussed in this chapter. *Conflict resolution, group mending,* and *confrontation* are techniques the practitioner uses when there are disruptions in the flow of the group process, or when it is necessary to redirect the flow of expression. The techniques of *data and facts* and *self-disclosure* are used when the members need information that is factual or affective. *Dealing with the unknown* and *taking stock* are used to help the group move to newer plateaus.

Each of these techniques has a relationship to the group interactions that actualize purpose. For clarification, see Table 7.1 below.

Conflict Resolution
(Bernstein, 1973; Deutsch, 1973)

Conflict is an essential feature of interpersonal relations. The successful expression and resolution of conflicts will enable a fuller intensity and greater depth in the group members' relations. Conflict consists of feeling and content about an issue members consider important.

Conflict resolution may be called into play in response to processes that are the product of experiences, programs, role rehearsals, and group interactions as well as interactions in environmental situations. This technique is used to define and bring to the surface conflict-causing issues so that differences are respected and worked on before

Table 7.1

Relationship of Techniques to Interactions That Actualize Purpose

Technique	Interaction
Conflict Resolution	Identify themes to be worked on Respect differences
Group Mending	Identify feelings to help group work on change
Confrontation	Identify issues for change Identify projections and self-fulfilling prophecies
Data and Facts	Identify themes to be worked on
Self-Disclosure	Identify feelings that help group work on change Foster sharing perceptions and feelings about each others' behavior
Dealing With the Unknown	Expressing role-enhancing behavior Help members work on change Identify projections and self-fulfilling prophecies
Taking Stock	Reflect and reinforce member and group change in order to replicate change

they fester, go underground, and reach the point of no return; this occurs when differences become so irreconcilable that they cause the dissolution of relationships.

The practitioner has to be prepared to use conflict resolution in and out of the group. Using this technique requires considerable quotients of self-awareness and self-discipline in exposing conflicts and dealing with them. The practitioner—like the members—is at risk of avoiding conflicts, thereby ultimately becoming unable to retrieve interpersonal relationships and establish truces.

Using this technique involves three interrelated activities. The first is *surfacing and defining* the conflict; the second is *clarifying themes, feelings, and stakes* in the conflict; the third is *offering new perspectives*.

The intent of surfacing and defining the conflict is to identify conflicts early enough to prevent the members from becoming engulfed in negative and hateful feelings. Rather than letting conflicts go deeply underground, the practitioner pursues them early on by identifying the issues and feelings that surround them.

The practitioner clarifies themes, feelings, and stakes in the conflict to help members view the issues through varied lenses and develop functional approaches. The practitioner probes through request and even through insistence, inviting the full participation of all members— whatever their alliances, or their intensity of investments in winning and in being right. Asking members for specificity around their feelings and stakes in a conflict, as well as checking for intentions and mis- perceptions, brings about clarification of issues and needs. This aspect of the technique helps members partialize their many concerns in an effort to provide flexibility where there once was rigidity.

The intent of *offering new perspectives* (Bernstein, 1973) is to help members to reexperience the issues in constructive ways. The practi- tioner reframes the members' experiences of the problem, building on the clarification of themes and feelings that has just occurred, by capturing and redefining its emotional and interactional dimensions. Reframing helps the members to identify and own the process toward resolving conflicts so as to gain perspective and enhanced interpersonal skills. The objective sought through offering new perspectives is to reestablish the "we" feeling in the group as a sign of work toward resolution.

The practitioner must view the signs of conflict as potentially posi- tive, and as opportunities to deepen norms that bring about individu- ality. The members can see that submerging conflicts and seeking indirect means to resolve them come from fear and anxiety, as well as from aggressive interests in power, control, and dominance.[1]

Illustration

A men's support group has been meeting for forty-odd sessions with increasing success in airing their concerns about vulnerability and feeling the need to dominate in their relationships at work—and recre- ation—with other men and women. For the last two months, the fabric of their process has been woven around communicating in areas where members disagree with one another. At times, there have been heated disagreements that so far have lead to valuable activities and discus- sions. The practitioner, Frank, has used various techniques.

At the end of a recent meeting the practitioner saw the two oldest members, Mitch and Norm, leaving together and whispering to each other. He noted that others saw this as well. Remembering that Mitch and Norm were central in the group's power struggle, having ultimately been rejected as group leaders early on, the practitioner decides to surface this dynamic in the next meeting.

As the members enter the meeting room, the practitioner notes that Norm and Mitch are uncharacteristically late. They arrive together, talking on their way in. The practitioner looks to them and points out the difference in their habit over the last sessions, indicating that it is reminiscent of behavior that occurred in the first few meetings last year: "Are you aware of it? Are others?" Others admit to having noticed it at the last meeting. With some furtive glances, Mitch and Norm agree to the pattern. The practitioner wonders if the behavior might not be in reaction to themes of domination and power that came up in the last meeting.

Talk begins, with some men seeing the common theme as being financial survival and success. Dave remembers that Steve in particular had been going over his struggles and feelings about this last week. Frank asks Mitch and Norm if this relates to them. Mitch becomes noticeably uncomfortable and, looking to Norm for nonverbal support, doesn't respond. Norm avoids answering also, saying "I don't have to answer you. You make such a big deal out of everything, the minute someone comes in late. Can't a guy just talk to a friend?" Sal says to Mitch, "I heard you say you're going to be out of work soon; that is lousy." Mitch tells him that it's none of his business: "I can handle it; Norm and I are working on it as we have always done." Members look at each other. Some retort glibly, while others offer advice and invoke caring attitudes.

The practitioner says, "What is happening here is very important to your agenda to reduce competitiveness and increase cooperation. Mitch, you bring to us a survival issue with its fears and anxieties. But affection and caring can go by the wayside when folks are involved in survival." Silence; dead silence. Then Norm says to Steve, "You've been showing off, despite the fact that you've been hurting these last few sessions." Then he turns and says to the practitioner, "And you haven't picked up on any of this, you've been getting off on being one of us. Fuck you all!"

The group seems stunned by the outburst. After a moment of silence, the practitioner says, "I guess you're right. I'm drawn to this, too. I look to you and Norm, and there's a lot I respect. I suppose that threatens my attitude about my role, so when I'm unsure I sometimes don't reveal my own vulnerability. I think vulnerability has been easy here around romantic relationships with lovers, but not in survival relationships or bread-and-butter issues." The members look at each other with the looks that imply they've heard the "truth."

Then a discussion opens up about showing vulnerability, especially when some of the men have experienced financial losses, unemployment, or business failures. Steve tells Norm, "I think you are helping Mitch hide his true feelings from the rest of us, and I think you're full of it." He then says to Mitch, "Many of us have been through financial ups and downs. Talk about it with us; don't act cool and in control of things when it's just not where you are." Mitch begins to talk about closing down his business, how he had tried to stay in, to keep the payroll going, but that it's not possible anymore. He is very down.

Sal begins to tell about the time he lost his job and the feelings of failure he experienced, the vulnerability, and the loss of masculinity that came from the inability to support his family. Members try to give Mitch hope by recounting their own prior struggles and telling him that they are there for him. Mitch points to Norm as a friend, but also acknowledges the others. There is a long and continuous attempt by different group members to share their feelings of vulnerability and fragility more openly, while at the same time attempting to learn that this sharing ultimately offers the support needed to go on.

The practitioner asks the group, "Does it help to talk about these things, to find another way to give support and show vulnerability? Or is it hard for you?" Steve says he feels these issues must be talked about, otherwise "my friend here, Norm, will just blow off crazy steam at me, and he'll have to tell you to fuck off again." The practitioner invites Norm to consider, "Does it help to just blow off steam? What if you hadn't accumulated all this pent-up frustration and anger?" Norm thinks and says, "I don't know if you guys can help. Mitch and I have a business deal going. But I must admit the support and encouragement takes a little bit off the worry." The practitioner says, "We can only help if you give us a chance."

Discussion

The practitioner first picks up nonverbal cues and decides to cite them in the forthcoming session. This is done directly, leading to a surfacing of difficult and painful feelings. The practitioner also offers some ideas on motives for the tension in the group, distinguishing between competition for affection and for survival.

The practitioner is included in the conflict; he cannot avoid his part in the interpersonal puzzle. By offering his own feelings of vulnerability to the group, the practitioner models honesty while at the same time attempting to offer clarification of issues and themes in the conflict. Through this, members are able to begin thinking and talking about their vulnerabilities and real issues that stretch the group's ability to talk about hard subjects.

This group appears to be on the way toward some sort of resolution that is more positive than negative. Members have not turned away altogether from conflict and painful feelings, but ability to show vulnerability openly will require further efforts. This group could easily have disintegrated had the practitioner not caused the conflict to surface. The focus of attention on the practitioner also helped the members by forcing him to respond directly, which created a jolt and provided the opportunity to restructure the group's thinking, perceptions, and attitudes.

Group Mending

It is a fact of group life that as the members move forward to meet their needs and interests they will encounter varying degrees of failure and success. Some of the members' experiences will result in feelings of vulnerability and ineffectiveness. Group mending is used to help members own and get beyond feelings of failure, rejection, and humiliation to restore the group's ability to function in an affirming, goal-oriented manner despite disappointments.

In the face of these reactions, the practitioner reaches for and actively initiates discussion of the interactions and feelings that are causing group members to feel hurt and uncomfortable. Denial, threat, and avoidance of talking about failures and negative reactions also are bound to occur; the practitioner helps bring about the talking-out of these difficult feelings while at the same time causing the group and members to examine and affirm their strengths.

Illustration

A group of 9-, 10-, and 11-year-old boys has been formed for socialization. They live in a group residence for children with severe social and emotional difficulties. The group has been organized with a goal of improving their success in social adventures and giving them opportunities for new and different experiences. Through their efforts—along with the energy of the practitioner, Randy—they have prepared for their first meeting outside of the residence. This requires leaving, taking public transportation for one half hour, going into a settlement house, and establishing their new meeting environment there. (Obviously much work has occurred between sessions among the practitioner, the boys, and the staff at the settlement house.)

Four of the seven boys and Randy are in the meeting room at the settlement house. Three have gone to the supply office for construction paper and scissors, which were supposed to be in the room but weren't. These supplies are to be used for making a group insignia that will be put up each time they meet in this room. Suddenly the door flies open, and the three boys are led in by an angry man who gives them hell for running in the hallways, saying, "You will not be able to come here again. I am going to tell the program director." While depositing them into the arms of the practitioner, he exclaims "Here they are!" and leaves, slamming the door behind him.

Silence and a mood of devastation ensue. There is shock. The practitioner holds the boys and duck-walks toward the others, beckoning them into his and each others' arms. He then gently nudges them to the floor, followed by more hugging and holding. Some boys are teary. The crayons, paints, and tape are around the floor. The silence lasts a long couple of minutes. Then the practitioner says, "Although the door is closed I feel that any moment that man will come back with the program director, and if this happens I will have them sit with us and talk. If they won't sit, we will stay sitting together."

Noting that much time has in fact passed, the practitioner realizes that no one is coming in. He says, "Boys, they aren't coming in, but we have to talk with the program director and the man who brought you back in to clear up things." The boys are listening intently. He continues: "Maybe there are misunderstandings, and maybe the three of you went off half-cocked. Whatever, this should not be the end of the world for us in this room. Randy asks the four boys who had been in the room, Joel, Eddie, Mike, Hal—should I or we all go to the program director's office?" They talk back and forth, with the practitioner keeping the exploration going. Randy then matter-of-factly addresses the three boys who had been returned to the fold, "What happened?" It is established that they went down a wrong stairway and had, after running into the man and his wrath, run away from him. The practitioner asks, "What are you feeling now, guys, about what is happening to us here?" There is talk now about how they felt wronged and misunderstood, as if they were bad people who could not be trusted. The practitioner wonders aloud, "How can we really show them that you all are trustworthy and respectful of the center?"

Discussion

The practitioner employs good professional judgment in immediately paying attention to the group as a whole. He engages in group mending in nonverbal, physical ways responding to the boys, his own shock, and to the boys' immaturity and fears. "I feel as though the man will come into the room" is his way of joining the boys in their feelings of hurt and humiliation. He does not interrogate, nor does he get caught up in what will happen. Rather, he stays with what their needs are for feeling safe, secure, and able to continue. By doing this, the group worker may well have avoided a subgroup conflict of blame placed on some of the members, or blame placed on the community center and its staff. The boys need to regain their emotional resources so they can figure out how to advocate for themselves in the center and be seen as responsible. The practitioner helps them to solve this problem, offering his own resources and support so that they can feel confidence in their ability to be eventually understood by the program director.

Confrontation

Confrontation is a very special technique used to change behavior as it is being expressed. It is used when the practitioner has judged that a member or the group as a whole has done considerable work on change and is ready to push through a doorway into a different form of expression.

The practitioner uses the technique by indicating that a form of interaction and expression in the present must be altered, right then and there, in the group situation. The practitioner identifies the dysfunctional expression and asks for and guides the desired replacement. Confrontation is done with respect for the members' rights to self-determination, their inherent capacities, and their developing abilities. Members cannot be forced against their wills to change the form or content of their self-expressions.

Illustration

In a parenting group, members have been talking about how they get caught between their spouses and their children when their children ask for things and seem to be playing one parent off against the other. Gerald says that he's noticed that he gets angry at his wife, Charlotte (who is sitting right next to him), "when I think you are being unfair to Sharon [their 15-year-old daughter]. But I'm having doubts right now; I'm not sure you're being unfair. But I guess I could take her aside and calmly talk to her." Before Gerald stops, Charlotte looks at him with a scolding air and retorts, "Yeah, there goes that 'Daddy's little girl' thing. You're always blaming me." He says, "But Charlotte, I am saying that I might be seeing it wrong, that maybe I am misperceiving." She looks away from him. He looks defeated. The other members have been struggling with this type of communication that comes up in parenting adolescents. Each time one of the couples tries to look at this, they get to a point in the process similar to the one Gerald and Charlotte are in.

The practitioner, Gary, asks Charlotte and Gerald to turn to one another. Then he says, "Charlotte, continue to be aloof and hurt. Give him the cold shoulder." "Now, Gerald," the practitioner continues, "play back to her what you said earlier, that you were misperceiving. But play it back to her loud and clear, so she can really hear you." Gerald says this to her directly, as instructed. Charlotte smiles, but doesn't change her pose. Gerald continues, "Hey, get off your high horse. You act like you're right and I'm wrong. That's not the case. You can be wrong, too." "In fact," he says, "maybe you play with Sharon's feelings like you play with mine." Charlotte shoots him an angry look. Gerald continues, "We're in this together, not in a battle." Charlotte tells him how difficult Sharon is to handle, that she can be manipulative and "you don't help." Gerald backs off. The practitioner says, "Don't back off, Gerald; each time you hear you're not helpful, you retreat." Gerald continues, saying, "Sharon is hard to handle and neither one of us can handle her all alone." Charlotte says, "I can't deal with her challenges and competitiveness." Gerald says, "Maybe you compete back," then backs off again. The practitioner says, "Come on, Gerald, stay with it." Gerald goes on, "You set it up so I feel like I'm her daddy *and* yours, like you're both sisters here. And I hate it." She responds, "I hate it, too."

Charlotte and Gerald talk more about how they have to back away from Sharon to their own private space to decide what to do when she tries to manipulate them. "What we do in front of her is terrible," Gerald says. Charlotte agrees. As they continue talking to each other, it becomes apparent to everyone in the group that this represents what goes on for all of them. The members start talking about how going aside and supporting each other in their relationships usually works and is valued by their children. The group worker joins in with this, helping the process of exploration and support to evolve.

Discussion

In this meeting, the practitioner seizes the opportunity to help both members of a couple change their characteristic way of interacting in an effort to help all of the group's members get past a characteristic stumbling block.

First, he uses confrontation to direct the couple in replaying a scene that was not effectively dealt with. He asks Gerald to repeat what he said to his wife "loud and clear so she can really hear you," implying that he was not heard before. Then he tells Gerald that every time his wife reacts to his forthrightness defensively, he backs away. This propels Gerald further. When Gerald retreats again, the practitioner uses confrontation again: "Come on, stay with it." The practitioner provides Gerald with very little room to maneuver out of the direct interaction with his wife. In essence, the group worker uses confrontation with Gerald, who gains impetus from it and uses the confrontation mode with his wife.

Throughout, the practitioner does not use confrontation with Charlotte. Rather, by confronting Gerald the practitioner enables him to be forceful and to use a broader range of self-expression and interaction with his wife. This holds the promise of strengthening the marital bond not only for this pair, but for the others, as they begin to see the relevance of this interaction to their own situations.

Data and Facts (Schwartz, 1961; Shulman, 1984)

The intent of this technique is to provide accurate information to help people carry out judgments based on the state of knowledge in the area, rather than biases that support other popular—albeit uninformed—viewpoints. One other aim of data and facts is to show that knowledge can be used by some as power to subvert interpersonal relations, rather than to support them. The focus here is on how expertness and "smarter than" positions can inhibit members from getting to the facts and meaning.

The practitioner is called upon to improve the members' knowledge base regarding relevant subjects. This is done through study, training, and consultations. The practitioner directly identifies and shares subject matter relevant to the group's purpose with the members. The practitioner also engages the members in their own efforts at gathering factual information and intelligent knowledge. The practitioner, having developed familiarity with the subject areas that underpin the group's purpose, is prepared to help clear up distortions based on incorrect information and biased knowledge. The practitioner carries out this technique within the group's process—in the meeting room as well as in the community.

Illustration

A human rights committee, meeting bimonthly, has been formed on behalf of a residence program for developmentally disabled people. The committee is composed of staff, residents, and community members. The social worker has been given the role of facilitator to assist them in insuring the humane treatment of the residents as well as the agency's relationships with the local office of Mental Retardation and Health. This meeting follows one in which representatives of the Human Rights Division of the local office did a training component for this group. There, the trainer spoke of reports of incidents of sexual abuse of the retarded by each other, and how difficult it is to help the retarded with their sexual urges.

At this meeting the committee is very involved with what the trainer said about sexual abuse. The group is moving immediately to develop regulations for the residence that would clearly limit the residents' opportunities for dating and cohabitation. Beverly, the practitioner, has done her homework in an effort to help them make a well-founded (rather than precipitous) decision that includes information gathered from a number of informed sources. The practitioner had read extensively about sexuality and the retarded, making it a point to visit more than five residences and speak with the various staffs in informal ways. She also has been involved in some phone consultations with a colleague who is studying this phenomenon and educating people who are retarded for sexuality.

The practitioner says, "Before we decide anything, I know people in other residences who are willing to have us visit to find out about their experiences with residents' sexual activity." There is more discussion, and a sense of confusion about how much information is needed to develop a well-thought-out policy. The practitioner says, "My experience in counseling some individuals who are retarded about romance has been okay, that people know their limits." Mary, the resident member, is shaking her head in agreement. The practitioner turns to her and asks, "Mary, do you know the woman from DMRH said she wouldn't go on an elevator with a client without others there? I heard her." Another member says, "I recall when we all went to the central office for training that first time, and she asked some of us to wait to go down with her." Mary says, "In the central office, they always think we are dangerous, but it's not true. They don't trust us." Beverly says, "This fellow, Marty, has a video of a group session on dating which I can bring to a meeting when you are ready. It will be easy to set up." People agree. She continues, "After gathering the information, then decisions can be made—no later than four weeks from now."

After lengthy discussion revolving around the sense of urgency to resolve the problem, the group realizes that they are anxious and do not have all the information. They agree to put off the decision. Some of the members volunteer to visit several residences. From the visits to several settings, members learn from informal chats with group home staff that when people who are retarded are passionate, they are louder and noisier than their nonretarded peers. The latter get anxious at the noise, and fear for the welfare of the noisemakers.

Discussion

This practitioner is aware of how prone group members can be to making quick decisions, especially when they believe that their actions are responsibly based. In this case, the members had two prior training contacts with state officials in the community; through those contacts they had come to believe a certain way about the proposed problem. In essence, they were prepared as a majority to make a particular decision—to limit the rights of retarded residents in the interest of their welfare. However, they were missing data from other sources. They had not spent time within the residences themselves, learning from informal sources and house staff about the residents' day-to-day activities and how sexuality had been discussed and managed.

The practitioner had to work against the group's desire to meet its obligations quickly while relying on only one source for data. She had to go against their tide, showing them in a nonconflictive way that there was other information to be gathered. By making these resources available to their scrutiny she was mindful not to hold her own and others' expertise over their heads.

In this process, the practitioner had to help the committee accept the frustration that comes from being unable to reach a decision because the problem has not yet been completely understood. However, by helping them include relevant facts and experiences, they avoided future embarrassment that could have resulted when the community and residents found out that the human rights committee's denial of residents rights had come about because its members had not gathered the necessary and relevant facts. Of greater significance, the members in making decisions for other human beings had to make decisions that respected the integrity and desires of those persons.

Self-Disclosure

Self-disclosure is used to convey humanness and fallibility. It shows the practitioner to be integrally related to and affected by the process. Self-disclosure is most often used in the group's middle phase; here, the members view the practitioner as unique and differentiated, with experiences and perspectives on interactions that can help them understand new aspects of social life and emotional expression. Before this phase, while the members are in struggles about their own power and control in relation to the practitioner, self-disclosure by the practitioner may lead the members to negative comparisons of their own abilities and successes. This puts the practitioner into the position of being a hallmark of special ability, often leaving the members feeling incapable by comparison.

The practitioner directly shares feelings and reactions toward members and significant others who are involved in the process. Self-disclosure of professional limitations and vulnerabilities is also useful; so is the request for help with certain difficult aspects of the practitioner role in the group. Self-disclosures occur both after reflective periods and in spontaneous ways. A request for help in solving the practitioner's personal problems is not appropriate, because it oversteps the bounds of the nature and meaning of the professional relationship.

Since humanistic group work is based on the group's externality, the practitioner often functions in real situations with the members. There the practitioner is observed as well, and these observations disclose his or her styles of expression and frailties. In this way the group worker discloses his or her handling of feelings, and of formal and informal role transactions.

In contexts where group members feel there is something wrong with them for having to be in the group, self-disclosure helps demonstrate the meaningfulness of interpersonal relationships and prevents one-upsmanships among members.

Because of its subjectivity and genuineness, self-disclosure is wedded to humanistic values and democratic norms of the method. One sees how the practitioner is called upon to develop self-awareness in all types of interpersonal situations, and to learn about mutual respect, cooperativeness, and taking care of others' needs. Furthermore, he or she does not violate people's boundaries, nor let his or her own boundaries be violated. Because these characteristics epitomize interaction in interpersonal relationships, it is clear why self-disclosure as a technique is used when group members are intently working on changing their own interactions in their interpersonal situations.

Illustration

Carla, Eunice, Michelle, Deborah, Eleanor, and Donna are discussing how defeated and angry they feel when they are the only women in mixed company at business gatherings. They have been meeting as a mutual support group of female managers, under the auspices of the company's employee assistance program. Eunice is saying, "So I cracked a prurient pun, and the men looked away as if they didn't hear me. I was ignored. They waited to interact again after I got the message. How screwed up; they were cracking lewd jokes left and right! It's like a variation on the time when women couldn't smoke, but men could!"

Michelle turns to Janet, the practitioner, and says, "It's the same for you most of the time. You sit in the cafeteria with other women, rarely with men except for business. We see that. What do you think? What is your experience?" Janet says, "At the risk of incurring your wrath, I want to hold off on talking about me right now. I assure you I will. Right now it's your experience, and I want to carry my role and make sure you know what you're working on. If I talk about my own reactions, I am afraid you will be too affected by my experience."

Some members retort, "You're playing games, Janet. You're keeping a distance from us. Tell us what it is like for you." The practitioner says, "I'm not keeping a distance; you're making me feel bad." Donna says, "Come on, you are a woman, too. You get something out of being with us each week. What do you feel out there at meetings and the like?" The practitioner says, "I feel caution and concern. I believe this is all happening because of the social psychology and politics of male and female relations. I look for ways to be me with men and women, and dislike feeling that I'm being stereotyped or not being able to say what I want. If I'm feminine with males it doesn't require assuming a submissive female posture. So I hate these situations, but I try not to personalize them, though at times I do anyway. I've had experiences like you, Eunice, where I might as well not have been in the room. But what will help you now is for everyone to have a look at what you all feel like when these kinds of things happen."

This explanation triggers the group members into questions and reactions about their own feelings and motives. Unfortunately, there is a sense of awe about the practitioner's grasp of herself in the situation, a sense that needs further work in the group.

Discussion

In this situation the practitioner does not choose to self-disclose on her own, though she may have a great deal to share with the group. When she is called upon to share her feelings, she does not at first. She prefers to have the group understand their own reactions to being rejected. In addition, for her to respond before members react to Eunice's predicament can serve as an avoidance for the members, making her too central to the process and them too peripheral. By not responding right away, Janet tries to help the members see that their issues matter more than hers, and that her resolutions can be helpful only as additional material for working on these problems.

Although she does not respond to what they are asking right away, she does trust them by giving them her genuine reaction, that they are making her feel bad, as well as her feelings about her professional responsibility with them.

On the other hand, the practitioner has to eventually respond to the request even though the risk is that the members will overidealize her. Not to respond is likely to cause the group to break faith with her. Telling them about herself undoubtedly stimulates many perceptions and feelings for the members; other dimensions of authority issues that are part of their present theme are stimulated. These signify the practitioner as special, and reflect submissive self-evaluations similar to those they experience with males.

Dealing with the Unknown

Dealing with the unknown is used to help the members take steps into change efforts and experiences when they are inhibited from moving forward. It is more often used when the members are considering their direction than when they are in the midst of an experiential happening. Use of this technique can lead to experiential processes.

Dealing with the unknown may be used when the members have run up blind alleys, or are not looking at realities because they are afraid to move toward them. The signs include random, undirected activity where there has previously been directed and purposeful activity. Another sign is the return to old forms of interaction and problem solving after a period of more effective and secure actions (Garland, Jones, & Kolodny, 1973).

The practitioner encourages the members to discuss their views about how change will unfold, what change will feel like, and what risks they imagine. Members are also asked to consider what fears prevent them from acting differently. This technique interfaces with the members' humanistic right to determine their own direction and destiny.

Illustration

A group of adolescent boys who are part of a drug-prevention group work program in their high school are complaining about the quality of parties and other interactions. It seems that whenever the high school has a dance, most of the kids hang out outside the school and do not go in. Many of them try to act "cool," as if going into the party itself is "uncool." It takes a toll on them because they never get to go inside to have fun; instead, they spend their time figuring out where they will go next—to the mall, the movies, or the pool hall—who will go with whom, and how to arrange the transportation. (Some of them have cars; some don't.)

At this meeting, several of the boys are admonishing each other for never quite getting anywhere together the previous Friday night. Jim says to Hank, "You said you were going to go to the mall, but when I went over there with Kelly and Joan, you weren't there. I bumped into Doreen, and she said you'd gone into the movies with the guys. Why didn't you wait?" Hank responds that the show was just starting. Pete retorts, "We should have stayed at the party. My mother was real mad when she heard we had left after she had dropped us off there."

The practitioner, Roger, says, "Let's look at what happened Friday night. How come you guys didn't just go into the dance?" Jeff says, "You can't go in, because you don't know if it will be a good party." Mike says, "If you're outside then you can see who is coming, and whether it's worth while spending money to go in." Greg tells the group, "I went in and they had a great DJ, but people who were inside really felt uptight because half of you weren't coming in. There were lots of girls there, too, and they were really mad at all of you for not staying." Kevin asks, "You guys who left, what did you do?" Several say they spent time looking for kids in the pizza joint at the mall, a couple went to the movies, and Jim and the girls went to the pool hall. "How was that?" asks the practitioner. Several mumble "okay" in response.

The practitioner asks, "What about the drug dealers, were they out there too?" The guys mumble "yes," and talk about what a drag it is to have to dodge those guys in the mall. "Given those guys in the mall looking to prey on you, what if you had stayed at the party with the DJ?" Roger continues. Hank and Jim begin to say it might have been better: "First of all, we wouldn't have to handle the dealers, and Greg said there were lots of girls there." Greg retorts, "You wouldn't know what to do with the girls anyway. You guys won't dance, you just like to act cool, but you won't go into a party and just party." The practitioner asks, "Does Greg have a point, guys? Is that true?" Mike sheepishly says, "Maybe."

Roger replies, "Come on, guys, let's look at this 'maybe' business." Jim says, "I had girls with me, I just didn't want to go in there." Hank says, "Yeah, but you're just friends with Kelly and Joan. I know you really like Doreen. And I think she was in the mall looking for you." There are jokes and laughter. The practitioner says, "It sure would have been easier to find Doreen if you all had stayed at the party, don't you think?" Pete says, "It's true, she left with Ellen when she heard us saying you had gone to the mall."

The practitioner asks, "What would have happened if all of you had stayed at the party like you had started out to do?" Pete says, "First of all, my mother wouldn't be threatening to ground me. And second, we might have found the girls!" Jim says, "Maybe Doreen would have stayed." Continuing, Roger asks, "What would have happened if you all had stayed? What would it have been like?" They talk about having to dance, and how some of them don't know reggae while others don't like disco. Roger responds, "So you guys are afraid that you don't dance so well." Hank tells the group that the girls are better dancers. Jim says, "Yes, at these parties the girls all hang together, laugh, look relaxed, and talk to each other."

The practitioner says, "Jim, just for the sake of argument, let's say there's another dance this Friday and you stay and you approach Doreen to dance. What would happen?" Pete chimes in, "She'd dance with you. Even if you're a lousy dancer." Everyone laughs. The practitioner says, "Well, Jim?" Jim says, "I don't know—she'd say she had to go to the ladies room and leave." "What if she did?" Roger asks. Jim says, "I'd be embarrassed." Roger says, "She could say no and you'd have to deal with it, but what if she said yes?"

Jim tells about how he feels shy and nervous. Roger wonders if other guys would feel that way. The group talks for roughly 15 minutes about feeling embarrassed, shy, and nervous with the girls. Roger supports their efforts by reminding them that "you never know how things will turn out until you try. If you don't try, you'll just be hanging out in the mall at the mercy of the drug dealers. Isn't that worse? Isn't it better to at least be at the mercy of your own feelings?" More laughter and good-humored discussion ensues. Then the boys start to talk about the local baseball team. The meeting ends with a resolve to go to the next party and to stay inside.

Discussion

Although the use of this technique revolves around dealing with the unknown, exploration and role rehearsal are also used to augment the technique. The practitioner stays with the content, directly questioning what is not clear and instructing members to listen and do the same. First, the practitioner asks the group why they did not stay at the party. This brings about some reporting—and hemming and hawing—about what the members actually did in their somewhat aimless search that evening. The member who remained at the party is enabled to talk about what it was like to be there.

The practitioner, knowing that the drug dealers hang out at the mall, wants to give them permission to talk about these concerns. He also wants them to know that he is aware they might go to the mall to buy drugs. This elicits their real feelings about their safety from the pushers and offers the alternative that dealing with the girls at the party is safer than dodging the drug dealers.

None of these issues could have been dealt with without the direct efforts of the practitioner. He moves along with the flow of the process, raising new issues for the group to examine. Concerns surface about maleness, shyness, and fear of rejection serving as rationalizations for not making a commitment to go into the party. Concerns about the unsafe environment also surface, and the drug issue remains one for future consideration. The boys support each other through this process. When they shift to baseball, the practitioner goes with the direction of the process, banking on the belief that the boys have gone as far as they are able in talking about their behavior, and that the next step involves going to the party with a different mindset—in touch with their fears and anxieties. Respecting the members' rights to learn from experience, the practitioner does not direct or encourage them to return to the subject, although he does wonder if this is not similar to the act of leaving the party in subgroups.

Taking Stock

This technique is used to help the group and members clarify accomplishments up to the present moment so that they can move into future goals. This may be done at the ending stage of the group, or during a natural transition to a stage with a newer set of working goals.

At the transition point in the process, the practitioner engages the group in a historical review of important events and crucial themes. The practitioner asks members to clarify the learning and experiences that have taken place, and to consider applications of this learning to future situations. This is done to heighten the group's awareness of the meaning of the accomplishments in the group at that place in time, and to offer members a chance to consider and integrate the various strategies, approaches, and affects that helped this meaning to come about. The practitioner asks for members to clarify, summarize, and crystallize prior events with a mind toward carry-over and the creation of new initiatives and alternatives.

Illustration

A group of young adults (ages 18 to 25) taking part in a support group in an urban college counseling office is ending after eight months. The group has faced many issues over the academic year. Included were issues of family, relationships, and academic achievement as well as various personal emergencies, including an abortion and a death. The members are talking about what it means to leave the group when the academic year ends next month. There has been a range of expression, from fear of leaving to some bravado about the ability to cope without the group.

Marcos and Alexandra begin to talk about how afraid they are to leave the group for the summer. They ask whether it is possible to reconstitute the group in the fall. The practitioner, Dawn, says that "we can talk about the fall later; I think right now it will help more for you to share what you are afraid will happen to you without the group." Marcos talks about how his mother and he get into battles about his stepfather, and how he and the stepfather don't get along. Reggie reminds Marcos how well he has dealt with his stepfather in recent encounters. Jackie also reminds him that he gets mad at his stepfather because he is really mad at his father for abandoning him. Marcos admits they are right, "but without you, I won't remember all of this." Alexandra talks about wanting to stay in the dorm rather than go home, because she doesn't want to face her parents' divorce. Marcos tells her, "You have to face it one day." She agrees, but says, "I would like to have the group to come back to."

The practitioner says, "Certainly we can form a group in September. Whoever wants to return to it, can. If you don't want to return, there will be no pressure. It will most likely have some new and different members, too." Several members shake their heads, indicating that they are not sure how they feel about new people joining. The practitioner once again says, "There's time to talk about a future group. I wonder how others are feeling about leaving this group now." Felicia, the mother of a two-year-old, says, "I welcome the chance to stop everything for the summer and have a chance to be with my baby." She talks about how the group has helped her accept her divorce: "Now I will try things out on my own." Mara supports Felicia's learning. The practitioner asks Mara, "What are your summer plans?" She volunteers that she has gotten a job in a resort for the summer where she will make a lot of money to help with tuition and books: "I hear there are some great guys at this place, so maybe I can test out making friends and not getting too intimate too fast." The practitioner asks Mara, "Can you clarify when you are in danger of getting too intimate too fast, Mara?" Mara talks about feeling sorry for herself when her father suddenly died, and leaning on men to help her feel better. She says, "I'm doing this less, and I'm making friends with women, too," acknowledging Felicia and others. Jose says, "But if you need me, you can call me, and I'll remind you. I'll be here all of June and July." Felicia says, "Mara, really, I expect you to call me anytime you feel down, but you better call me when you feel good, too! I know I will call you." Mara thanks everyone for their special support. The practitioner reminds Mara what a hard year she had with her father dying. "Mara, you learned that your mother is not weak, and neither are you. You didn't have to sacrifice schooling, and you and your mom were able to work out a way to come through for you. You turned out to be stronger than you thought." Mara considers this and agrees.

Dwight talks about how hard the summer without the group will be, and his fears about being drawn into a local gang he doesn't want to associate with. Fred says, "Stay away from them, that's all! Do you have a job yet?" Dwight says, "I don't, and it makes me uptight." Others advise that it will be easier for Dwight to handle these guys if he is too busy to be seen by them, and is involved with college friends. The practitioner asks Dwight how he feels about seeking a job. Dwight talks about how he usually has let things happen on their own, and that he learned in the group that this is not a good idea: "I've gone for jobs, and I've even asked people I know for leads." The group supports him for taking the initiative. The practitioner reminds him how taking the initiative with his parents and sister helped the family face his sister's drug habit: "You did the hardest job on them you could have done, and it worked. So of course you can do it for yourself now," Mara says. The practitioner says, "It seems the more you've all been able to talk openly and face things here, the easier it has been for you to deal with important problems."

The members talk more about how it will be not to see each other during the summer. A couple of members are relieved that they will have a chance to get away from everything related to school. Several are pleased to know they have the option to return in September; some are ambivalent about coming to a different group, still wanting the practitioner to redefine the terms for next year.

Jose tells the group he is going to see his relatives in South America in August. The practitioner encourages the members, saying, "Talk more about how you think the summer will be. What have you learned here to help you handle the summer?" The members talk about patterns of behavior they have been working on.

The practitioner reminds them that there are four meetings left in which they can continue talking about future options. Felicia asks the practitioner what she herself will be doing in the summer. She volunteers, "I have a three-week trip planned with my husband and children to a lake resort. And I look forward to time off, for sure!" Everyone laughs, and jokes about how she must be "relieved to be rid of us for a while." She chides back, "No, you're not that bad, honest. I like this group. We've been through a lot together. And you've put in lots of great work. So it's real hard for me to end, too."

Discussion

The practitioner uses the technique of taking stock in a way that is organic to the group's process. The fears of some members about ending the group surface through their initial desire to reorganize the group for the fall term. The practitioner engages them in talking about the meaning of leaving each other for the summer, and the possibility of ending the group. She also involves them in talking about their specific fears, and how they have handled them in the past. This enables her to help many of the members appreciate how they have been handling difficult issues and feelings.

The practitioner reinforces the learning of members in cases where it is apparent that special support from her is needed. For instance, she is mindful to help Mara, who having lost a parent exhibited much dysfunctional acting-out behavior throughout the year. The practitioner responds to the situational aspects of Mara's behavior, although it is possible that her problems with men and her mother will require further work. For the moment, however, Mara seems to enjoy the support from the group necessary for her to continue her studies, and to stabilize her relationship with her mother as well as with men. On a latent level, the practitioner uses her own parental ability to reinforce Mara's current strengths.

Members like Marcos, Felicia, and Alexandra have been experiencing personal losses that leaving the group may rekindle. On the other hand, each of these members has demonstrated an ability to handle difficult interpersonal relationships through their mutual helping efforts. Acknowledging the efforts and gains made by them proves useful. Special affirmation by the practitioner is necessary especially for members who seem to need extra support.

The practitioner makes sure to validate the feeling some members have of wanting the group to end. She is careful not to yield to the desire of several members to continue, which might serve as pressure for others to return in September. Thus the practitioner is careful to say that the group can be offered in a different form in September. Members then are able to share a sense of freedom that comes from leaving the group, leaving school, and going on vacation. The practitioner, too, validates this feeling by sharing her vacation plans with the group. The humor at the end provides a helpful way for the members to gain perspective, and to work on further issues in the remaining sessions.

SUMMARY

This chapter discussed seven techniques used by the practitioner to help the group actualize its purpose:

Conflict resolution, group mending, and *confrontation* are means for working out differences of opinion, and hard and painful feelings about relationships, in the group and in the members' individual or collective experiences in their life situations.

Data and facts and *self-disclosure* are used to give the members objective facts and materials, as well as empathically derived experiences and supports, to use in their own efforts.

Dealing with the unknown and *taking stock* focus the members on what they have come to be able to do, and on how people feel and handle feelings of anxiety and fear as they move on to new aspects of situations and relationships in and out of the group. They are also employed when the group is preparing to end.

The next chapter will describe the techniques used throughout the humanistic group work method to achieve both of the dual objectives—developing the democratic mutual aid system and actualizing purpose.

NOTE

1. When conflict arises prior to the group's normative crisis, similar strategies help the group develop norms. At that time, it is useful to draw upon the technique of *decision making*, which is parallel to conflict resolution for the development of the democratic mutual aid system. This technique provides a strategy for coping with the power dynamics that tend to surround conflict during the normative crisis. When conflict occurs after the normative crisis, the members have an opportunity to add a new dimension to their differentiation.

Chapter 8

DEVELOPING THE DEMOCRATIC MUTUAL AID SYSTEM AND ACTUALIZING PURPOSE

The following techniques represent the practitioner's attempts to help members express an array of feelings, ideas, actions, and attitudes. In the actual group process, the worker will notice that some members need encouragement toward open and genuine behavior, either as a result of unfamiliarity with humanistic ways of participation or out of fear of disapproval. These techniques are used throughout the group process to bring about a variety of social and emotional interactions in relation to the humanistic group's dual objectives. They are *demand for work, directing, lending a vision, staying with feelings, silence, support, exploration,* and *identification.* They are generic to social work practice itself and are interwoven in full and partial forms with the other techniques. For clarification, see Table 8.1.

Demand for Work (Schwartz, 1976; Schwartz & Zalba, 1971)

This technique is used to encourage and motivate members to examine process and purpose issues, as well as related tasks. From a humanistic perspective, while respecting the equality and uniqueness of each member, the practitioner is aware that people may be reluctant to engage with one another. This is true in part because of the newness of

Table 8.1

Relationship of Techniques to Interactions That Develop the
Mutual Aid System and Actualize Purpose

Technique	Interactions
Demand for Work	Includes all experiences
Directing	Develop democratic norms Respect differences Create activities in the milieu Express & identify feelings to work on change Express & identify feelings to heighten group awareness
Lending a Vision	Includes all experiences
Staying With Feelings	Develop affective bonds and cohesion Help members express feelings toward each other Help members express feelings toward practitioner
Silence	Identify group process issues and heighten group awareness Test group's autonomy
Support	Includes all experiences
Exploration	Develop affective bonds Expressing and identifying feelings that help group and members work on change Identify themes to be worked on
Identification	Enhance goal setting Respect differences Express and identify issues for change Identify themes to be worked on Identify group process issues Identify projections and self-fulfilling prophecies

the group situation at the start, and the ambivalence members face at
new junctures in the process when an increase in risk and effort is called
for. In addition, members may become fearful about expressing their
personal issues because they anticipate group pressure, stigmatization,
or scapegoating.

Through the demand for work, the practitioner emotionally encourages and sometimes insists that the members move forward into the
work at hand. The practitioner holds the group to its focus and directly
recognizes when the members' tangential processes may be an "illusion
of work" (Shulman, 1984). The practitioner also takes into account
times when tangential subgroup processes are useful for restimulating

thinking and new efforts. Furthermore, when the group rests on its laurels, the practitioner acknowledges their accomplishments but reminds them that there is more work to be done.

The demand for work is used throughout the group's life. Further along in the process, it is used when members get bogged down in fears about moving on, or in conjunction with the technique of dealing with the unknown. It is also used empathically to deal with resistant attitudes that surface when confrontation is used to help members move into new experiences.

Illustration

A teen program planning group is meeting to carry out its effort in programming for the Monday night lounges. Early on in the meeting some of the vocal members accuse the practitioner, Vanessa, of bossing them around, of not really letting them make their own plans. The practitioner asks, "How am I bossing you around?" and awaits a response. Charlotte says, "Each time we throw out an idea you lean forward, and you look at us." Maureen says, "You ask us questions and give us your opinions." Others chime in, "We feel like you are all over us." The practitioner says, "Maybe I am in some ways," and trails off into thoughtfulness. The members continue to raise objections to the practitioner's involvement.

As this topic tapers off and they disengage from the practitioner, they move back into putting out ideas and arguing among themselves. After some time the practitioner begins moving in, and the group becomes uptight again. Noting this, Vanessa says, "I'm just joining with you. Yes, I do have a concern; I notice that you all react to each other as if the other is trying to have the ideas or be the boss. When this happens you do not move ahead, but get tangled up. Come on, get past this; it won't hurt you to come out the other side and see what you can create."

This demand jars the girls into activity and they plan a list of programs with high energy and nonverbal signs of satisfaction, moving to put them on a flier. No one remarks about the practitioner's push, and she just continues with the flow of the process, joining in and being gregarious with them.

Discussion

The practitioner here is faced with a challenge to her authority. She values this within the frame of the members' right to challenge and question her. She also encourages this because she actually believes that she is probably doing some things that are inhibiting them. As she listens, she notes that the girls view one another within the same frame, too. Given this, the practitioner sees that they are reacting to power and control issues, and to resistance to moving ahead. Not excluding the possibility that her behaviors are inhibitory, the practitioner chooses to stay with the process and her most immediate observations. She identifies the teens' interactions, and in the same breath moves ahead to demand that they work. She does this with full affect, keeping focused on the task at hand and hoping that it works out, but not necessarily needing it to work out. She sees this process as useful for self-determination whichever way it turns out.

As a result, the members move ahead, and the practitioner moves into interacting with them in the experience of planning. This has the potential of taking the group up onto another plateau of accomplishments.

Directing

Directing is closely aligned with the demand for work because it calls upon the practitioner to be interactive and expressive rather than reflective and neutral. The group worker's tasks in directing are derived from the metaphor of the director's role tasks in the world of drama.

The practitioner verbally or physically helps the group enact new behaviors or interactions. Directing calls upon the practitioner to actively instruct and move group members from location to location and position to position within the group environment. It can involve asking the entire group, subgroup, or individual members to physically move to different locations. Directing also aims to assist people in communicating directly with one another when they have interpersonal issues to deal with, rather than avoiding the necessary face-to-face interaction.

Illustration

Johnny, Carl, Paul, Richard, and Saul—boys in a group of 11- to 13-year-olds—are running around the room. Maurice is blindfolded, trying to find them. The practitioner is moving in and around the interactions of this game, trying to stay out of their way while encouraging them. The boys laugh and push each other, fall, and make sounds. Maurice grabs one, holds him, touches his face and body, and identifies him correctly as Richard. Off with the blindfold; they fall to the floor—with the practitioner laughing, too—and just as the boys start putting the blindfold on Richard, talk develops. Carl and Richard are heard to say that after group they are going to a "talented and gifted" meeting for the first time, that they have to go, and that they hate meeting new people.

The practitioner, Andre, grabs the moment and says, "Up and at 'em boys, Carl's and Richard's new experience fits right in." While he is talking, he is blindfolding Richard: "When you meet new people for the first time, it is just like finding out who they are when you can't see them, like in this game—except you *can* see them. Richard, run after the others. Boys scatter, but let him grab you; slow it down. Good! Richard, you've got someone. Don't take off the blindfold. Hold him." The boys are instructed to watch and listen. To Richard, he says, "Say to him, 'Hi, my name is Richard. What's your name?'" The other boy says, "Johnny." The practitioner says, "Okay Richard, ask him an identifying question, like 'which school do you go to?'" He does, and Johnny answers.

After several interchanges, Richard says (imitating the practitioner's tone), "Why are you wearing that stupid blindfold and listening to that stupid bushhaired monster?" pointing to Andre. Everyone bursts out in wild laughter, falling all over one another. Then they calm down and bow to each other stiffly faking polite "hello, who are you?" greetings.

Discussion

In this illustration the practitioner is using programming activities as age-appropriate forms of communication with youngsters. He is able to seize the moment to use a game to help some members work on a specific need—learning how to find out who a stranger is. The practitioner recognizes the analogy between the game and the situation the two members will be in within an hour's time. The practitioner quickly directs the boys in a form that allows the game to assist in clarifying a situation the members are facing. Their esprit de corps and their previous history allow the members to move into this activity easily, following directions well. The practitioner believes in the outcome of the process as the lesson, and does not teach about what is and what did happen; he just lets it unfold. The process develops to where there is a denouement. The boys enact "getting to know you," which appears as though it will carry over for Carl and Richard as well as to the others.

Lending a Vision (Schwartz, 1961)

The practitioner calls upon the special knowledge base he or she has developed through being a professional with many groups in order to provide perspective, hope, and a sense of faith about the group's ability to achieve its objectives. The technique is used at new junctures in the group's evolution, or when the group is feeling let down. At the start of the group the practitioner lends a vision by giving the members ideas about in what areas and how they will work together. While using this technique the practitioner draws upon his or her professional experience, education, and emotional perspective concerning the nature of the life experiences of people in groups and in other community-based real life situations. In addition to reading and empathizing, the practitioner seeks out other colleagues and allied professionals in order to develop the wisdom necessary for the philosophical perspectives provided when lending a vision.

The practitioner directly offers hope regarding the special importance of learning in a democratic mutual aid system, as well as the special importance of accomplishing group purpose together. Drawing from the group's experience, the group worker recognizes what is happening, and provides motivation to continue work by pointing out what can happen between people. He or she approximates a reasonable picture of reality, its unpredictableness, and its ups and downs. The practitioner communicates feelings of passion and commitment about the future to help members gain faith in their abilities. The vision lent is a red—*not* yellow—brick road upon which the members can establish a solid footing as they move ahead into what feels like uncharted territories of interaction.

Illustration

County jail prisoners in a group for maintaining sobriety are talking about how they will have a hard time going back to their neighborhoods. All agree that it will be difficult to see old friends who will be "wet," luring them back into drinking. Some are also talking about the characters they know in the streets who are selling drugs and making big money. Frank says, "It is hard for me to see my brother, who is a drinker. We come from an alcoholic family and we are close." More talk ensues about how they would like to help their families and friends. Then the talk shifts back to their own fear of returning to their communities.

Ed tells them, "The last time I left jail I ended up coming back because I got involved with drinking again, stole a car, and was caught drunk." Charles responds, "I don't want to go through that scene of being in jail again." "Once is enough. But I get afraid, because everyone has stories like yours." The practitioner, Rick, asks, "What are you afraid of? Do you know?" Charles responds, "I am afraid I won't make it, because the temptations out there are too great." Others agree that there are too many temptations on the outside.

The practitioner says, "Hey, wait a minute. I know there are lots of stories about going out and coming back because people get into the same bad scene. I know it's hard, but there are also the other kinds of stories—of success, where people left here and kept sober, went to school, got jobs, and made a life for themselves. Those are usually the people who planned good and hard for themselves to have things work out. Come on, don't just get into a bad place. The temptations will always be there. But you don't have to give in to the streets. Not if you have a plan." Sal retorts, "Come on, man, prove to me I'll have more money going straight, that it's worth it to stay sober and make a plan." The practitioner says, "Maybe this is not about money. Maybe it's about having a life for yourself that's a real life, not acting cool in the streets, living from minute to minute just to have the best car you can get!"

Obviously, the practitioner makes his mark, as the group falls back into quiet pensiveness. Finally Sal, now fighting to hold back tears, says, "It's just that I'm afraid I won't make it. It seems easier not to try." Charles tells him, "You have to remember how much it hurts to be in jail." Sal agrees. The group begins to talk, with each member locating a feeling of hope that will enable personal efforts. Charles encourages Sal to use the time in jail constructively by taking high school courses. Ed agrees, "The last time I did not make any plans while I was in jail, so when I got back to the neighborhood, there I was back with the same losers again." The members continue talking in this vein.

Discussion

While the group talks about the kind of social environments they will each have to confront upon release, the practitioner does not minimize their difficulty. A practitioner with this type of group must recognize that going back to unsupportive communities represents an awesome challenge. Yet the practitioner wants to remind the group that, in spite of difficulties, some have waged successful efforts.

The practitioner has to balance his understanding of the difficult tasks at hand with his desire to give the members further impetus, hope, and faith in themselves to continue the uphill battle to regain ownership of their lives. Rick does this by empathically acknowledging the realities they face in returning to their neighborhoods, while at the same time letting them know that obstacles can be overcome by planning and development of options. When members challenge him, asking if it's worth it to try to plan at all, the practitioner has to become more passionate in his involvement with the group, reminding them that all does not have to be lost—that all is lost only to the extent that members give up on themselves.

Lending a vision requires a communication of passion and faith in peoples' wills. It also requires sharing a belief that planned strategies can be used to overcome obstacles. By sharing his faith in their abilities, the practitioner helps the members find the hope and fortitude to continue in the face of actual obstacles.

Much more work will be needed in this group. Each member will have to specifically identify his personal obstacles. The topic of helping families and friends will also have to be worked on before members are about to be released.

Staying with Feelings (Middleman & Goldberg, 1974)

The expression of feelings is one of the hallmarks of human interaction, along with the ability to interact with awareness. Thus group interaction needs to include opportunities for members to express their feelings, to feel comfortable expressing them, and to express these feelings in ways that are considerate of others. Humanistic values support this. Each person's emotional and intellectual contributions are sought in a humanistic group. Furthermore, it is recognized that when interpersonal relations are affected by sanctions on the expression of ideas, actions, and emotions, the content and form of expression become noticeably devoid of emotional language. Because of this, the technique of staying with feelings is important throughout the entire process of group life. It serves to help members express their feelings rather than to conceal or block them, thereby facilitating an emotionalized (rather than intellectualized) process in the group.

The practitioner carries out this technique by serving as a model for the expression of feeling, speaking in the language of emotions. In addition, he or she asks members to identify what they are feeling, while at the same time acknowledging and identifying feelings as they are being expressed by the members.

The practitioner can learn early on how uncomfortable or defensive a group is by sharing his or her own feelings of anxiety due to the group's newness and the ongoing demands of group life. Judging from the response of discomfort or spontaneity, the practitioner can learn about the group's ability to stay with feelings. When processes emerge that are leading to deflection or suppression of feelings, the practitioner assists the members by activating and valuing their emotional expressions.

The technique is also carried out by staying emotionally, aurally, and visually tuned in to the verbal and nonverbal expression of affects. These expressions include manifest forms such as happy, uncomfortable, glad, disgusted, and the like. Nonverbal forms are evident in facial expressions and body language. Tones of expression are attended to as well. The emphasis is more on overt forms than on inferences a practitioner can make about covert feelings. Working on inferential feelings can overstep the members' abilities, causing more defensiveness and the risk of assumptions on the practitioner's part. Feelings are evident enough in the verbal and overt nonverbal processes in the group. By asking about feelings freely, and acknowledging members' feelings, members are helped to develop and sustain an atmosphere of comfort, while learning about the values that accrue from leading with their emotions when interacting.

Illustration

A group of single mothers who have been involved in abusing or neglecting their children is meeting to focus on the difficulties of single parenthood without assistance from spouses, lovers, and families. The group has come a long way. They have set up a phone network with each other, and have gotten support for this as an experimental part of their entitlement income. (They keep records of their calls and submit them monthly.) The practitioner, Gloria, is also the DSS worker, and many concerns about her role in the child protective services bureaucracy have been raised and dealt with in earlier meetings.

In this meeting, the members are talking about the experience of picking the children up from day care centers after work, training programs, or schools, and having to mother children. Annette says, "I'm just wiped out. I plop down on the couch, tell the boys to give me thirty minutes, close my eyes, and some times I have to shoo them. But they are learning." Maxine chimes in, "Sara and David jump all over me—I'm exhausted." Sally blanches and says softly and with great intensity, "I slapped Joel, backhanded him with my knuckles; his nose bled. I called Carol afterwards, but I had already done it." There is a stunned silence.

The practitioner, Gloria, says, "Oh—oh! I feel for you, Sally. It must have scared the hell out of you and frightened Joel. Wow!" There is silence. The practitioner says to the group, "Say something to Sally." Others say they feel sorry. Annette says she feels scared for Sally and herself. Carol strokes Sally's hand. Margaret starts crying. The practitioner says, "Wow, this really gets to all of us." Then she says to Sally, "I don't want to tell you what you are feeling or to ask you what you are feeling, but I guess I would like to know where you are at emotionally." Sally says, "I'm horrified. I feel like a nasty bitch, like I did when I yelled at Joel saying he was just like his father, a fuckin' failure." Most of the women huddle around her, listening intently. There are tears, then silence. The practitioner remains quiet.

After a while, Gladys breathes a sigh of relief and smiles. Sally says to the practitioner, "Report me for abuse." Gloria says, "I feel that under the circumstances of who you are, what your pattern is, that this is an odd happening. You know that my colleagues and I deal with these judgments all the time. We are aware of the discomforts we feel in this role, and also aware of how you stay in touch with and on top of your feelings in the difficult situations you're in."

Discussion

It is evident that this group has been working on and through their issues of being single parents for some time. In this meeting, the group is in one of these states. Their effectiveness comes from their trust in one another and the worker, which centers on the anticipation of acceptance of each other's feelings.

When Sally indicates that she hit Joel, the group does not expect retaliation from the members or the practitioner. In fact, this concern has already been dealt with. In this situation, the practitioner's relating to feelings through example and direction is a normative occurrence in the group. She clearly responds to the intensity of the moment with her exclamations of "Oh!" and "Wow!" This supports the group's ability to stay with feelings, and validates the intensity of the experience for each of the members as well as for Sally.

The practitioner then asks Sally directly to share what she is feeling. After Sally shares her reactions, the practitioner does not rush in with a response. Rather, through her silence, she allows the members time to experience their many feelings and to sort out their reactions. Breaking in with a sigh of relief, Gladys reflects the group's readiness to shift the mood and examine the event. Sally then begins to deal with her own judgment of herself by asking the practitioner to report her for abuse. Gloria tells her honestly that she does not feel this is warranted. Her assessment is based on the intensity of the mutual aid in this group (as evidenced by their ability to accept and deal with each other's feelings), the telephone support network they have created, and the infrequency of the act of striking her child.

Silence

Silence is a technique that is to be used to convey respect and support for the struggles and capabilities of the members. It is used to help and encourage the members to be themselves despite the actual and perceived social pressures to conform to expectations. The practitioner's silence offers a way for members to reflect, rather than to immediately react to internal (psychological) and external (social) stimuli. It may also be used to assess the group's relative autonomy from the worker by noting the group's degree of comfort with the practitioner's silence, and its capacity to work on its own in the face of it.

Silence is a technique that can often be misused by a practitioner to create a condition of anxiety in the group with the intent of spurring the members to work. Certainly this objective has its place, but only in a very technical and precise way as a type of confrontation; that is, silent confrontation. However, it is by no means the main purpose of silence as defined for use in the humanistic model of social group work.

To enact this technique the practitioner remains silent. The body language is relaxed; the look on the face is attentive, curious, and empathic. It is neither neutral nor distinctly emotional. When noting that the members are working productively in the process toward developing mutual aid and actualizing purpose, the practitioner may choose to remain silent because what he or she would say would not add anything to the members' processes. In fact, if the practitioner is questioned about his or her silence, a brief explanation of the silence and encouragement of the members to continue is warranted.

Illustration

A couples' group run out of a community mental health clinic is meeting. "Carl," a member addresses the practitioner, "you've been quiet for so long today." "I'm listening to you," the practitioner says, "and taking in what you're all working on. Don't worry, when I feel I have something to contribute, I will." He then falls back into empathic and attentive silence.

The members continue interacting. Vince turns to Maurice and Corinne and says, "You two have to stop blaming each other." He acknowledges his spouse, and says "I feel almost contaminated by your battles when Maria and I leave here. I'm not blaming you. But it's like Sherri said a few weeks ago, we carry each other home with us after group, don't we?" Others nod their heads.

George and Terri turn to Maurice and Corinne, saying they feel uncomfortable and worried for them. Maurice and Corinne express positive feelings that the group is caring about them, but also show that they feel concerned and confused that the group is blaming them. George looks at the practitioner (who remains silent), and then continues talking to Maurice and Corinne. The members appear to become more comfortable with Carl's silence, and as the meeting progresses no longer look in his direction for input or permission after members' seemingly charged reactions.

Discussion

This illustration represents the effective use of the technique of silence. When asked to intervene, the practitioner begs off, explaining to the members that he is listening and has nothing to contribute at that time. He does use a nonverbal directive for them to continue; they do so, with the practitioner listening attentively. When George looks in the practitioner's direction for participation, Carl continues his attentive silence. This gives the members the impetus to work on their collective issue—taking responsibility. It enables them to effectively work on this with the practitioner in the background, rather than the foreground, of their process.

Support

Support is used to reinforce forms and content of interpersonal expressions that affect the caring milieu of the democratic mutual aid system and working on purpose. To use support, the practitioner needs awareness of the ways in which people interact that permit open and undefensive transactions, which in turn foster give-and-take and the exploration of alternatives as well as learning about choices and change.

The practitioner verbally and nonverbally directs positive cues and comments to encourage these types of interactions. This is done by pointing out to the group when and in what way members' intentions, activities, and processes are useful to the group's objectives. Support is an empathic statement by a practitioner highlighting a part of the process as helpful. Brief comments and nods of agreement are also useful. There is an element of expertise in the use of support, since the practitioner highlights and underlines particular means as helpful alternatives for achieving certain conditions.

Illustration

Elena, Tom, Roberto, and Douglas, members of an elderly group in a community center, are discussing how to insure that they have good medical coverage. The other members, Nancy and Roseanne, are listening attentively. Douglas says he is concerned that he is spending too much out of his budget. Others talk about the high cost of doctors' visits. Douglas falls silent, shaking his head.

The practitioner, Betty, notes to herself that Douglas has retreated and says, "Douglas, you are on the right track; isn't medical care expensive whichever way you cut it?" This revives Douglas, who says, "I read in the paper that the elderly either haven't enough or have too much coverage. Maybe I have too much. But when I ask my caseworker, she says I have just the coverage I need." Elena says, "The senior services workers are good people. But they make mistakes. When I worked I would shake my head 'yes' out of habit because I was so overworked. Maybe your worker did that, Douglas?" The practitioner says, "That's a good track to be on. Your money is limited, and focusing on whether you have too much coverage is one good direction. Why spend unnecessarily?"

The group continues talking about how they will find out if their coverage is adequate or not. Roberto says, "Look, we will each put what we have on a list, right now, and I and anyone else who wants to come with me can go to the federal building to get advice. We have lots of time on our hands to wait," he adds sarcastically. The practitioner responds, "Isn't it a pain, how you have to wait and wait?" Roberto says, "I will probably die right in the chair." The members laugh. Roseanne says, "I can laugh and cry. It's hard at our age. You would think people would appreciate us more. My insurance agent told me my premium was late." The practitioner says, "Douglas, didn't you say that there was something in the paper about too much medical coverage? Wait a minute, I'll go get my newspaper from my office."

Betty runs out to get the paper and returns. They all look at the article, which gives them further impetus to delineate their varied medical insurance plans to determine overlap and overspending. Roseanne and Douglas agree to go with Roberto to the federal building. Betty volunteers that she will go with them if they feel they need her. After some talk they decide to go without her, saying, "If we strike out this round, you can come to our rescue."

Discussion

The practitioner's intent in this excerpt is to be supportive of the members' efforts. She is aware that members are focusing on the realities of their situations with persons who have power over them. The practitioner supports their efforts, recognizing that it may be difficult to sustain these efforts toward clarifying with appropriate bureaucrats what kind of coverage is suitable. First, she shows support to Douglas by restating his perception and reaction. Second, she does not ask the group to share their feelings, for fear they will slip into their ambivalence. Rather, she is very direct in supporting the track they are on, one of trying to ascertain and clarify what is appropriate medical coverage.

By responding to Roberto's sarcasm, Betty reinforces the feelings of frustration and dehumanization they feel when bureaucrats make them wait. As the group begins to gather momentum toward learning more details about their benefits, the practitioner spontaneously reintroduces the newspaper article on medical coverage to help further focus the members' efforts. Going to her office for her newspaper is also an act of support. She shows further support by stating her availability to go with them to the federal building.

Exploration

Exploration is a technique used to involve members in free-flowing expressions of feelings and perceptions about process and content issues. It is used to highlight the members' curiosities, and to enable the suspension of judgment for the sake of expanding awareness and understanding of emotional and ideational nuances. Exploration stimulates a process that surfaces and considers the pragmatic and emotional values of perceptions and feelings. Exploration also ties in with the norms that respect people's experiences and intellectual voices, as well as those that help them to determine their unique existences.

Through open-ended remarks or questions to members or the group as a whole, the practitioner stimulates the expression of perceptions and feelings. The practitioner shows curiosity regarding affects and ideas without projecting any sense of accusation, interrogation, or closure. When using this technique the practitioner does not presume to have right answers. The practitioner directly asks the members to look at different perspectives concerning themselves, others, and situations as they are examining interactions. In effect, the practitioner shows that by being inquisitive with one another members can share and develop abilities as well as different approaches. Through exploration, the practitioner models how to be appropriately curious about others, how this helps to overcome feelings of intrusiveness.

Illustration

A group of disabled men (mostly in their forties and fifties) who have been outpatients in a long-term hospital for persons with chronic and disabling diseases have been involved in a socialization group for many months. Some live with their families, while others live alone or in nearby group residences provided by the hospital. Most are wheelchair bound; some need special assistance in getting to these meetings.

The group has been a vital experience for these members. One of the issues has been the planning of a show at the hospital for the children's ward. Moe says, "It's hard for some of us to communicate with each other, and to plan events like this for the children without our aides helping us." Marilyn, the practitioner, says, "What do you mean, Moe?" He continues, "I guess I feel frustrated. We need other people to help us, and I want us to do this show, even though we need your help and our aides' too." Marilyn asks, "Anyone else got any thoughts on this?"

Gabe says, "Yes, I feel frustrated too. But I'm getting a touch phone since I can't dial. Now I will be able to call everyone more often. Listen, I have an idea for the show. I want to get my nephew's band to entertain. Do you think we could do a thing like that? The hospital would have to pay them; I couldn't ask them to come for free. I have a beautiful tape he gave me from weddings they play. He's also a magician, and I know they entertain at children's parties, too." Henry says, "I like it." The practitioner says, "Come on, let's hear more about this show."

More members start to talk about this. Xavier suggests they get some of the nurses and social workers to do a skit with the group for the children in the hospital: "Or, if that doesn't work, we could get a local comedian." The practitioner says, "These are all good ideas; can you go on?" Gabe then says, "Forget it. They won't come. And besides, I can't call to ask for a favor." He continues, "My brother, his father hardly comes to see me—the bastard." Marilyn wonders, "What would it mean for you to call? Say more, Gabe." Gabe talks about not wanting favors from others. Marilyn wonders if others have similar feelings. Xavier and Willy acknowledge these feelings, with Willy adding that "it's hard to be disabled and to feel you need people's help all the time." Willy then says to Gabe, "I've heard you play that tape of your nephew, and he is really good." Then he says to the practitioner, "Marilyn, does the hospital have a budget for this stuff?" Marilyn says that it does. Willy then tells Gabe, "Then it wouldn't be a favor. He'd get paid. You would be doing *him* a favor. Come on, I'll call him for you if you want!"

After some thinking, Gabe says, "No, I'll call him. It has to be me. You're right. I have to work on my own feelings of pride. But maybe he'll be pleased. Besides, I've got my new phone." After some more enthusiastic talk, Gabe says to the group, "Hey, you guys, if my nephew says yes, you owe me for this one!"

Discussion

There are several types of exploration used by the practitioner in this illustration. She uses exploration with all the members to generate a clarification of feeling; again with all of them to generate a flow of ideas; and finally with one particular member to generate a flow of understanding.

At the start, the practitioner tries to help all of the members to examine the feelings of frustration they are having regarding their disabilities, especially as these feelings relate to their current objective of running a party for hospitalized children. Once Moe talks about his own frustration, the practitioner uses exploration by posing an open-ended question to the others; this allows more expressions of frustrated feelings by several members. Then the group spontaneously goes on to talk about the party rather than about their own frustrations. Gabe is so excited by the idea of asking his nephew to entertain that he bypasses his frustrations, focusing on his new phone and his new capability for communication with others. The practitioner connects to members' desires to generate a flow of ideas and processes for the children's party, and further helps them bypass feelings of limitation and frustration.

"Come on, let's hear more on the show" is a further use of exploration. This use of exploration focuses on and stimulates members' capacities to generate creative ideas. One must note that the practitioner does not work with the group on the hows of lining up entertainers or writing skits with the staff. To do so at this time would stymie a group whose members seem to need help in generating ideas more than they need to dwell on what they can or cannot do. Once possibilities are flowing, there is enough time to make plans.

In her use of exploration with one particular member, Gabe, the practitioner helps him to examine specific feelings. Her pointed but open-ended question, "What would it mean for you to call your nephew?" helps him look at his pride, as well as his angry feelings toward the brother who does not visit him often. Although Willy gives him the option not to call his nephew, Gabe's choice is to override his anger and pride to help in the group's efforts.

Identification

Identification is used to specify repetitive aspects of self-expression or process that are related to the group's purpose or norms, that the group or member are not aware of as significant. These may be patterns of behaviors that—once labeled and understood—can offer group members other viewpoints concerning events and their reactions to them. (Identification may be used as a precursor to the technique of confrontation by focusing on significant behavior.)

The practitioner specifies and characterizes directly specific patterns and expressions that are becoming evident in the group, asking the group and/or individual members to connect these behaviors to their current issues as these relate to process or purpose. The practitioner may also metaphorically label behaviors so that the symbolic demarcation may expand awareness of emotional expressions in the future.

Illustration

The members in a young adult women's socialization group are talking about why they have been striking out with men recently. Tracy goes on and on, becoming more enamored with her own ideas than with hearing what others are saying. Members in the group begin to tune her out. Finally, Susan interrupts, expressing her own upset with the man she met last week (who turned out to be married and looking for a fling): "I never got the point until the end of the evening that he was just interested in fooling around, not in finding out about me." Jennifer jumps in, saying she had similar problems, and "I can't figure out how I pick them." Tracy begins to talk again about how she avoids these kinds of men by not going to the usual singles places. Gladys pipes in, "That's why you haven't been with anyone lately, you don't even try." Jennifer impatiently says, "It was not at a singles bar where I met this guy. I met him when I did a consultation for a computer company." Susan says, "You should see what happened to me! I did a presentation on personnel, and this guy was in the audience and asked me questions. He was the only live one there."

There is more talk; a lot of it seems to reflect impatience with each other, as well as some hostility. The women are having trouble hearing each other, and seem to be more intent on ventilating than listening. The practitioner, Inez, says, "Wait a minute. You're all doing something now that isn't helping you. You're all talking, and no one is listening." There is a silence. Then Jennifer says, "It's true, I was so stuck on telling my story that I don't remember a thing about what Susan said. I think it had something to do with meeting a live wire in a personnel conference." Susan says, "Something like that." The practitioner states, "Maybe it would help to try to figure out what this means." The members begin to talk about how disappointed some of them are. This leads to more discussion about how angry some of them become when they are disappointed, and how much they want to hide the anger and disappointment by talking their way out of these feelings.

Later in the meeting, the topic of being able to listen clearly for cues from the men they are with begins to come up. The practitioner asks, "Isn't this connected to what was said earlier about listening to each other's cues in here?"

Discussion

The practitioner here identifies a pattern of behavior that is very close to the surface and pertains to all the members, giving the collective the opportunity to note and to figure out the meaning of the behavior (not listening). There is much more to call their attention to; however, merely identifying the absence of listening points the group in the direction of thinking about how this behavior is being enacted in their relationships with men, and in other social situations. Through the surfacing of the issue of not listening, the members are able to move ahead and examine their current behaviors.

By asking the group later in the meeting how their issues of listening to cues from men relate to what was said earlier, the practitioner helps them to distinguish patterns in their forms of presentation from a variety of angles. At no time does the practitioner override the group's process. She gives the members ample opportunity to find out for themselves what the expressions of hostility are all about. She also gives them ample room to conduct their own feedback with one another. She does not interpret their behavior, but lets the interpretation emanate from them.

Focusing on "listening" rather than hostility, anger, and disappointment reflects the use of the technique of identification (whereas focusing on hostility and anger would represent the use of interpretation).

SUMMARY

This chapter has discussed eight techniques the practitioner uses throughout the entirety of group life to achieve both of the dual objectives—developing the democratic mutual aid system and actualizing purpose. These techniques are not merely specific to group work; they are generic to social work as well.

Demand for work is used to help the members remain on track in all aspects of achieving their objectives. *Directing* is used to move members into new situations, environments, or experiences that promise to help them to meet their objectives. *Lending a vision* provides expanded perspectives for the group, and offers hope about future endeavors. *Staying with feelings* validates and emphasizes the fundamental significance of emotional interaction.

Silence is a technique used primarily to encourage the group's and individual members' reflection and autonomy; silence is *not* used to create debilitating anxiety. In using *support*, the practitioner reinforces the development of a caring milieu and fosters the members' efforts to meet their needs. *Exploration* uses curiosity and interest to help members look at the nuances of feelings and actions. The denotation of repetitive actions and feelings through *identification* is used by the practitioner to help members comprehend their meaning and importance.

In the next section, attention will turn to viewing and assessing the significant feelings and patterns of the individual members within the changing phenomena of stage themes.

Part III

DIFFERENTIAL USE OF TECHNIQUES

Chapter 9

ASSESSING THE MEMBER IN THE GROUP

Assessment as a habit of mind is present from moment to moment as the worker "listens" to make sure his interventions are responsive to client concerns. (Germain & Gitterman, 1980, p. 19)

Assessment of the member in the group makes use of the practitioner's perceptions and empathy—as well as knowledge and values—to guide the use of techniques. The practitioner considers the meaning of unfolding events and interpersonal expression, in order to empathize and interact with the member as he or she works on participation and purpose in the professionally guided social work group. The practitioner considers the stage of development of the group, along with salient group needs and member commonalities that enable cohesion.

The practitioner judiciously accepts his or her intersubjectively developed observations. These are reworked in the process of helping the member take part in the group. The practitioner's stream of consciousness includes several steps: (1) naively perceiving the group phenomena; (2) suspending judgments in order to empathically understand the members' concerns; (3) and creating conceptual lenses. These are used to comprehend and intuit the meaning of members' interactions. As the last step in the assessment, the practitioner tests out these perceptions, and tentatively accepts or revises them.

ASSESSMENT ACTIVITIES AND THE GROUP MEMBER

Stage theory has been used to understand the changing behaviors of different types of members—including children (Garland & West, 1983) and psychiatric patients (Garland & Frey, 1976)—during the group's evolution. The guiding assumption is that change in member behavior is in some ways shaped by the stage of development the group is in, and that member behavior is not to be viewed apart from the stage context.

Furthermore, psychological and sociological constructs are necessary in order to provide the practitioner with conceptual lenses that may sharpen professional assessment. Sarri and Galinsky (1967) have delineated guidelines for assessing the group member. These include environmental and cultural factors, as well as personality dimensions that affect members' participation in the group's development as a helping milieu.

Illustration. During Stage Theme 1 ("We're Not in Charge") Rochelle, one member of a group for pregnant prisoners, supports many of the norms that the practitioner presents. At the same time, Rochelle assertively stops other members from weakening her opinions. The worker takes note of this highly unusual differentiated behavior so early in the group's inception. At the end of the meeting, Rochelle approaches the worker and asks him to write a letter formally attesting to her meaningful participation and regular attendance. Rochelle says, "This can help me transfer to a prison with better services for pregnant prisoners, and a better nursery." The practitioner judges the request as a positive reflection of survival, and movement to Stage Theme 2 ("We Are in Charge"). He agrees to write the letter, hoping that this act will have a neutral or positive effect on the member and the group.

By the next meeting, the women have heard about the letter; they open up by defensively questioning Rochelle about her motives. The practitioner takes center stage and universalizes the value of Rochelle's behavior to avoid putting her on the spot as the group begins to move toward the normative crisis and Stage Theme 3 ("We're Taking You On"). The practitioner asks the women to give examples of how each member is pursuing her own survival agenda in the prison.

Rochelle listens attentively. She cautiously borrows some of the practitioner's actions, lets others speak, and maintains her poise. The practitioner observes a strength of presentation as well as Rochelle's ability to use her ego functioning.

The practitioner also becomes aware that Rochelle does not consider the sociopolitical significance of her race (she is black). He conjectures that she and the others are not yet able to openly deal with the effects of racial stereotyping and discrimination in and out of prison. He thinks about what the members' responses will be if he acknowledges the racial and ethnic differences among the members. He thinks, too, about their view of the racial and gender differences between himself and the group.

ASSESSING THE MEMBER IN THE GROUP

This chapter will present ways of observing group member behavior that make use of stage themes in relation to psychosocial frames of reference. As the group moves through its stage themes, the members react to and contribute uniquely to the process. Stage themes reflect members' subjective reactions to their sense of the practitioner's authority and their own potency in the group experience. A member's stage theme reactions generally vary from slightly intense (tempered by age-appropriate judgment) to more intense (affected by significant quotients of unreasonable reactions in comparison with the benign actualities of the process). Timing and pace in developing a mutual aid system and actualizing purpose are related to members' personal capacities of emotional and cognitive expression, their previous group experiences and skills, and to the difficulties presented by the group's purpose.

The stage theme reactions of "We're Not in Charge," "We Are in Charge," "We're Taking You On," Sanctuary, "This Isn't Good Anymore," "We're Okay and Able," and "Just a Little Longer" can be tempered by the practitioner's use of technique. Throughout the process, the humanistic method lodges authority and leadership in the hands of the members along with the practitioner. Paradoxically, the open and accepting quality of the values and norms of this milieu can cause stage theme reactions to dominate a member's experience as he or she reacts with anxiety to the freedom for self-expression that is fundamental to this form. At the same time, these thematic subjective reactions interfere in the members' and the group's work (Bion, 1959); their manifestations also provide opportunities for changing how members handle themselves. Stage theme reactions are grist for the mill; in the process, both the practitioner and the member can consider how the member's participation is being affected by his or her external circumstances, as well as by the group experience itself.

PSYCHOSOCIAL LENSES FOR ASSESSMENT

The approach in this chapter stresses interpersonal criteria for assessment in the situation of the group process, interweaving sociological and psychological forms. When attention is drawn to interpersonal issues in the group, the practitioner can see how an emotionally disturbed member will play out psychosocial limitations in the here-and-now interaction of the group. This helps to discern the difficulties the member is having in his or her actual experiences. Furthermore, the practitioner can note when social deprivation is the fundamental cause of difficulties in psychosocial expression in and out of the group.

The practitioner focuses on the following guidelines which provide lenses for assessing the member's behaviors:

- capacity toward mutual aid and purpose
- ego abilities and sense of self
- social institutional environment
- stereotypes and self-fulfilling prophecies
- symbolic representations of practitioner and group

These five psychosocial parameters for understanding the member are used throughout the process in varying degrees to help the practitioner develop empathic sensitivity to the member. Differences between the parameters are drawn in relation to how closely each of them keeps the practitioner connected to the member's immediate interactions in the group. Observations focused on a member's abilities to contribute to mutual aid, or on the member's symbolic representations of the practitioner and the group, are less apt to draw the practitioner's stream of consciousness into tangential considerations, causing a drift away from the process during the meeting. On the other hand, focus on ego abilities and social institutional factors draws the practitioner's thinking to historical and political considerations, which are used to complete the practitioner's perceptions of the member's presentation in the here and now.

To insure that these criteria for assessing the individual member are connected to the evolving process of the humanistic group, each of these criteria will be considered within the context of the group's stage themes. For further clarification, see Table 9.1.

Capacity Toward Mutual Aid and Purpose

Garvin (1985) defines processes as "those changes occurring in activities and interactions . . . that are related to goal attainment [actualization of purpose] . . . and . . . group maintenance [developing the mutual aid system]" (p. 211). Examination of members' capacities to carry out the tasks called for in the social work group is a necessary part of the practitioner's skill. The abilities identified with mutual aid and democracy include caring, sharing, listening, decision making, and respecting differences. In this framework, the practitioner perceives how each member is joining with the others. He or she observes how the member learns about and appraises norms and values other participants bring to the experience, and how each member reacts to the practitioner's support of humanistic values and democratic standards. The practitioner discerns the extent to which the members express themselves in personally oriented or group-oriented ways, rather than blending both forms. The extent to which the member's behaviors are process or purpose oriented is also considered, along with flexibility and expansiveness in role repertoire. The member's orientation toward power and efforts to control (rather than to influence) is viewed.

Abilities identified with achieving group purpose call for taking risks toward changing dysfunctional interpersonal patterns as well as situational factors. Also called for is the expression of an increasingly broad range of feeling, and a clearer communication style that reflects empathy and mutual respect. The practitioner considers how the member expresses and enacts his or her reasons for being in the group.

Stage Theme 1: We're Not in Charge

The practitioner assesses the member to support his or her autonomous functioning, and to broaden the member's problem-solving and role-taking abilities. Some members will need more support for autonomous functioning than others.

At the start of group life some members are silent, and others take part cautiously. The practitioner considers the extent to which each member expresses process, purpose, or self-oriented behavior. The practitioner looks for preliminary enactments of listening, empathy, cooperativeness, and the ability to communicate clearly.

Table 9.1

Assessing the Member in the Context of Stages of Group Development

	Stage Theme 1 "We're Not in Charge"	Stage Theme 2 "We Are in Charge"
A. Capacity Toward Mutual Aid & Purpose	Democratic process: listening, communication, level of group skill, view of difference	Democratic process: inclusion, exclusion, decision making, respect others' rights
B. Practitioner Assesses to:	Help member autonomy	Enable democratic norms, mutual aid, cooperation
C. Ego Abilities and Sense of Self	Clear vs. diffuse self-worth level; accuracy of self-perception	Reactions to ambiguity and freedom; withdraw or rebel; anxiety level
D. Practitioner Assesses to:	Know if to lend, repair, or support ego	Validate, universalize perceptions & feelings
E. Social Institutional Environment	Effective or ineffective environmental supports; level of testing of group	Nonnurturing milieu may bring out anger, disappointment, powerlessness
F. Practitioner Assesses to:	Help alter environment in future	Show empathy & validate member's feelings, needs
G. Stereotype & Self-Fulfilling Prophecies	Member vulnerability to stereotyping; how member enters group, is seen in group, stereotypes others	Does stereotype pervade self-presentation; is member angry, frustrated, isolated?
H. Practitioner Assesses to:	Enable entry into group	Guard against repeated stereotyping or stigmatizing
I. Symbolic Representations of Practitioner & Group	Member view of worker as group standard bearer; view of worker as social control agent	Extent of desire for worker to control; expecting disappointment
J. Practitioner Assesses to:	Enhance trust, neutralize screens	Help view expectation of worker to demystify

(Continued)

Table 9.1

Assessing the Member in the Context of Stages of Group Development
(Continued)

Stage Theme 3 "We're Taking You On"	Stage Theme 4 Sanctuary	Stage Theme 5 "This Isn't Good Anymore"
Democratic process: extent of joining others in taking on worker; ability to work out negative feelings	Democratic process: takes part freely in mutual aid; Purpose: work starts; sees ability to grow	Actualizing purpose: side-tracked from task in face of difficulty
To foster sharing of power toward developing future purposes	Develop movement to problem solving toward purpose	Remind member of commitments to change
Ability to demystify practitioner, over idealize, or challenge, and fear	Challenged or fearful in intimacy; forward movement & hope or new crisis	Extent of hopelessness, reluctance, fear; are these chronic or crisis?
Offer acceptance of critical member; affirm boundaries	Offer corrective relationship though group	Help member reach beyond; inquire as to chronic or crisis
Member may fear co-optation and words	Member may see group as second chance; or reinforcement of current supports	Is loss of hope due to overwhelming environment? Consider prior strengths
Affirm concern about sincerity	Pave way for altering environment	Clarify futile feelings; validate reality; find alternatives
Member may not take part in challenge; may not be overly dependent	Member's latent or direct messages to air stereotype	Assess how stereotype feeds futility and avoidance of risk taking, challenging group
Notice absence of challenge; probe for stereotypes	Help correct prior negative experiences	Affirm difficulty of change; offer hope
Now interaction is salient; test for anger; form relationships with member	Through what familial lens is worker seen? Other lenses?	Ascertain member disappointments that prevent forward movement
Reach for direct feedback from member; develop expectations for future relationship	Work through salient screens; establish here and now trust	Offer one's own vision of group's future; be empathic

(Continued)

Table 9.1

Assessing the Member in the Context of Stages of Group Development
(Continued)

Stage Theme 6 *"We're Okay and Able"*	*Stage Theme 7* *"Just a Little Longer"*
A. Actualizing purpose: able to change vs. sidetracked in the face of adversity	Actualizing purpose: can member take stock of growth & future?
B. Help member own goals & blocks	Help continuation of growth in future
C. Hopeful or hopeless regarding change; risk taking or fear of failure	Temporary loss of mastery; level of denial or flight
D. Enable situations for mastery	Enable confidence in gains made in group
E. Does member see options for changing environment & supports or economic factors?	Does member see options at group's end?
F. Enable change in environment	Enable plan of future actions in milieu
G. Level of need to deal with obstacles of stereotype	Fear of future stereotyping
H. Help deal with long-term effects of stigma	Enable mastery of new approaches
I. Meaning of practitioner to member: role model or teacher; how much does member take in?	Reactions as abandoning; able to accept reality of relationship
J. Strengthen bonds to enable change	Maintain perspective on relationship

Showing empathy and appreciation for the mutual aid nature of the group experience, as well as tolerance for individual differences, are significant indicators of the member's ability to solve problems with others. The practitioner watches and experiences how each member reacts to his or her explicitness about humanistic values and democratic norms, and observes the member's skills in democratic participation. Members, because of age or institutional or subcultural experiences, may not be familiar with democratic modes and ethics; or they may be reluctant to apply them for fear of repercussions (for instance, as in the case of refugee groups; Glassman & Skolnik, 1984).

Considering the member's abilities to develop mutual aid and democratic processes is more significant at the start than defining the member's ability to work on purpose. The practitioner tests out the assessment by trying to provide the member with alternate ways of interaction to see how rigid or flexible his or her self-expressions are in interactions with others. By offering a preliminary clarification of democratic process and mutual aid, the practitioner develops more clarity about the member's potential in this interactive capacity.

Illustration. A group of child care counselors is in the third session. Up until the halfway point in the meeting, most of the members are looking to the practitioner and imitating her comments, exhibiting Stage Theme 1 ("We're Not in Charge") behaviors.

The practitioner notices that Rick has been silent and watching with a disturbed look on his face, fidgeting in his seat. She asks him, "Rick, you look disturbed by what is going on. What's happening for you?" Rick tactfully begs off; the practitioner empathically insists. Rick finally says, "I don't see things the same way you are putting them. I feel uncomfortable because the others seem to agree with you. Yet I don't believe this group can belong to the members alone. They just look to you for advice now, so they are all very much looking for approval."

After Rick's presentation of his views and disagreements, the practitioner says, "Rick, your differences with me and everyone else's differences with each other are what will make this group worthwhile and challenging. I do give my views, too. I consider them to be different, though not necessarily better than yours." Rick says, "Thanks; I really thought you'd be inflexible." The meeting continues, with members now looking to Rick and one another more, and less and less to the practitioner.

Group Theme 2: We Are in Charge

Faced with the saliency of the autonomy rebellion, some members actively take part in the power struggle while others withdraw, preferring not to take sides. Affect is often intensified in the form of competitive feelings, while others try to hide such feelings by turning them into dependency or submission. The practitioner assesses the member's abilities to offer nurturance, respect, and inclusion to the variety of different individuals who compose the membership.

Some members may try to exclude others and show inflexibility for tolerating differences. Some will attempt to preserve others' rights and foster inclusion by directly inviting their participation. However, cooperative modes usually are not responded to at this time; those efforts tend to be ignored. The practitioner has to tune into and empathically address the disappointments or disillusionments of these members so that their input is not withheld from the group.

The roles the member takes give indications of how he or she reacts to the ambiguity of the normative crisis. Some members try to avoid or deny the crisis by becoming rigidly task oriented. Some show interest in other people's feelings. Some seek power over others in order to maintain feelings of security and position.

The practitioner tests out his or her assessments by offering invitations to isolated and individualistic members that support their right to be different. The practitioner also interprets members' anxieties, power plays, and leadership attempts as manifestations of the search for group norms. The practitioner offers support to the member who becomes noticeably anxious in the throws of the group's ambiguity.

Stage Theme 3: We're Taking You On

The practitioner assesses members' ability to join in directly expressing feelings about the practitioner. The practitioner assesses each member's ability to use feelings toward authority constructively within the group's democratic context.

The practitioner must discover the extent to which each member needs opportunities to deal openly with his or her feelings about authority in this group. Some members are motivated toward dominance, and disapprove of the group's developing democratic power structure. The member's ability to acknowledge competitive and cooperative feelings with the practitioner helps work out stumbling blocks toward cooperation and functional cohesion. Members need to be assisted in handling their negative feelings in the interest of the group's forward movement.

The practitioner tests out members' abilities for sharing power by gauging to what extent each member is willing to engage cooperatively with others and the practitioner. An invitation to share power and position with the practitioner also helps the member who may be anticipating a strained relationship with authority figures.

Stage Theme 4: Sanctuary

The practitioner is conscious of each member's ability to handle closeness. The practitioner notes when a member is experiencing pressure to conform to the high affect of this period. He or she assists the member in recognizing that the price of belonging is not conformity.

The democratic mutual aid process is cresting as the most useful means the group will have for achieving its purpose. The practitioner considers the extent to which members see themselves as both helpers and receivers by looking at how actively or peripherally each member participates. The practitioner considers how supportive or guarded members' expressions of feelings are, and how deviant members are from the group's salient modes of expression. Effort is focused on helping members develop role behaviors suitable for this stage. Note is taken of the degree to which members have given up their needs to control, and the degree to which each member is using the group as a sanctuary.

The practitioner considers how each member views himself or herself in the helper-receiver roles. The practitioner supports the validity of skeptical members' feelings, which may be picking up on negative factors in the group.

Stage Theme 5: This Isn't Good Anymore

Some members' abilities for achieving purpose are not well developed. This type of member may give up when confronted with difficult and frustrating situations that result in threatening feelings. The practitioner notes the degree to which members lose their connection to the processes of mutual aid developed earlier. The practitioner weighs the effect of disenchanted members' feelings on others.

The practitioner reminds members of their commitments to work on the group's purpose with others, and helps each member identify the emotional and situational roadblocks to involvement in this effort. The practitioner helps members reconnect to others, strengthening fragile bonds when necessary, and calls upon the group's spirit of mutuality to solve problems.

Stage Theme 6: We're Okay and Able

The achievement of purpose is salient in this stage, and is represented by members' capacity to work on effectiveness and change. Consideration is given to each member's relative ability to develop an agenda for broadening self-expression in and out of the group. The practitioner's focus is also on the relative capability of each member to use the feedback process in the group, and to deal with interpersonal and defensive barriers that sidetrack or inhibit change. Furthermore, the practitioner takes into account the member's ability and willingness to participate in helping other members achieve their purposes.

The practitioner observes how each member handles tension and difficulty in interpersonal relations, with interest in how openly members are able to change maladaptive communication patterns, try out varied role behaviors, and develop broader ranges of affective expression in the group. Consideration is given to how cognizant members are of risk and change processes, as well as to how connected or disconnected they are from fellow members and significant others.

Stage Theme 7: Just a Little Longer

The practitioner considers how each member may continue to grow after the experience. At the time of ending, members are often noted to have flattened or fickle affects.

Each member's ability to plan future agendas in the face of ending is crucial. Not being able to do so may show a pattern of avoiding feelings of dependency and rejection that prevent members from moving on to their next steps. Finding supportive relationships that foster members' continued growth is important. A feeling that some member may have to "go it alone" is a clue that these members may feel mistrustful of other situations and supports that may be offered.

The practitioner explores the importance of prior losses in relationship to the loss of the group experience as a place for support and accomplishment. Members are helped to consider how to continue work beyond the group through creating and pursuing necessary supports.

Ego Abilities and Sense of Self

Assessment can be shifted toward members' characterizations of self and abilities for self-expression. The assessment focuses on members' ego functioning in their interpersonal environments. Conceptions of ego functions (Goldstein, 1984) such as the ability to employ reality testing and judgment, the capacity to tolerate frustration and control impulses, the ability to develop and sustain object relations, and the use of defense mechanisms that inhibit or enable emotional expressions are used to observe members' presentations in the group process. The practitioner considers if each member's presentation aligns with his or her age and physically appropriate abilities, or reflects impoverishments in the member's sense of self and the uses of his or her ego functions.

The practitioner also considers the extent to which members present distinguishable or diffuse identities (Erikson, 1963), express self-worth or impoverished self-images, present feelings of mastery, demonstrate relative accuracy of self-evaluation, and manifest the ability to accurately discern their impact on others.

Stage Theme 1: We're Not in Charge

Ego functioning abilities are noted at the beginning, when each member is getting his or her bearings. The extent to which members present clear, diffuse, or rigidly defined pictures of themselves may offer the practitioner a preliminary impression of how the group will unfold. The members' demonstrations of feelings of self-worth and mastery regarding prior and current situations, as well as abilities to hold to feelings of identity, integrity, and equilibrium, are considered. Judgment, reality testing, memory, frustration tolerance, impulse control, and guardedness are taken into account. Although the members' accuracies of self-perception may not be clear to the practitioner at this stage, he or she gathers impressions by focusing on how the members hear and respond to each others' cues. A high level of resistance to efforts at curtailing a monopolizing member's input may indicate a covering over of anxiety and lack of self-perception. Exhibiting intense anxiety when attempts are made to clarify a member's statements or feelings may be an indication of the member's identity confusion and fears about rejection and persecution.

Stage Theme 2: We Are in Charge

The practitioner assesses each member's emotional equilibrium in and psychological perspective about the group process when there is conflict and anxiety. Some may withdraw, or become overactive, in the face of disorientation and anxiety. The practitioner also gauges the extent to which each member takes on leadership with other members and the worker. He or she considers if members' presentations are consonant or in conflict with their ages and physical abilities. Prior hurts and anger with authority are apt to be expressed through passive or aggressive hostility toward members and the practitioner.

The practitioner offers acceptance to the anxious member and universalizes the feeling for all who are feeling varying intensities of inhibitory anxieties and social disorientation.

Stage Theme 3: We're Taking You On

In the context of challenges to authority, the practitioner considers each member's ability to view and react to the practitioner's authority more realistically. The practitioner should be neither idealized nor denigrated. Fear of freedom from control—or anxiety about destruction of the authority object—may underlie members' difficulties in challenging the authority figure in order to come to know about the practitioner's fallibility and humanness. The overchallenging and critical member may fear the practitioner's power. Distortions are often transferred from experiences with and perceptions of other significant figures.

The practitioner offers acceptance to the member who idealizes authority. When necessary the practitioner does not challenge the idealization, because this issue will reappear later on and can be used by the group to help the member. The member who is afraid that a positive relationship with the practitioner will result in the loss of integrity is helped through an affirmation of the boundaries and differences between the member and the practitioner. The overattacking member will need help in dealing with and rechanneling these misdirected feelings. By neutralizing members' negative reactions, they can be enabled to join the group and maintain appropriate distance from the practitioner.

Stage Theme 4: Sanctuary

The practitioner considers the members' ego abilities and anticipatory anxieties in order to offer opportunities for corrective relationships through the group's resources. Each member is also offered protection and permission to set an individualized pace, particularly if the group is moving too fast into intimacy for the member, causing him or her to feel identity confusion.

Some members may feel competent in intimate and interdependent situations; others may feel threatened and fear losing controls and boundaries. Intimacy should offer a renewed chance to develop and to feel self-worth, rather than stimulate emotional and identity crises that lead to avoidance of other members and the practitioner.

When noting that a member is fearful, the practitioner may respond directly by empathically reflecting these feelings, or indirectly by universalizing the fearful feelings about intimacy experienced in varying degrees by all members. The practitioner tries to decrease intense levels of anxiety by insuring the right of any one member to proceed at his or her own pace.

Stage Theme 5: This Isn't Good Anymore

The practitioner assesses members' ego abilities for dealing directly with interpersonal obstacles, in order to assist in attaining mastery and success rather than disturbing periods of difficulty and failure in relationships. Attitudes of inferiority, incompetency, identity fragmentation, isolation, stagnation, and despair (among others) can draw members into anxieties and inabilities that were reflected in earlier struggles with the worker as well as with other members. Caught in negative attitudes and feelings, a member will have difficulty conquering defensive barriers in order to work on significant interpersonal issues.

Consideration is given to whether or not—and to what degree—hopeless and fragmented feelings are due to present stimuli, crises, or to chronic psychosocial conditions. The practitioner empathically points out hopeless attitudes, and works with members to engender hope and involvement. Actions in new experiences and interactions counter negative feelings developing feelings of pride through accomplishments.

Stage Theme 6: We're Okay and Able

As the members actively engage issues related to purpose in the group process, the worker attends to the members' presentations of attitudes, interests, wishes, motives, and plans. The normative age stage crises (Erikson, 1963) bring about periods of disequilibrium in each person's character, which are resolved with a predominance of synthesizing and comforting emotions through engaging experiences. When these age stage crises are not resolved, individuals experience ego dysfunctioning, problems in self-esteem, and identity distortions.

The practitioner assesses ego functions to support and accentuate change in interpersonal relationships. A member's positive or negative self-image influences how he or she is viewing the group's purpose. The chronic inability of a member to set or follow through on personal agendas may indicate ego dysfunction and low self-esteem.

The practitioner gauges the extent to which members use their own ego abilities to undertake new experiences without the need for sustainment by the practitioner. The worker also considers how aware members are of their own shifts in patterns of self-expressions in interpersonal relations. Active awareness is a sign that a member is able to use the group as a helpful medium of change. When this is the case, conscious ego functioning—including interaction and feelings of self-awareness and identity—is manifest on a streambed of emotions.

Stage Theme 7: Just a Little Longer

As the group comes to a close, the practitioner is interested in how aware members are of their regressions in social and emotional interactions. A member who discerns this pattern recognizes the necessity for the regression, and does not become lost in it or overanxious because of it. The practitioner also assesses how members use their wills to refocus on identifying the external supportive frames of reference and situations each is in and will join. The practitioner attends to the members' effective uses of judgment, reality testing, and memory as means of gauging the value of new environments and relationships.

The practitioner also considers the real and fictionalized references each member makes about the practitioner's image. The more fictionalized, the less the member is owning his or her experience in the group; the less fictionalized, the better able the member is in handling fear of the unknown.

Prior traumatic losses are rekindled as the group comes to an end. The practitioner takes into consideration that recall of prior losses may interfere with ego functioning to the extent that members lose confidence in their gains in the group.

Illustration. Maurice is recounting his experiences on a date a few nights earlier. Earlier, during Stage Theme 5 ("This Isn't Good Anymore"), Maurice experienced great difficulty moving forward. The group is now in Stage Theme 6 ("We're Okay and Able") and the members are confronting him. He is acting attentive and connected, but Victor sees Maurice swallowing, and sees him roll his eyes in disdain. Victor questions, "What's up, Maurice? You have a defensive attitude on." Maurice's Adam's apple moves again; he fidgets and starts to sweat. The practitioner alters the course of the process by saying to the group, "Give Maurice room to breathe, to get his bearings. None of us moves at the same pace."

Later on, as the group is coming to a close during Stage Theme 7 ("Just a Little Longer"), Maurice, looking distraught and anxious, is encouraged by members to speak up. He tells the group about how difficult it is for him to leave old friends, because he still becomes upset when he remembers how sad he felt in moving to a new neighborhood when he was 11 years old. The practitioner helps him to express his feelings of childhood loss and to consider the ways he can manage his feelings about leaving the group, as this brings up reflections of the past. The members offer support, and some share similar feelings. Throughout this process Maurice is becoming more comfortable, his anxiety dissipating through the discussion.

Social Institutional Environment

The member's connection to the social institutional environment, through his or her primary and secondary socializations—stemming from family sources (of primary socialization) and institutional sources (of secondary socialization) (Berger & Luckmann, 1966)—the socio-cultural and political dimensions of social class, race, ethnicity (Devore & Schlesinger, 1971), educational level and access to upward mobility, historically and currently determined, will influence the member's view of the group and his or her membership in it. Each of these dimensions will affect the member's values and interactions.

Furthermore, the degree of environmental supports that members experience from family, friends, networks, workplace, and community institutions such as schools, religious groups, and social agencies will shape their involvements in the group. The kinds of resources and opportunities for mobility that members have in the community will relate to how they need and use the group.

Stage Theme 1: We're Not in Charge

The practitioner assesses with an eye toward assisting members in altering their social and political environments, as well as their perceptions of them.

Manifested in the members' early behaviors in the group is the degree to which they are part of supportive or unsupportive external environments. A member with effective environmental supports, or a member seeking a change in environmental affiliations, may demonstrate fuller connections toward the group experience and the practitioner while testing less. On the other hand, anger and unbridled expressions of frustration may be indicative of ineffective environmental supports and limited access to social mobility.

The practitioner validates members' judgments and experiences of their impoverished and rejecting environments. The practitioner is careful not to blame members by denying the power of deprivations, further reinforcing their feelings of victimization and hostile aggression or self-denigration.

Stage Theme 2: We Are in Charge

A member who has experienced a long history in nonnurturing milieus may react with cynicism, anger, and frustration toward the practitioner. Lack of confidence in the environment can carry over into the group. The barriers to social mobility and the feelings of powerlessness indicative of this group stage heighten members' frustration, hopelessness, and anger. The degree to which others and the practitioner can act with sensitivity toward such members, whether or not they themselves have had effective environmental experiences, is crucial.

The practitioner validates members' anger, frustration, and feelings of powerlessness with the aim of directing the energy from disappointment into the will for problem solving. All members benefit from this, learning the truth about the relationship between social and political deprivation and personal survival in the sociopolitical environment.

Stage Theme 3: We're Taking You On

The practitioner assesses the extent to which being deprived of rights and entitlements leads members to suspect the group to be a depriving environment. A member experiencing deprivation will value actions much more than words, despite the fact that a concerted use of both is necessary. The member may be suspicious of the group's dialogue with authority for fear that the members are being co-opted by the "power structure" through its words, without concomitant acts and deeds.

The member who is necessarily suspicious of words is useful in the group's process. The practitioner affirms this suspiciousness, and brings its critique into play so that its perspectives become part of the group's effort to affect authenticity. Through this type of affirmation, the member—having real reason to be suspicious—is helped to develop the means to deal with those who have power and control over his or her circumstances through the uses of strategies that include self-awareness, empathy, reality testing, social coalitions, and political compromise.

Stage Theme 4: Sanctuary

Where a member's external environmental supports have been ineffective, the safety of the group may provide an opportunity for the member to experience the group as a secure, effective, and valuable social and political milieu. The group may also provide the member support in gaining necessities from his or her social environment. For a member who is in effective social milieus, closeness in the group may gird his or her feelings of caring and communion through adding to the member's abilities to be and become with others.

The practitioner affirms the member for whom the group represents an effective and nurturant milieu in juxtaposition to his or her current sociopolitical environments.

Illustration. In the early life of a sobriety group, Joe is being quiet, keeping a distance even when members are gathering their strength during Stage Theme 2 ("We Are in Charge"). The practitioner is cognizant that this member has virtually no other sustaining networks and is using the group as his sole source of support. The dominant concern for the practitioner is whether or not the members will help Joe belong. Furthermore, by focusing on social institutional factors, the practitioner becomes aware that Joe's lower educational level (in relation to the other members)—as well as his distinct status as the lone welfare recipient in the group—might be making it more difficult for Joe to become a part of the group. At the same time, the practitioner notices that several of the members have driven Joe home to his modest rooming house after the last two meetings, despite his objections.

During Stage Theme 4 (Sanctuary) the members, as if realizing the special importance of this group to Joe in meeting his need for environmental resources, form a supportive net for him by driving him to the sessions and meeting him for refreshments. This marks the beginning of Joe's ability to share his pressing concerns with the members at future meetings.

Stage Theme 5: This Isn't Good Anymore

The practitioner now considers if any member's loss of hope and fear of failure is due to factors outside the group. Consideration is given to whether or not members are struggling with environmental factors such as poverty, homelessness, joblessness, racism, or family illnesses that cause overwhelming obstacles which suppress hopefulness and will. Members' prior abilities to deal with environmental stresses are taken into account as well.

The practitioner helps members to develop their feelings of assertiveness and will in relation to the actual realities that are causing feelings of futility. The practitioner validates futile feelings and supports assertive acts in order to stimulate movement toward alternatives.

Stage Theme 6: We're Okay and Able

The practitioner is interested in helping members to develop personal approaches and political attitudes that will enhance their effectiveness in dealing with environmental obstacles.

Consideration is given to the approaches that members develop for confronting their current circumstances, and to the ways in which members deal with cultural, racial, and economic dynamics. Each member's abilities to behave in different ways in these circumstances is also noted in relation to the counterforces of hurt, anger, and frustration, as well as others' attempts to suppress the member's actions. The practitioner also identifies and helps members to secure opportunities and concrete resources.

Stage Theme 7: Just a Little Longer

The practitioner considers how the members are carrying out specific actions in their social environments. Separating from the group's nurturing milieu is especially disappointing for members whose immediate environments are unsupportive and dangerous. Such members will have to take the initiative in creating new options, including opportunities for their own social mobility and securing of concrete resources.

The practitioner explores members' anxieties and concerns about surviving in their current circumstances without the group's support. Alternative helpful situations are considered to replace unsupportive ones. Before the group's end, the practitioner takes special steps to insure that each member has become connected to supportive situations provided by the agency and community institutions.

Stereotypes and Self-Fulfilling Prophecies

Stereotyping and self-fulfilling prophecies in the members' presentations—centered on race, class, gender role, ethnicity, sexual preference, physical condition, or psychological state—provide the practitioner with another lens for assessing significant aspects of interpersonal relations in the group's process. The social psychological factors of stereotyping and self-fulfilling prophecies interact with members' intrapsychic factors to bring about impoverished social relationships, identity confusions, restricted ego functioning, and experiences of dominance and submission in social relationships.

Stereotyping and self-fulfilling prophecies interfere with members' experiences of self and others in the group. However, with effort, the toxic effects of these dynamics can be neutralized. The humanistic group fosters a process that is inhospitable to character assaults and discrimination. The injuries sustained through stigmatization create pain and anticipation of rejection, which—along with the group's acceptance—may paradoxically increase a member's testing of the safety of the group.

The practitioner remains attentive to the effects of stereotyping. The practitioner considers how stereotypes and stigmas affect members' senses of belonging and acceptance in the group. The practitioner looks to the circumstances of stereotypes to provide grist for the mill for changes of self and other in the process.

Stage Theme 1: We're Not in Charge

Since stereotyping is likely to occur during periods of first impressions, the practitioner considers how each member is characterized by others and characterizes them. This is done to safeguard members' initial entries into the group, and to prevent judgmental or stereotypical perceptions of one another.

The practitioner uses his or her awareness of a member's class, ethnic, and racial affiliations as signifiers of potential negative stereotyping. He or she takes note of the conflict-free or negative, self-fulfilling, stereotypical image the member may bring to the group. He or she looks for the ways the group members are perceiving the individual and how the member is reacting to the group's stereotypical and nonstereotypical expectations. People who anticipate being the brunt of stereotypes approach groups wanting to know if they will be accepted. The practitioner responds to these cues, opening up the issue of acceptance and expectations, empathizing with issues related to self-fulfilling prophecies as well as racial, ethnic, and gender stereotypes.

Stage Theme 2: We Are in Charge

Some members may view the practitioner and peers as people who dominate others. These fears are aroused as the members grapple with using democratic norms and humanistic values that run counter to those in their actual life situations.

A member's conscious awareness about his or her possible stereotypes, and others' reactions to these, will assist the member in functioning in the group. These stereotypes may pervade members' presentations of self in the form of self-fulfilling prophecies. A member bearing a stigma may pose an indirect challenge to the others to react by displaying negative attitudes about the group's activities, or by sulking.

As cliques vie for leadership, the practitioner is alert to any member's use of stereotyping to dominate or exclude others. This guards against the development of covert undemocratic norms, which undermine humanistic values. The practitioner paves the way for everyone to look at stereotypes, stigmatizations, and resultant self-fulfilling prophecies in order to develop the group norm of inclusion.

Stage Theme 3: We're Taking You On

A member who has been stereotyped by other members, but not stereotyped by the practitioner, may not become involved in challenging the practitioner. This member will need help and support from the practitioner to challenge the members who are doing the stereotyping. He or she will also require help in challenging the practitioner's authority, so that the member can experience his or her own leadership qualities in the group.

The practitioner is not immune from stereotyping members. Accepting this, the practitioner looks for evidence of his or her acts of overt and covert stereotyping. Owning one's part requires a direct question: "Am I misperceiving you and offending you?" Furthermore, the practitioner should give an authentic response to the member's answer. The practitioner affirms and supports the member's feelings, acknowledging and apologizing for any distortions. The practitioner may also ask the other members what they have perceived about the practitioner's behavior, eliciting their reactions to his or her acts and perceptions.

Stage Theme 4: Sanctuary

During this time of safety and closeness in the group, values and norms that promise humanism and democracy result in a feeling of safety and relaxation. This may be more pronounced for the member who is treated as an object of derision and discrimination in the external environment. On the other hand, a negative reaction to the atmosphere of the Sanctuary that tests its reliability is also not unusual. In some instances, members can band together, assuming superior attitudes toward others and stereotyping and rejecting others in and out of the group.

The practitioner considers how to help members change the negative anticipations they have developed in prior social experiences. Effort is also turned to raising the group's collective awareness about the toxic effects of stereotyping, so that the quality of sanctuary can serve as a safe haven in which to develop individual and group efforts to confront stereotyping and discrimination.

Some members may send out signals that they wish to discuss stereotypes in order to test the group's willingness to accept them. The practitioner should attentively develop this theme because it offers a chance for deepening acceptance among all the members. All members will be helped to broaden their social skills and connections by dealing with stereotyping.

Stage Theme 5: This Isn't Good Anymore

The practitioner considers how to help members deal with their feelings of futility in reaction to others' inabilities to inhibit stereotyping. The member who is losing faith in the group's capacity to view him or her as a real person, rather than in the frame of a stereotype, needs to be brought back into the interaction to confront the stereotypes and to appraise the kind of interactions he or she is having in the group. The member who moves away from group life because of concerns about stereotyping challenges the group to prove itself once again as a milieu that is able to transcend acts of discrimination and stereotyping that are prevalent in the external environment.

Stage Theme 6: We're Okay and Able

At this time, members are motivated to work on the real life issues that brought them into the group. The practitioner assesses the way stereotyping impacts emotionally, causing interpersonal barriers. The practitioner evaluates the degree to which members retreat from social and political interests and involvements for fear of rejection and suppression. Consciousness of the ubiquity of "isms"—ethnocentrism, racism, sexism, ageism—is brought to the fore to help members work on these issues through comprehension and action.

The practitioner attends to how members, by means of innuendo or direct appellations, distort others' personalities and actions. Members are assisted in engaging specific individuals in order to develop constructive ways of challenging and overcoming the use of stereotypes and discrimination.

Illustration. A group is composed of pregnant prisoners in an urban prison with a large majority of nonwhite populations. At the first meeting, the practitioner has just finished introducing the group experience "as a place for mutual support and survival for pregnant prisoners, your babies, and your families while in and out of prison." A member asks in Spanish if the practitioner can speak Spanish. The practitioner, a white male, is about to say "no" when an African-American group member emphatically says, "We don't want no people who can't speak English in this group." The group worker responds, "In this group, people who speak any tongue have membership. And if some of you aren't bilingual, or don't wish to translate, I will find a way of keeping it going." Two people move forward and begin translating.

Later on, during Stage Theme 2 ("We Are in Charge"), the nonwhites begin to challenge the worker's way of observing their interactions. As the challenge continues they become more and more fearful, because whites are dominant in the prison power structure; this mirrors the political and economic situations in their communities. Out of this fear the members start raising their hands to speak, like school children asking the teacher for permission. They will not respond to the practitioner's questions of this; he lets it go and recedes into the background, hoping they will be less fearful. Still they raise their hands. Eventually, the practitioner sits on the floor, below the members and out of their line of sight. This helps the members' face-to-face interactions. They begin to talk about how to interact in the group, and how to share strategies for survival in prison. Eunice instructs the practitioner to "join in, and give your opinions, too," adding as an aside to the others, "He's okay." Others nod in agreement.

Moving into Stage Theme 4 (Sanctuary), the members talk about how well-off they are compared with other prisoners who don't have the group. Attitudes of superiority and racial epithets about other women prisoners that reflect the power structure in the setting are heard. The practitioner wonders, "How will you handle this special view of yourselves back in the cell block? You are putting yourselves on pedestals." This brings about further discussion about being victimized by the system.

During their work together at Stage Theme 6 ("We're Okay and Able"), the women move into talking deeply about the stigmas of racism and sexism they face and will face, along with overcoming obstacles of having been in prison. The creation of opportunities in the context of discrimination is considered.

Stage Theme 7: Just a Little Longer

Separating from the group may rekindle fears of being stigmatized. This may be expressed by denials of the group's value and loss of the sense of mastery gained in the group as the members reestablish interpersonal defenses to survive in rejecting and denigrating environments.

The practitioner explores the denials of the group's significance by members to determine if they are related to fear of being seen and dealt with stereotypically in future social interactions. The practitioner considers to what degree the members own effective approaches and attitudes to defend themselves and to seek support from others in situations that are characterized by values and norms shaped by stereotyping and discrimination.

Symbolic Representations of the Practitioner and Group

Assessing the reactions of members to the evolving process is done by considering how frequently and with what intensity members attach symbolic significance to the role of the practitioner. Reactions to the practitioner will depend upon each member's frame of reference (Garland, Jones, & Kolodny, 1973) regarding authority and the meaning of group life. The practitioner and members may be seen as harsh or benevolent authority figures, familial parental or sibling figures, or as representatives of social institutional control. Members may attach parent and child symbols to themselves or to the practitioner, because the small group can be reminiscent of the family. These subjectivities, if not age appropriate, distort the realities of the relationships and the potential for productive accomplishments in the group. The practitioner will have to consider the relative fluidity and rigidity of these frames of reference, and how these affect each member's participation in a productive process.

Stage Theme 1: We're Not in Charge

The practitioner formulates a tentative assessment of the members' perceptions of him or her, enabling members to deal with distortions that interfere with the trust necessary for involvement in a full interpersonal process.

Members perceive the practitioner's reactions and the group's affiliation processes in relation to other helpers and groups they experienced (Shulman, 1984). This will be expressed to a greater or lesser extent depending on their anxiety about membership in the group and the type of authority the worker will use. Some members may perceive the practitioner in the capacity of standard-bearer of the group, or may view the practitioner's image of the humanistic group with skepticism.

The practitioner considers the extent of the members' willingness and abilities to engage with him or her directly. The practitioner may be responded to with trust or mistrust, as an enabling expert or a depriving agent of social control. The members' symbolic views of the practitioner also skew and shape their perceptions of other members.

The practitioner can test out his or her assessments by inactivity, seeking to note changes or confirmation. Then the practitioner may engage symbolic distortions to alter the member's perceptions by restating the practitioner's role or the group's purpose. If clarification of these factors becomes difficult, then the subject has to be dropped until later on in the process to avoid recalcitrant attitudes that may bolster further symbolic reactions. The practitioner hopes that the member's experiences in process will be corrective without confrontation.

Stage Theme 2: We Are in Charge

The practitioner assesses each member's perceptions of the power of the authority role to help in clarifying distortions and expectations attendant to it. This enables members' fuller ownership of and responsibility for the group process.

Members who are feeling powerless during the normative crisis may express desires for the practitioner to assert control. Such members may question the practitioner's ability to meet their needs. This may be done by cloaking the worker in the garb of a "good, all-knowing person" or an "obstacle and enemy to the process" (Bion, 1959). At this juncture in the process, the practitioner may be symbolized as an agent of a depriving and repressive social institutional structure. This may be expressed by expectations of disappointment about the worker and the group ever being helpful.

The practitioner tests out the assessment of the members' realistic and unrealistic expectations by creating opportunities for dialogues so that actual interactions can pave the way for truer images of the practitioner.

Stage Theme 3: We're Taking You On

The practitioner here is interested in helping the members experience him or her as an actual human being with a specific role and expertise in the group.

When taking the practitioner on, each member is attempting to clarify his or her perceptions and feelings about the practitioner as an authority figure, while asking for reactions from and dialogue with the practitioner in return. Interactional realities are the salient material to engage around, rather than those that are historical or intellectualized. This juncture in the process is the practitioner's opportunity to reach the member who is most distant, angry, or disappointed, to begin the process of forming a relationship that is based on current interactions and changes in behavior rather than on projections from the past. The practitioner invites the member's feedback, responding in a way that helps the member develop a direct and meaningful relationship with him or her.

Stage Theme 4: Sanctuary

At this stage, the practitioner and group are usually symbolized through a familial lens (Garland et al., 1973). Given this, much data may emerge about what interferes with members' age-appropriate abilities to interact. The practitioner can be cast into the image of an all-knowing parent who can develop the best group, or as an ignorant failure of a parent who is incompetent and will not experience good feelings. He or she also runs the risk of being perceived as a political collaborator who should join this special group as a sibling against parental figures, or as someone who can never join in because his or her lifestyle is "so different." These parental and politicized symbolizations may cause the member to defensively seek the protective comfort of the group's sanctuary.

The practitioner works on engaging distortions of these sorts by acknowledging the members' feelings and working with them to clarify perceptions of the practitioner's behavior. Some transferential material can be left unexplored by the practitioner if it shapes the member's style of appropriate characterization.

Stage Theme 5: This Isn't Good Anymore

When the group is feeling down on itself, the practitioner deals with the members who express this viewpoint most often. He or she openly explores the reasons that members feel unable to move forward, focusing on the members' particular disappointments in the methods of the practitioner, other members, and the group as a whole.

The practitioner recognizes that he or she is called upon to offer corrective experiences, as an authority figure that differs from those in authority with whom the members have had negative experiences. He or she actively helps the members examine their pessimism deriving from the expectation that someone in authority will be a source of frustration, rather than a source of support for meeting needs.

Stage Theme 6: We're Okay and Able

The practitioner considers how he or she uses the worker role to create bonds with the members that enhance their abilities to work on change while minimally encumbered by symbolic distortions. When a member wittingly juxtaposes and alternates distorted and realistic perceptions of the practitioner and the group, he or she shows signs of knowing the symbols for what they are—masks that interfere with relationships. Members actively engage in the process, identifying symbolic distortions as obstacles to their work in the group.

In the change process, members may utilize the practitioner as facilitator, role model, or teacher. Members borrow abilities and take recommendations from the practitioner more often as they accept the practitioner as a separate individual. The practitioner considers the amount of direction each member is able to take, and the degree of palpable connection each member has to him or her. When not symbolically distorting, the member connects to the practitioner as an authoritative enabler.

Illustration. At the tenth meeting of a teen parent group, Jessica asks Helen, the practitioner, "What makes you so special that you can help me out?" Helen responds, "Jessica, I have my training to help me, and my desire to help all you young women and men try to rear your children, and to enjoy yourselves with others." John says, "It's so hard to come home, get the kid from day care, and feel connected. Forget it! And on Saturday night, when I know all my friends are out, and I have r-e-s-p-o-n-s-i-b-l-i-t-y!" John turns to Helen and asks, "You were a teen once, how did you handle the desire to be with your friends?" Francie cuts in, "Don't tell yet, Helen, because you're not the teacher. Just write it down." Helen says, "Okay, let's all write down how we handle responsibility. Then we'll all go around and read what we wrote." The members agree. "Don't cheat, Helen," is heard from Francie. They laugh. Helen says, "This is good stuff for role playing. By the way, let's not forget the picnic in a couple of weeks for the children and grandparents. Another responsibility to plan and to enjoy."

After the discussion of responsibility, Jessica comments, "Helen, you make us feel good. You are nicer to us than anyone else." Helen feels misunderstood and suffocated by the "good parent" label of this perception. She is aware that Jessica and the others are fickle; twenty minutes earlier, Jessica had tested her ability, a phenomenon that happens regularly in this group.

At later meetings, after a year of work together, during Stage Theme 6 ("We're Okay and Able") the group is talking about how they feel so old and so young at the same time. They are alternately caught between trying to meet their responsibilities, and resenting them as well. After talking about wanting her mother to help her with her daughter, Jessica says to Helen, "I wish that I could go back to school." Helen, aware of Jessica's special need for support and her sensitivity when she experiences rejection, chooses to respond directly before eliciting the group's response: "That sounds like a fine idea. What did you have in mind?" Jessica gathers up her strength, and talks about becoming a nurse. Helen supports her and universalizes her experience for the group: "Alice and Inez, when you went back to school, it seems to me you felt good." This gives the cue to Inez who responds directly to Jessica, "It's true, Jessica,

I like it. It's hard, but I like it. Why don't you come down to the school, and I'll show you around; we'll get some booklets and you can spend the evening, if your mom will babysit." Jessica says, "Oh, for school, my mom will babysit," and looks at Helen. Helen responds with a smile of approval.

Stage Theme 7: Just a Little Longer

When the group moves toward ending its process, a member's perceptions of the practitioner can shift from experiencing the practitioner as realistic and enabling to perceiving him or her as all-comforting or all-rejecting. This will be evident by attitudes and activities wherein the member moves back to earlier ways of depending upon or challenging the worker.

Members in this stage experience feelings of comfort or abandonment by other members, as well. Each member needs to view the practitioner and group experience through significant frames of reference that serve as realistic models for future relationships. The practitioner assesses how intensely each member remains lodged in the midst of perceptual distortions. This is done to gauge what type of emotional and social issues may be obstacles for the members in future situations, and how able the members are in working through these feelings as they move on. The practitioner identifies the extent to which these are stage specific or fundamental to the character, pattern, and personality of each member. If the latter is evident, confronting these distortions at the end will be counterproductive for the member, stimulating regressive attitudes and activities.

SUMMARY

This chapter has focused on psychosocial parameters and perspectives for assessing the member in the group. The habit of assessment helps the practitioner empathize with and observe the member as a distinct person in the process. The following dimensions of members' behavior were considered: (1) ability to take part in processes that develop democratic mutual aid and that actualize purpose; (2) ego abilities and sense of self; (3) the social institutional environment; (4) stereotypes and self-fulfilling prophecies; and (5) symbolic representations of the practitioner and the group.

To shed light on the changing nature of member behavior during the group's development, these dimensions were delineated in the context of each of the seven stage themes. Each parameter casts a different light on the perceptions the practitioner experiences when observing and assessing members. The task of the practitioner is to shift from one type of lens to another, and to be aware of the effect these lenses have on his or her perceptions, empathy, judgments, and acts of engagement with each member.

Part IV

CONTINGENCIES

Chapter 10

PRACTICE VARIATIONS

GROUP MEETING ENVIRONMENTS

A *group meeting environment* is the physical space that the practitioner and group members use for their meetings. This environment is important because it is composed of physical spaces and objects that have logistical as well as symbolic significance. Logistically, it has to be accessible to the members. The route used for getting to the meeting area has to be easy to map out or, if not straightforward, mapped out in advance so members can navigate their ways to it. Members with physical difficulties have considerations that will have to be accounted for when they are given directions on how to get to the meeting room. Once in the environment, chairs, tables, sufficient lighting, ventilation, and space for movement need to be considered as significant factors to be attended to by the practitioner.

The meeting environment also has symbolic significance. Its condition, implements and objects, location, and where it is in relation to its surroundings may affect the members' and practitioner's views of themselves. A neatly furnished lounge communicates a different message than a room with cast-off furniture that is not well kept.

The practitioner at the outset has primary responsibility for being involved in the selection, logistics, and symbolic dimensions of the group's meeting environment (Kurland, 1978). This may be done before the first meeting or later on, with or without the group's input. The practitioner must become familiar with both the symbolic and logistical aspects of the environment, in order to be prepared to assist the members with their reactions.

In selecting the environment the practitioner may also choose to reorganize it. Tables can be moved to the side, to better accommodate a circle that invites people to look around at one another, to move around, and to use the floor. It is very difficult to set up role plays when people are seated around tables; this kind of arrangement mitigates against the creative energy that can flow from groups. It is also difficult to see and relate to people sitting along the sides of rectangular tables.

Children's groups may require a large room with tables to one side and floor space on the other, suggesting a range of possibilities for experiences, programming, and interpersonal relationships. By way of contrast, a room with a one-way mirror suggests a particular view of the nature of the relationship between the members and the practitioner—an us-and-them framework that should immediately be explored in the group. A refreshment table suggests that some provision will be made to accommodate members whose journey to the meeting might be stressful. Large name cards (that can be read across the room) used at every one of the early meetings may help people tune into one another and the practitioner, avoiding the embarrassments that can occur in group situations.

PREGROUP CONTACT

Pregroup contact refers to formal and informal interactions the practitioner might have, by design or chance, with prospective members. The formality of pregroup meetings will vary with the agency's function, the group's purpose, and the amount of time the person will be asked to wait before the first meeting.

Whether meetings are formal or informal, as the agency representative the practitioner is expected to respond directly to questions asked by prospective members, offering a view of the group's purpose as well. The practitioner elicits the member's view of how his or her needs might be met within the context of this group, and lends a vision about how the group might work. Some members will have questions about how group work technically functions. Others will have ambivalence about taking part; this, too, will call for a direct but uncomplicated response. Providing an orientation to the nature of group participation by describing and discussing the give and take of group life, the processes of mutual aid, and the democratic modes to be used helps allay people's fears by giving a framework within which to understanding and experience the means to be used.

The practitioner's response to questions and discussion of group purpose, followed by encouragement to try a meeting and see how the experience feels, usually facilitates initial entry. Sometimes a prospective member may not be certain that group participation will be useful in meeting his or her needs. In this case, more time spent with the person in examining the group's possibilities in light of the person's unique needs may prove to be helpful.

Some agencies conduct complex intake interviews for all new clients, whether they are interested in joining a group or participating in individual counseling. This format is not recommended as a necessary prerequisite for group participation. However, a formal intake procedure does not necessarily have to be detrimental to group membership. There is no reason why a psychosocial intake process that is a routine aspect of agency practice cannot be used constructively to facilitate entry into a group. The practitioner is called upon to design the contact in such a way as to effect an understanding of group experience as *membership* within the mutual aid system. The practitioner talks about how group method helps people help themselves and one another through the membership role with its tasks and responsibilities. The practitioner also seeks to find out about the potential members' previous group experiences, and what they anticipate.

In formally meeting with each prospective member, the practitioner is tuning in to the members' interpersonal abilities, considering what their entries into the first sessions will be like, and what their capabilities and problems in membership might be. The general aim is to find ways of assisting each of the different people to fit into the beginning process. Also considered is whether or not there is good reason to dissuade a person from group membership, either because the individual does not need it or because he or she will not be able to make effective use of it at the present time. In these situations, the practitioner helps the person find other more suitable resources.

Illustration

In trying to set up a group in the Women to Women program for the initial meeting, the practitioner has been on the phone a good number of times in the last three weeks with prospective members. She has also received calls from potential members who have questions and doubts. As she gathered information from different women, she was able to talk in general to them about the various issues some women face—divorce, economic independence, career, and children.

One conversation with Lucy quickly moved into the prospective member's talking about the details of her problems with her former husband, who she says is having great difficulty accepting the divorce. He wants a reconciliation—as she puts it—"inducing guilt for the sake of the children." The practitioner interrupts when Lucy takes time out to catch her breath: "Boy, Lucy, that is a difficult spot. I appreciate how upset it makes you. It's not uncommon, either; I've found that there've been a good number of women in the program who've had similar problems with themselves and their ex-husbands, and these groups have been quite helpful to them." Lucy responds, "That's good to hear." The practitioner also responds to the guilt Lucy is feeling and says, "Guilt is also an issue that has come up in these women's groups, so I doubt that you will be alone with those feelings. In fact, one of the women interested in joining this group has mentioned how guilty she feels about her kids." Lucy now begins to ask questions about the other members. The practitioner tells her there is one more divorced woman, and another who is separating. She also says there is one who is remarried, and has to deal with the mix-and-match of children. Lucy tells the practitioner she has a friend with that problem. Lucy seems satisfied and able to hold off talking about her issues. The practitioner says "goodbye" and "I look forward to meeting you on Tuesday."

During the start of the first meeting, the practitioner opens by saying, "I've had opportunity to talk with each of you in the last few weeks by phone and have gotten a sense of why you thought you'd come. I've also given you a general sense of what others are coming here for. Why don't you just start by going around, giving your name, and stating what brings you here to the group, or anything else you want us to know right now." After they spend 15 minutes in these introductions, the practitioner says, "I hear some common as well as different issues. What I hear that is similar is a desire to get to know yourselves a little better and to develop skill in standing up for yourselves. Some of you want to clarify relationships with ex-husbands, children, parents, bosses, or lovers. This certainly gives us a start, doesn't it? What do you think? What would you like to get out of this?" Members now begin to talk more about what they want out of the group.

Discussion

This illustrates a clear-cut example of group practice without formal pregroup interviewing. The practitioner uses the pregroup information she received on the phone to center herself in the group, to develop a sense of the members' issues and gauge their reactions. Pregroup contacts of any type are aimed to motivate actual participation in the first session. They are designed to stay away from working on issues in the one to one mode. Thus the practitioner does not probe Lucy's feelings about her husband, nor does she relate to the possibility that Lucy might also be having difficulty accepting the divorce. Rather, she universalizes Lucy's concerns and redirects Lucy's effort toward thinking about membership in the group. The practitioner lends a vision for the group at this very early premeeting stage, and connects herself to Lucy in an effort to motivate her interest in the first meeting.

At the meeting itself, having already talked about their goals and interests in the individual phone contacts with the practitioner, the members are prepared to enter into a beginning process of searching for commonality and examining the potential of mutual aid processes.

INFORMAL BETWEEN-SESSION CONTACTS WITH PRACTITIONER

Once the group is underway, meeting with the practitioner between sessions may be a positive continuation of the group's work efforts. This is especially true when programs are being planned, tasks are being completed, roles are being rehearsed, and decisions made in the group are being followed through by the members. In such instances the members may call upon the practitioner to help gain access to agency resources and personnel. Contacts with the practitioner represent a continuation of the type of between-session interactions members are having with one another.

In some situations, contact occurs when members frequent the agency setting for more than the group meeting—either for leisure-time activities, therapeutic communities, or residence. Whether the practitioner is approached for advice or supportive intervention, the principle of humanistic group method is to shape the contact so that the member can bring relevant concerns to the group members at the forthcoming meeting. If many members try to talk to the worker outside of sessions about issues directly related to the group, this suggests that the group as a whole is having difficulty dealing with some aspect of itself. The practitioner redirects the issues back to the group, without becoming overly involved in out-of-meeting problem solving.

While it is generally recommended that members use the group as their central arena for work related to group purpose, from time to time members will require opportunities to meet with the practitioner in between group meeting times. Members may have particular crises or needs that depart from group purpose. Some purpose-related problems cannot wait to the next meeting, or will not get enough attention unless the group meets more than once a week. Scheduling an extra group meeting is optimal, though not always possible. Therefore, seeing members between sessions to deal with the realities and anxieties of particular problems and to direct the members back to the group for more work can be an imperative. Although the hope is that members have enough supportive networks among themselves to speak to one another between sessions, there may be times when this is not possible.

Illustration

The practitioner, Herb, in a cancer support group hears that Paul, a group member, has left a message that he hopes the practitioner can see him that day. Herb calls him back, saying, "Hi, Paul, I got your message. What's the matter?" Paul answers, "The cancer came back, man. I don't know what to do. It's too much to handle." Herb responds, "I'm sorry, Paul, really sorry." Paul says, "It's now back in the lung. Damn it. I knew it. I felt it. I just didn't want to deal with it again. I have to go back for treatments. I hate the whole thing." The practitioner asks, "Have you told anyone yet?" Paul says that he hasn't because he is too uptight to even think about it, and that it's too much of a blow.

The practitioner says, "It sure is a low blow; I agree. I'm here and I'm listening. I have another 5 minutes right now, but we can talk later." Paul says thanks, and the practitioner continues, "Go on with what you were saying." Paul says, "I told my wife, of course, but I can't deal with this enough to tell anyone else." "Does that mean the group, too?" asks Herb. Paul answers, "Yes, for now. I wanted to talk to you first, to get my head together. I don't want to upset them either. They're all going along, hoping they won't get it back. I can't tell them this." Herb says, "What about one person in the group for now, since we don't meet again until next week?" Paul says, "Not yet." The practitioner responds,

"Okay, whatever you want. Paul, I have half an hour this afternoon or one hour tomorrow when I can see you. What's your preference?" Paul decides to wait until tomorrow.

When Paul sees the practitioner the next day, they talk about his illness, his anxieties about his job, treatments, dying, and how to tell his sister and brother-in-law. The practitioner listens, is supportive, and points out how hard it is for Paul to bring bad news to people. The practitioner is also aware how difficult it is for Paul to ask for help, but he appropriately chooses to let that issue surface in the group. They talk again about telling the group, and Paul decides that he will call his friends in the group, Tony and Lenore, whom he talks to frequently enough.

Discussion

The member has had some devastating news. First, the practitioner offers clear-cut support and affirmation, as well as his own reaction of upset to Paul's bad news. Certainly this news is completely within the purpose of the group, and will have to be expressed there. At this time, however, Paul needs the opportunity to talk with the practitioner. This is in part because he is experiencing some difficulty reaching out to the group members, but also because he is in crisis.

The practitioner tests to see whether a gentle nudge will help Paul make a call to a group member; he finds out that Paul is not ready. This message confirms the need for the meeting with the practitioner, who quickly offers it. Seeing that Paul is willing to wait one day shows that the brief phone work may have already offered some support. The practitioner does not probe for feelings beyond those that are manifest.

When seeing Paul the next day, the practitioner permits him the opportunity to share his concerns and fears about the recurrence of the cancer. What becomes evident is that Paul is also having difficulty telling his sister and brother-in-law. The practitioner helps Paul make the connection to being afraid to tell the group. This gives Paul the impetus to tell two trusted friends in the group before the next meeting. The practitioner is careful not to diffuse Paul's future work in the group by dealing with the latent issues concerning his reluctance about asking for help that goes along with telling the group. This, being a very difficult time for Paul, would be an inappropriate time to work on changing behavioral patterns.

FORMAL BETWEEN-SESSION
CONTACTS WITH PRACTITIONER

These types of contacts occur when a practitioner works individually, in family or marital sessions, or in a community organization committee with group members. Each method has somewhat different objectives and processes, and clients, patients, or members also have different qualities whose boundaries and parameters need to be respected. The mutual judgment of the practitioner and member is called for regarding how the member can integrate the group meetings with the other sessions. This will open up opportunities for the practitioner and member to make relevant comments in the group about the issues without violating the boundaries of each experience.

Illustration

Maria is in a casework process with the practitioner, David, as well as in the group. During the meeting Maria says, looking directly at the practitioner, "This issue between Celine and me is just what I was talking with you about in our sessions." The practitioner says, "This crossed my mind, too. Looks like you are about to bring it up, so go ahead." After explanation and discussion of the issues she has been working on individually with him, David asks Maria to look at ways this issue is playing itself out in the group. Members begin to look at the pattern in the group from different angles.

Later on in the session, Bonita says "David, can I be in individual with you, too?" David says, "It's possible for any of you to be in individual if you and I explore our views on its value for you. Also, we all have to be careful to look at the many aspects of this possibility. For instance, one issue to consider is if it is really good for you. Another question to ask is if you want it because another group member has it, and you are envious. What are you thinking and feeling?"

Discussion

This illustrates a not-so-rare occurrence that places the practitioner in the situation of having information about a member that is not in the group's domain. In addition, the practitioner runs the risk of being the subject of group competition, and the member runs the risk of group envy. In this meeting, raising the issue of envy directly helps all the members examine their needs and irrational feelings that come about when they think one member may be getting something special in the relationship with the practitioner.

POSTGROUP RESPONSIBILITIES

Much necessary work will occur prior to and during the very last session of the group. However, following the last session the practitioner may remain involved with group members in effecting referrals, entitlements, and communications about their situations. Particularly in settings where daily contacts occur, there will be interactions with group members. Some extra time may be needed to end the contact with the practitioner.

If ongoing professional contact continues after the group's ending, there may well be opportunity for references and allusions to the group experience. These allusions should not be allowed to break the boundaries of propriety by violating the person's and others' confidentiality. It may come about that the former member needs guidance and counsel that properly fits with the professional's role. If this is the case, time should be set aside for help or referral, but not to open up or explore issues that were manifest or latent in the person's group experience.

There may be some persons who need further opportunity for contact with the practitioner after the last session. Appraising what the person is asking for and considering how to assist is useful. This stance acknowledges differences among members in approaches to handling endings. The practitioner may have to indicate that it is not possible to be as deeply and frequently involved with the former member, pointing the person toward other sources of assistance.

What professionals tend to call "loose ends" at the group's conclusion are really part of the process. The practitioner needs to insure that referrals have been effected, and that former group members know how and when to move on to other resources. The practitioner is available to colleagues to help them contact and understand the needs of former group members. Finally, the practitioner finishes off the process by updating professional records and statistics.

SHORT-TERM GROUPS

Short-term groups are those that will meet from between three to a dozen sessions, more or less. The short-term group is usually developed by the agency around a particular theme, or to deal with a special issue. Many of these groups are education or growth oriented rather than for remediation purposes. Groups for parent effectiveness, psycho-education, discharge planning, postmastectomy patients, or women in transition are examples of short-term groups. In developing and defining a technology of practice for these groups, the assumption is made that the short-term nature of the group's professionally guided life is a function of a thoughtful discussion and planning process.

In short-term groups, the limitation of time will not permit a detailed working on and through of complex needs. Some objectives, processes, and techniques of the humanistic method are curtailed, while others are magnified within the confines of time (Alissi & Casper, 1985). The shortening of time does permit telescoping of particular needs, and can be used to highlight a particular issue.

In the short-term group, the practitioner is called upon to partialize areas of concern in order to predetermine which purpose-related needs to address, which goals might prove functional for the members, and which issues to avoid. Developing the democratic mutual aid system and actualizing purpose are accelerated by either collapsing them, directly providing for them, and/or bypassing other processes altogether. Developing programs and opportunities for role rehearsal may be heightened, whereas dealing directly with some aspects of the practitioner's authority and the surfacing of most conflicts is avoided.

Assessment skills are important in the short-term practice situation. Practitioners need to rely on knowledge of stage theme behaviors and issues to shed light on the group's movement, where to collapse processes and where to telescope them. Lang (1986) has developed a framework for assessing social work groups lacking certain properties. In this framework, the short-term group is a type of "collectivity." The six variables Lang uses to assess these groups are: temporal variables of frequency and duration; contextual variables; individual variables; entiative variables such as fit of members, their interactional skills, and stability of attendance; and professional variables centering around the practitioner's framework and skill.

In a short-term group, temporal variables (Lang, 1986) mitigate against the group's ability to work in depth on many issues. Thus those few issues selected for work have to be the most consonant with members' needs. In making these selections, the practitioner is called upon to stimulate the group's efforts by explicitly lending a vision concerning how the issues will be worked on in the group and away from it. During pregroup contacts and the first session, the practitioner may present the group's goals within the confines of instruction, rather than lengthier time-consuming discussions, in order to focus in so that work can begin. Throughout the group's short existence the practitioner will need knowledge of the fit of members, their interaction skills, and their stability of attendance, especially with regard to the members' interpersonal processes of group mutual aid. The practitioner will also need to know about the members' individual variables—life cycle factors and limitations as these interact with group's issues.

In the short-term framework, explicit professional knowledge (Lang, 1986) and the technical skills for guiding members' work on process and purpose in an abbreviated structure are required. Therefore, another factor is evident regarding the degree and level of practitioner activity. Lang (1972) has provided a framework for addressing the relationship between members' capacities and the practitioner's activity. In short-term work, while member capacity has some effect, time leaves the practitioner in a circumstance where he or she must be more active than usual (Lang, 1986). The practitioner asks for more interactive, experiential, and didactic activity in the short-term group. Visual and aural aids are used. In addition, experiences related to the techniques of role rehearsal and programming with significant others are of great value in a short-term group.

In the long-term group's process, more of an interplay between experiential and reflective modes occurs. In the shorter process the members need interactions that help acquaint them with themselves and their activities in their roles. From this point of view, the group worker quickly partializes the phenomena in the first session and focuses on those aspects of interaction that will help the members carry out actions. Then the practitioner develops role rehearsal to help in immediate interpersonal expressions.

Illustration

This is the first meeting of a neonatology group for parents of newborns in the intensive care nursery. The mothers have just given birth to these babies, and have been here from two to four days; the infants will remain for several weeks after the women are discharged. The intent is for this group to continue meeting two times a week while the mothers and fathers are returning to the hospital to visit and care for the infant, for a total of eight sessions. This is the first meeting. Four

women and two men are present; the practitioner has also asked a nurse
take part.

As they gather, the women especially begin to talk about how
difficult it is for them to see their babies looking so frail, with tubes
attached to them. One man seems to respond when his wife talks,
sharing fearful feelings as well. The practitioner suggests that this is a
difficult time and, that "we wanted to get you together, so you can talk
about your feelings and get support." Mazie asks, "Why don't they let
me go in to see my baby when I want to?" The practitioner says that it's
usually because they are doing something for the baby. The nurse nods
agreement. The practitioner continues, "But I know how hard it is to be
told you can't see the baby right now." Felicia tells the group how hard
it is for her to go in when they are poking and bothering her baby, and
how she doesn't understand it all. Lou, Felicia's husband, says he hopes
they know what they are doing. "I have to trust they know what they
are doing," he adds. Dina tells how awful she will feel about going home
tomorrow "empty handed." Felicia agrees that she will feel the same
way. Her husband tells her, "Let's try to be patient, and hope they can
get our baby's lungs working on their own."

After 25 minutes, the practitioner notices that Anna and her husband
Kenny have not spoken yet. She directs her attention to them saying,
"You've been so quiet; what are your reactions?" Anna, with much
hesitation, softly talks about her sister losing a baby after 3 days and
how terrified she is of this. Kenny looks so choked up he can't talk. The
rest of the group falls silent. The practitioner says, "I guess this hits
home, doesn't it." All agree. Mazie says that she sometimes has a hard
time being with the baby, because she is so afraid of losing her that she's
afraid of loving her too much. Anna admits that she had a difficult time
even going to see the baby, and how awful and guilty she feels. The
practitioner says, "This is not unusual; that's one reason for having this
group, so you can talk about these feelings."

Felicia talks about her own difficulty seeing the baby and tries to
reassure Anna. Anna reaches for Kenny's hand. She says, "I get so
upset, because we don't know what the outcome will be." Kenny says,
"I don't know what to tell Darryl at home about his baby sister. And
Darryl hasn't even seen her yet." The practitioner asks the group, "What
do you think Kenny can say?" Felicia says that he can tell Darryl that
the doctors and nurses are taking care of the baby because she's not
strong enough yet to come home. More discussion ensues; questions
are also asked about how to help siblings at home cope with a baby they

haven't seen yet. After some more talking, the group is of the opinion that the children at home should be talked with, but not frightened "even though we feel scared." Kenny says, "I feel better just knowing how to approach Darryl." The practitioner says, "Boy, we've said and done a lot today."

Vivian, the nurse, says, "I just want to tell you that the infants start out looking so weak and vulnerable. But we've seen them thrive in intensive care and, you know, they're tough little buggers, too. And they respond to you. So if you want to know what to do, just holding them can help."

As the group is winding down, the nurse and practitioner suggest they all go to the ICU together to look at the babies. This is met with much enthusiasm. As they are walking over there, the practitioner begins to tell the group about the ten-year reunion they had recently of the ICU babies, and how wonderful it was to see them now. The members "ooh" and "aah," and the practitioner asks if they can meet in three days. Most of the women will have been discharged by then except for Mazie, who had a cesarean section and was staying an extra day. "But we'll be spending a lot of time here," says Anna. "Any time you say, we can meet," Felicia chimes in. The nurse and practitioner set the time and everyone agrees.

As they walk down the hall, the practitioner encourages the members to ask her and the nurse questions. They begin to ask various questions about tubes, support devices, and the babies' appearances and coloration. The nurse answers many of them; both the nurse and practitioner encourage the members to ask their doctors as well. The practitioner takes the time to ask Mazie if her husband can come next time, and if Dina's boyfriend is available, too.

Discussion

This illustration shows the partializing, focusing, and programmatic interventions the practitioner uses. Because at the start the members spontaneously talk to one another, the practitioner does not intervene to talk about group purpose or structure. She answers a question directly and undefensively about why they can't see the babies when they want to, then acknowledges the frustration and anxiety they must be feeling so as to provide a further catalyst for talk on a feeling level. Once the group has gotten off the ground and talk about the babies' apparent frailty surfaces, the practitioner supports their expression of feeling.

This is a short-term group of people in crisis situations. There is no time to wait for the group members to draw out the quiet members. After giving it 25 minutes, the practitioner asks Anna and Kenny directly how they are feeling. This surfaces their concern about the loss of a sister's baby, which is presenting extra difficulties for them. Also, in talking about their fear of losing their baby, they were surfacing another very hard issue for the parents to deal with—making the commitment to the baby. The practitioner is quick to universalize the ambivalent feelings. This enables others to talk about how fearful and ambivalent they are about seeing their babies. In two instances she weaves the group's purpose ("to get support") into the content presented.

When Kenny asks what to say to the child at home, the group shifts into its next level of process and problem solving. Together, the group decides that the child at home should not be alarmed. Here the father is an important figure, because he is the one in the house while the mother is in the hospital.

The nurse is an important member of the team, and she uses herself prudently through the vantage point of her expertise. Her presence communicates the need for medical understanding, and her support and caring of the women comes through. The meeting comes to a close with a group activity, visiting with the babies. As they spend this time together, the parents will have a chance to raise questions and think about new things to talk about. Talking about the reunion of the ICU babies is calculated to lend a vision and give hope to the parents.

The men become increasingly involved, and by the end Kenny is responding to someone other than his wife. This poses good potential for including the men at future meetings. The practitioner informally sets up inclusion of two missing men at the end of the session.

Short-term groups like this one need focus and clearly conceived issues to deal with; this one has them. The past is not dealt with, only the present situation. People are permitted to be with each other in whatever way is comfortable. One man is permitted to use his wife as the main connector to the group for the time being; this is acceptable.

OPEN-ENDED GROUPS

In agency practice, some situations and programs develop in which people congregate in subgroups and collectivities with fluid boundaries. The open-ended group gives people the opportunity to take part in group life while entering and exiting at their own pace. Membership in these types of groups changes over various time periods, usually with some definable nucleus maintaining the group's continuity and history over time. The open ended format offers a group opportunity to meet needs and solve problems, without members being required to make a commitment to attend all the time. This is good for people whose life demands require more flexibility, who may feel overcommitted, and for people who can't commit to more than several meetings. Examples of these groups include the divorced and separated parents at a community center, the hearing-impaired group at a nursing home, and a teen rap group at a family center clinic.

Recently the various phenomena and practices of open-ended groups have been identified, discussed, and researched by Galinsky and Schopler (1985, 1987) who have been in the forefront of creating understanding of these groups. Open-ended groups all seem to have entry and exit rituals (Galinsky & Schopler, 1985) in common, with the nucleus of members usually assuming the responsibility for orienting new members and helping others tie up loose ends before they exit. In some instances groups experience a constancy of change, with one or two members leaving and coming every week. This format poses the most difficulty for the practitioner (as well as for the members) because of the amount of time and tediousness of the effort spent in never-ending orientations and departures. On the other extreme there are groups whose members leave only at infrequent intervals, with new ones also entering every so often (Galinsky & Schopler, 1987). In such situations the group and the practitioner will have to orient the new member to the group's culture, while being aware of culture-related group phenomena the member will not understand when they appear. Advance warning will have to be given to new members to ask for explanation of processes they do not understand. However, responsibility for this ongoing orientation remains with the practitioner and the group's nucleus, not in the hands of the new member. For instance, a member who is puzzled by an apparent shortcut in a decision does not know that one month prior the group spent time on this issue. Having to be sensitive to these processes places pressure on the practitioner—who most often is the carrier of group history—to interpret and translate.

Some open-ended groups have been found that will experience long periods of stability during which there is no change, followed by periods of great flux during which many members leave and new ones come in a cluster (Galinsky & Schopler, 1987). This structure is most helpful to the practitioner and members, because the period of stability permits them to experience the group as a well-structured and strongly cohesive entity. Many of the practices used in long-term groups apply during this time; work that is done has continuity for members, and it is possible to carry the work from meeting to meeting.

In working with open-ended groups, the practitioner's effort is toward applying the fullest range of group work technique with all the members, trying to motivate each member's potential and capability. Sometimes the nucleus will carry responsibility for conducting programs and events that others will participate in who will not be involved in preparation for them. When using the technique of programming the practitioner will work with the nucleus, poll everyone who is there for input, and help them include as many others as possible in the delegation of tasks. At times, as with the short-term group, the practitioner will have to compress the process or telescope issues in order to build a beginning, middle, and end to the meeting.

An aspect of the practitioner's role is also to reach outside the boundaries of the current nucleus—to those members who come and go—in order to expand and recruit others into the boundaries of the nucleus. Working with the members of the nucleus to recruit new members is another typical process in the open ended group situation.

The dysfunctional form of the open-ended group is the product of a process wherein professionals and agents with formal power to sanction group experiences will not allow a full membership group to exist, for fear that power will be taken away from them. At the same time they will impose sanctions against specifying, requiring, or taking steps to identify new people who will benefit from the experience and come regularly. This comes about as a result of personal discomfort with power, projections, and fear of danger in the group. The practitioner in such situations is at risk of being seduced into maintaining the illusion of an open ended structure and a "pseudo-open" group. Skill is required in recognizing the phenomena, working with the group, modifying its structure, and enabling the inclusion of members within the framework of a closed-ended humanistic group method.

Illustration

Each week at the same time, Carrie, the practitioner, goes into the women's cell block to work up a list of group members for that evening's meeting of the women's support group. Simultaneous factors influence the open-ended nature of this group: women come and go, depending on their sentences; women are in different moods from day to day; and who comes very often depends on whose attendance the prison officials encourage and enable. Carrie wishes the culture of the group experience to disseminate into the culture of the cell block. She figures that over time she will get to work with many of the women and the cell block culture.

Once again, 15 women sign up to march past the guard a half hour later, get a pass, and meet Carrie a few hundred feet (and four gated checkpoints) away in the group meeting room. And once again, six of the women on the list are the regulars—the nucleus that is "always" in attendance, although over a six-week period the nucleus changes. The remaining nine are either new, or women who came to some sessions and then skipped several meetings up to now.

By 7 p.m., nine of the women who signed up arrive—five of the nucleus, and four of the new members and "rotators." Carrie welcomes them warmly, invites them to sit, and politely waits for the process to start. This night Mona says, "What's this group for?" Elvira, of the nucleus says, "It's a talk group. We give each other advice on how to survive in here." Silence. Paula says to Carrie, "So you're like a teacher; teach us." Carrie says, "Not exactly. I join you all in raising issues that bother you so we can see how you can help yourselves and each other."

Brenda plunges in, saying that she isn't sure she wants her kids visiting her in prison: "They frisk the baby's diaper!" There is anger and frustration expressed. Then the women talk more about their feel-ings, and the pros and cons of their children and families visiting them. Carlotta says that her cousin is in another cell block "right in this place, and I can't get to see her." The practitioner validates how difficult this must be for her. The women discuss several approaches Carlotta can take with the guards. Carrie volunteers, "If you want, I'll see what I can find out about policies they have about this, without rocking the boat for any of you in here." Carlotta asks her to wait another week. Carrie continues by asking, "What are some of the other troubles the rest of you are having with visiting or in other ways?" Vera, new to the cell block, asks about how someone finds out about visiting. Several mem-bers explain to her.

The session continues, with the women talking about how others in the cell block are curious about what goes on in the group. Several members say that it is not just curiosity; it's also a feeling that some of the group members have a clique that the others are not a part of. Carrie interjects, "Sometimes it helps if you let them know they can come." Many of the women are trying to talk at once; Carrie is conscious of encouraging the interweaving of process between the members in the nucleus and the new members, and helping those in the nucleus direct the process so people don't monopolize it. (The women are so in need of attention, and lonely, that they will talk on and on.)

At the good and welfare at the end of the meeting, Carrie is the last to speak. She expresses her reactions and says she hopes "to see all of you, and others, next week—pass the word about the group." The practitioner accompanies the women to the first checkpoint, consciously and actively interacting with the core and the new members, continuing to encourage their participation. She assures them they will see her next week at 6:30 "scaring up names for the list."

Discussion

Several contextual factors are important dimensions for this group. One is the informal structure of the guards who help decide when and which women will attend the group meetings. The other aspect of the informal structure revolves around the culture of the women's cell block, and how participation in this group affects participation there. The practitioner is very conscious of the group's place in the system; by consistently reminding members to invite others to attend, she insures that women in the cell block do not feel closed out of the process. This could create feelings of jealousy or anger if women did not feel the group was available for all of them. Carrie exhibits her understanding of this dimension when she volunteers cautiously to find out about the policy governing visitations within the prison itself among family members, if the member wants her to.

The practitioner expects to be challenged by new members, who are prone to wonder why this practitioner would want to come to a prison to help these women survive. Although this concern is not expressed directly to Carrie, a challenge is almost immediate from one new member. The practitioner, with the help of the members, is able to put the new participants at ease so that work can begin.

The process is accelerated by Carrie's intervention, which moves the group beyond her but does not avoid her centrality, either. She helps all members participate in airing their concerns about visiting, especially with regard to children. She also invites collective participation, which is aimed at helping the women talk to each other within the group and in the cell block.

Members turn to talking about how they are affecting the cell block by attending this group. The practitioner encourages them to invite others to attend; this reminds members that they didn't close out others by participating. The opportunity is clearly available for all.

Before they leave, the practitioner uses the good and welfare at the end of the meeting to help provide closure for the evening. This is especially important in a group that may feel fragmented, and in which members may not return the following week.

As they leave the room, the practitioner escorts them to the first checkpoint. She interacts with all of them, and she again asks them to invite others. She promises to return, firming up the usual time and place, as they walk away talking together.

COPRACTICE (Papell & Rothman, 1980c)

Copractice is the situation in which two persons assume equal responsibility for work with a group. This model of professional involvement can lend itself effectively to the objectives, processes, techniques, values, and norms of the humanistic method. Copractice has the potential of adding an ingredient to the group process that is not present when there is one practitioner. This ingredient gives the members a chance to take part with two practitioners who interact with one another and who may have different styles in the group.

The practitioners in this arrangement are not ranked (Levine, 1980). Asking a line worker or student intern to work with a senior practitioner in the group to enhance learning is not copractice, because of the unequal distribution of power and authority (Herzog, 1980). While this format may enhance some aspects of learning (although this, too, is questionable), the added person is never allowed the position of experiencing himself or herself in the group with the full responsibilities, obligations, and sanctions of the professional. What usually happens is that the junior partner takes an inordinately long time to become effective in the process and to take risks that are group oriented. The junior partner tends to talk to members one at a time, rarely focusing on or raising those group process issues that are in the domain and authority of the group practitioner. Also because they feel like they are being watched by a supervisor, these practitioners have great difficulty relaxing and getting into the situation. Practice is thus stilted and narrow, rather than expansive and creative.

The decision to copractice thereby is usually a practical one based on what benefits members might derive from two practitioners. Sometimes a mix of gender is thought to be helpful to a group, either for role modeling or to serve as a symbolic parental pair. This can be true in a teen group, a residential treatment group, or a children's group. Sometimes a racial or ethnic mix is thought to be useful as a symbolic way of connecting oppressed minorities with the mainstream (by enabling trust from the members via the modeling of trust between the pair). Also, in some settings where the connection to a professional is central to the change process, two practitioners are thought to provide more emotional choices for members whose interpersonal connections are weak. In some settings, especially institutional ones, copractitioners from different disciplines are thought to enrich the treatment process, such as a nurse or psychologist practicing with a social worker. At other times, the group's work itself is felt to be too draining for a single practitioner—as in some cancer support groups, where certain feelings of the practitioner have to be siphoned off outside the group in order to help the members. In some community or work groups, the copractitioners provide more opportunities for members to make connections to necessary tasks.

The decision to copractice with a group also needs to be based on whether these colleagues can carry out the activities and emotions necessary to the undertaking. Two practitioners cannot go into a group unprepared, from session to session, to develop the method and its processes. First, they need to have a prior history and relationship with one another that is not conflictive. Two people with differing styles and approaches to a group cannot be put together for the sole purpose of creating a balanced experience for the members. Copractice is not a question of balance created by parallel play. Actions of practitioners need coordination, which requires added time and effort. Time is needed each week for debriefing after the group and a premeeting collaborative session, along with the inevitable unplanned contacts that take place when colleagues work together.

Pre-session meetings aid the practitioners in sharing their perceptions and feelings about one another, and examining the nature and characteristics of their relationship in the practice roles with the group. The process they will use together will be a reflection of what they expect to happen in a group. Focusing on the group's stage themes (see

Chapter 3) and sharing their personal reactions to the members and to each other with regard to these themes is a helpful approach to framing the copractice issues. They all have to consider the extent each practitioner is feeling invested in the group during Stage Theme 1 ("We're Not in Charge"). During Stage Theme 2 ("We Are in Charge") the process centers primarily on the members, not the practitioners. A copractice model here might adversely affect group autonomy if the practitioners collude to maintain their power by preventing the group from taking them on directly. In the members' views, two people presenting a united front are capable of controlling the group; they are hard to beat. In this model, two people—not one person—will be in authority, and both will have to be dealt with by the members, which interferes with independence and autonomy. As the members move toward the stage of "we're taking you on," the practitioners are called upon to present their interaction for scrutiny and engagement to assist the group into becoming a democratic mutual aid system. The members may attempt to divide them into "one of us" and "not one of us," perhaps to diffuse their power; one practitioner may move to protect the other from the confrontation. These concerns and issues require honest exploration between the practitioners in the interest of strengthening the members' autonomy and development in the democratic process. Upon some resolution of authority issues, the copractitioners will be more favorably viewed as the group accepts the positive aspect of copractice—having two professionals helping them.

During Sanctuary the pair will have to display closeness with each other in the group, rather than being afraid to let the group see their professional bond. Showing the group their relationship opens up opportunities for the members to explore group fantasies about their relationship as friends, lovers, or "mom and pop" (Garland, Jones, & Kolodny, 1973). These wonderments need not be dealt with directly at the time; they may be useful to explore later on. As the group turns its effort toward actualizing purpose—with its ups and downs—how the practitioners react when the members reach the roadblocks of Stage Theme 5 ("This Isn't Good Anymore") is important to focus on: how responsible are they feeling for the group? When the group feels "We're Okay and Able" in Stage Theme 6, the practitioners should provide each other with latitude and support to interact in their creatively unique ways with any of the members. They should answer questions put to them by the members.

Copractitioners will also share their reactions to each other's use of techniques throughout the group. In addition to examining their own relationship, they need to share their observations and reactions to members in order to consider the helpful or dysfunctional effects their collaborative effort is having on the members. Copractitioners must examine the roles they play in terms of who speaks primarily to whom, and for what reason. They also might consider who has better access to particular members, and which of them becomes activated by particular members. The techniques of the method serve as a guidepost for examining their own propensities to use certain interventions and omit others, thereby providing helpful self-awareness for both practitioners.

How they intervene in the group process will affect how the members perceive the professional power and authority of each practitioner. Certain acts of initiative and confrontation are perceived as having more potency. When members look at the two practitioners, one may be seen as a taskmaster, while the other may be viewed as a confronter, or as the peacemaker. Copractitioners must consider what stimulates these perceptions.

Differences of race, ethnicity, and gender between the practitioners will be viewed differentially by members (Davis, 1984; Garvin & Glover-Reed, 1983). Often, women and members of minority groups will be seen as less potent "junior partners," regardless of prior training and skill. The group members view through lenses that are distorted by stereotypes. Dealing with this phenomenon explicitly in the group enhances the humanistic values and democratic norms of the method and utilizes the method to enhance members' social functioning with different types of people in authority roles. However, the issue of stereotyping must be aired regularly between the pair.

Finally, the copractitioners may be called upon to handle interpersonal conflict between themselves. One practitioner may take issue with an approach the other uses in a meeting, or the two of them may find themselves going off in different directions; the conflict may be reflective of stage issues. The type of honesty and forthrightness required to copractice will tax and stretch the practitioners' personalities, knowledge, and skill. The professional rewards from these efforts center around receiving the validation, feedback, and critiques that group practitioners rarely have the opportunity to get unless they are supervised through videotapes.

Illustration

Ted and Doris are copracticing with the socialization group in the day hospital program. The group has met for seven sessions. This meeting continues on the theme of members being spontaneous with each other in informal encounters during the day. Ted and Doris are sitting away from each other, a decision they made from the start to avoid being focused on as a "powerful force," and to be able to interact with members in small talk before the meeting starts.

Cynthia says, "Hey, Jack, I like coming over to gab and joke with you; I'm a social person and I like it." Jack smiles saying he likes it, too, and notices that Ted and Doris do also because, "when you two see each other, you acknowledge each other—and us, too." Doris says, "I like to do that, even though I get so busy and single-minded sometimes."

As this goes on, Chester is scowling more and more. He mutters to himself frequently, finally lurching forward in his chair and exploding to Ted, "You are watching the group and taking notes for Dr. Carmichael!" Everyone, including Ted, is stunned. Ted says, "Chester, these are just my papers I carry around here; look at them." He passes the papers around through the members to Chester, who just holds them limply. Doris says, "Ted, go over and show him the papers." Ted follows her direction and, crouching in front of Chester, shuffles through the papers, reading parts to him. He shows them to others across the room as well. Doris and several others get up and walk over to chat with Chester. "Come on, man, don't freak out," Cynthia says, now sitting next to him. Echoes of "Ted's not playing with you, honest," can be heard from the others. Chester mumbles slowly as he handles the papers, then calms down and gets in a better mood. In the shifting around, people have changed seats, with Ted on one side of Chester and Cynthia—the most gregarious of them all—staying on the other side.

After the session the copractitioners walk out of the day room, with people around as they start to debrief. They do not feel it is secretive, so they talk about what was satisfying and effective. Ted says, "I'm glad you told me to go over to Chester; that was great. Once you said it, a light bulb popped up. I thought, that's his way of asking for interaction. It worked out. And that Cynthia, she *said* she was a social butterfly. She gets them out of themselves when she's like that." He turns and smiles at Cynthia, who had been standing around overhearing. They both smile and nod to her as she runs off to get a hold of Chester. "We did a good job, eh?" Ted says.

Discussion

What is crucial here is how the practitioners follow each others' instructions. This comes from their pre- and post-session meetings, where they have discussed what they see people doing and how they themselves are interacting. Following directions in this way comes from their abilities to hear and listen to each other without being defensive. It is obvious that their interaction is not stilted; if it were, Doris could not take the risk to ask Ted to move over toward Chester. And even if Ted did follow Doris' direction, it might be less likely to be effective because of the power struggle he would be having with Doris. These copractitioners have sufficiently discussed and worked on their different perceptions of the group so that when their own conflict-laden issues are present, they are not acted out before the group. Ted is able to trust Doris' lead. Neither of them is afraid to fail in the other's eyes. There is enough flexibility available so that they will work to find a different route for reconnecting to members who need them.

Another important feature is that Doris and Ted sit apart. This nonverbally communicates to the members that they will not use their supportive dyad to protect themselves in uncomfortable situations.

SUMMARY

This chapter has presented some special considerations for practitioners. The time frame and physical location of the group will affect its process. The types of formal and informal contact with members the practitioner has between sessions will be determined by agency structure and member need; these will affect the group. Meeting with some members after the group has terminated may be required to insure effective referral processes.

In some agency settings, short-term groups are developed to meet specific and singular needs of members. The practitioner in these cases will selectively abbreviate and bypass some of the processes of developing a mutual aid system, filling in with them when they are not all fully developed. The practitioner will also help the group actualize a singularly attainable purpose within that time frame.

Open-ended groups are convened to provide flexible opportunities for people to participate in group life. These groups tend to develop with a nucleus of steadily attending members. The coming and going of some members places extra responsibility on the practitioner who, along with the nucleus, orients new members and says goodbye to the departing ones. Open-ended groups will tend to have varied patterns and time frames as well—some more stable in membership, and others less stable.

Copractice as an approach is recommended only for professionals with equal status and the ability to develop forthrightness and mutuality with each other. In this way, they can model cooperative behavior, following each other's lead and sharing openly in the group. Copractice can have negative consequences for the group when the practitioners have minimal rapport. Without cohesion in the copractice relationship, the members will not be able to work on their authority issues, for fear of taking sides in a pair that has covert conflicts.

REFERENCES

Alissi, A., & Casper, M. (Eds.). (1985). *Time as a factor in group work.* New York: Haworth.

Asch, S. (1965). Effects of group pressure upon the modification and distortion of judgments. In H. Proshansky & B. Seidenberg (Eds.), *Basic studies in social psychology* (pp. 393-401). New York: Holt, Rinehart & Winston.

Bennis, W. (1964). Patterns and vicissitudes of T-group development. In L. Bradford, J. Gibb, & K. D. Benne (Eds.), *T-group theory and laboratory learning* (pp. 248-278). New York: John Wiley.

Bennis, W., & Shepard, H. (1962). A theory of group development. In W. G. Bennis, K. Benne, & R. Chin (Eds.), *The planning of change* (pp. 321-340). New York: Holt, Rinehart & Winston.

Berger, P., & Luckmann, T. (1966). *The social construction of reality.* Garden City, NY: Doubleday.

Berman-Rossi, T. (1987, October). *Empowering groups through understanding stages of development.* Paper presented at the Symposium for the Advancement of Social Work with Groups, Boston.

Berman-Rossi, T. (1988, October). *The tasks and skills of the social worker across stages of group development.* Paper presented at the Symposium for the Advancement of Social Work with Groups, Baltimore.

Bernstein, S. (1973). Conflict and group work. In S. Bernstein (Ed.), *Explorations in group work* (pp. 72-106). Boston: Milford House.

Bion, W. R. (1959). *Experiences in groups.* New York: Basic Books.

Boyd, N. (1971). A definition with a methodological note. In P. Simon (Ed.), *Play and game theory in group work: A collection of papers by Neva Boyd* (pp. 141-148). Chicago: Jane Addams School of Social Work.

Bradford, L., Gibb, J., & Benne, K. (1964). *T-group theory and laboratory learning.* New York: John Wiley.

Clark, K., & Clark, M. (1965). Racial identification and preference in Negro children. In H. Proshansky & B. Seidenberg (Eds.), *Basic studies in social psychology* (pp. 308-317). New York: Holt, Rinehart & Winston.

Cooley, C. H. (1956). *Human nature and the social order.* Glencoe, IL: Free Press. (Original work published 1902)

Coyle, G. (1978). *Group work with American youth.* Reprinted by *The Journal of Sociology and Social Welfare.* (Original work published 1948)

Davis, L. (Ed.). (1984). *Ethnicity in social group work practice.* New York: Haworth.

Deutsch, M. (1968). The effects of cooperation and competition upon group process. In D. Cartwright & A. Zander (Eds.), *Group dynamics* (pp. 461-484). New York: Harper & Row.

Deutsch, M. (1973). *The resolution of conflict.* New Haven, CT: Yale University Press.

Devore, W., & Schlesinger, E. (1971). *Ethnic sensitive social work practice.* St. Louis: C.V. Mosby.

Dewey, J. (1923). *Democracy and education.* New York: Macmillan.

Erikson, E. (1963). *Childhood and society* (2nd ed.). New York: Norton.

Falck, H. (1988). *Social work: The membership perspective.* New York: Springer.

Galinsky, M. J., & Schopler, J. W. (1985). The patterns of entry and exit in open ended groups. *Social Work with Groups, 8*(2), 67-80.

Galinsky, M. J., & Schopler, J. W. (1987, October). *Group development in open ended groups.* Paper presented at the Symposium for the Advancement of Social Work with Groups, Boston.

Garland, J., & Frey, L. (1976). Applications of the stages of group development to groups in psychiatric settings. In S. Bernstein (Ed.), *Further explorations in group work* (pp. 1-33). Boston: Charles River.

Garland, J., Jones, H. J., & Kolodny, R. (1973). A model for stages of development in social work groups. In S. Bernstein (Ed.), *Explorations in group work* (pp. 17-71). Boston: Milford House.

Garland, J., & West, J. (1983). Differential assessment of school age children: Three group approaches. In N. Lang & C. Marshall (Eds.), *Proceedings, 1982 Symposium, CASWG, Toronto* (pp. 130-148). Toronto: Committee for the Advancement of Social Work with Groups.

Garvin, C. (1985). Group process: Usage and uses in social work practice. In M. Sundel, P. Glasser, R. Sarri, & R. Vinter (Eds.), *Individual change in small groups* (2nd ed., pp. 203-225). New York: Free Press.

Garvin, C. (1987). *Contemporary group work.* Englewood Cliffs, NJ: Prentice-Hall.

Garvin, C., & Glover-Reed, B. (Eds.). (1983). *Groupwork with women—Groupwork with men.* New York: Haworth.

Germain, C., & Gitterman, A. (1980). The life model of social work practice. New York: Columbia University Press.

Gitterman, A., & Shulman, L. (1987). Mutual aid groups and the life cycle. Itasca, IL: F. E. Peacock.

Glassman, U., & Kates, L. (1983). Authority themes and worker group transactions. *Social Work with Groups, 6*(2), 33-52.

Glassman, U., & Kates, L. (1986a). Techniques of social group work. *Social Work with Groups, 9*(1), 9-38.

Glassman, U., & Kates, L. (1986b). Developing the democratic humanistic norms of the social work group. In M. Parnes (Ed.), *Innovations in group work* (pp. 149-172). New York: Haworth.

Glassman, U., & Skolnik, L. (1984). The role of social group work in refugee resettlement. *Social Work with Groups, 7*(1), 45-62.

Goldstein, E. (1984). *Ego psychology and social work practice.* New York: Free Press.

Herzog, J. (1980). Communication between co-leaders: Fact or myth. *Social Work with Groups, 3*(4), 19-30.

Hollis, F. (1972). *Casework: A psychosocial therapy.* New York: Random House.

House Plan Association. (1965). A group work program for college students. City College, City University of New York.

Klein, A. (1953). *Society, democracy and the group.* New York: Women's Press and William Morrow.

Klein, A. (1970). *Social work through group process.* Albany: State University of New York.

Konopka, G. (1963). *Social group work: A helping process.* Englewood Cliffs, NJ: Prentice-Hall.

Konopka, G. (1978). The significance of group work based on ethical values. *Social Work with Groups, 1*(2), 123-132.

Kurland, R. (1978). Planning: A neglected component in group work. *Social Work with Groups, 1*(2), 173-178.

Lang, N. C. (1972). A broad range model of practice in social work with groups. *Social Service Review, 46*(1), 76-89.

Lang, N. C. (1981). Some defining characteristics of the social work group: Unique social form. In S. L. Abels & P. Abels (Eds.), *Social work with groups: Proceedings 1979 Symposium* (pp. 18-50). Hebron, CT: Practitioner's Press.

Lang, N. C. (1986). Social work practice in small social forms: Identifying collectivity. In N. C. Lang & J. Sulman (Eds.), *Collectivity in social group work* (pp. 7-32). New York: Haworth.

Lang, N. C., & Sulman, J. (Eds.). (1986). *Collectivity in social group work.* New York: Haworth.

Levine, B. (1979). *Group psychotherapy, practice and development.* Englewood Cliffs, NJ: Prentice-Hall.

Levine, B. (1980). Co-leadership approaches to learning group work. *Social Work with Groups, 3*(4), 35-38.

Lewin, K. (1951). *Field theory in social science.* New York: Harper.

Lindeman, E. (1980). Group work and democratic values. In H. Trecker (Ed.), *Group work foundations and frontiers* (Re-released edition, pp. 13-25). Hebron, CT: Practitioner's Press.

Lowy, L. (1973). Decision making and group work. In S. Bernstein (Ed.), *Explorations in group work* (pp. 107-134). Boston: Milford House.

Middleman, R. (1981a). *The non-verbal method in working with groups.* Hebron, CT: Practitioner's Press. (Original work published 1968)

Middleman, R. (1981b, October). *The values of social group work.* Paper presented at the Symposium for the Advancement of Social Work with Groups, Hartford, CT.

Middleman, R. (Ed.). (1983). *Activities and actions in group work.* New York: Haworth.

Middleman, R., & Goldberg, G. (1974). *Social service delivery: A structural approach to social work practice.* New York: Columbia University Press.

Milgram, S. (1963). Behavioral study of obedience. *Journal of Abnormal and Social Psychology, 67,* 371-378.

National Training Laboratory (1966/1967). *Manual for participants.* Washington, DC: Author.

Papell, C., & Rothman, B. (1980a). Social group work models: Possession and heritage. In A. Alissi (Ed.), *Perspectives on social group work practice* (pp. 116-132). New York: Free Press.

Papell, C., & Rothman, B. (1980b). Relating the mainstream model of social work with groups to group psychotherapy and the structured group approach. *Social Work with Groups, 3*(2), 5-22.

Papell, C., & Rothman, B. (Eds.). (1980c). Co-leadership [special issue]. *Social Work with Groups, 3*(4).

Sarri, R., & Galinsky, M. (1967). Diagnosis in group work. In R. Vinter (Ed.), *Readings in group work practice.* Ann Arbor: University of Michigan.

Sarri, R., & Galinsky, M. (1985). A conceptual framework for group development. In M. Sundel, P. Glasser, R. Sarri, & R. Vinter (Eds.), *Individual change through small groups* (2nd ed., pp. 70-86). New York: Free Press.

Schwartz, W. (1961). The social worker in the group. In R. Pernell & B. Saunders (Eds.), *New perspectives on services to groups: Theory, organization, practice* (pp. 17-28). New York: National Association of Social Workers.

Schwartz, W. (1976). Between client and system: The mediating function. In R. W. Roberts & H. Northen (Eds.), *Theories of social work with groups* (pp. 171-197). New York: Columbia University Press.

Schwartz, W., & Zalba, S. (Eds.). (1971). *The practice of group work.* New York: Columbia University Press.

Seitz, M. (1985). A group's history: From mutual aid to helping others. *Social Work with Groups, 8*(1), 41-54.

Sherif, M. (1965a). Formation of social norms: The experimental paradigm. In H. Proshansky & B. Seidenberg (Eds.), *Basic studies in social psychology* (pp. 461-470). New York: Holt, Rinehart & Winston.

Sherif, M. (1965b). Superordinate goals in the reduction of intergroup conflict. In H. Proshansky & B. Seidenberg (Eds.), *Basic studies in social psychology* (pp. 694-701). New York: Holt, Rinehart & Winston.

Shulman, L. (1981). *Leading a first session* [Videotape]. Montreal: McGill University.

Shulman, L. (1984). *Skills of helping individuals and groups* (2nd ed.). Itasca, IL: F. E. Peacock.

Theodorakis, M. (1973). *Journal of resistance* (G. Webb, Trans.). New York: Coward, McCann & Geohegan.

Timerman, J. (1981). *Prisoner without a name, cell without a number.* New York: Knopf.

Trecker, H. (1972). *Social group work.* New York: Association Press.

Vinter, R. (1985). Program activities: An analysis of their effects on participant behavior. In M. Sundel, P. Glasser, R. Sarri, & R. Vinter (Eds.), *Individual change through small groups* (2nd ed., pp. 226-236). New York: Free Press.

White, R., & Lippitt, R. (1968). Leader behavior and member reaction in three social climates. In D. Cartwright & A. Zander (Eds.), *Group dynamics* (pp. 318-335). New York: Harper & Row.

Whittaker, J. K. (1985). Program activities: Their selection and use in a therapeutic milieu. In M. Sundel, P. Glasser, R. Sarri, & R. Vinter (Eds.), *Individual change through small groups* (2nd ed., pp. 237-250). New York: Free Press.

Yalom, I. D. (1975). *The theory and practice of group psychotherapy* (2nd ed.). New York: Basic Books.

LIST OF ILLUSTRATIONS

INDEX

ABOUT THE AUTHORS

URANIA GLASSMAN, M.A., M.S.W., is Assistant Professor at the Adelphi University School of Social Work, where she teaches social group work, social work practice, and a seminar for field instructors. She has practiced with groups and individuals, providing services to refugees, youth, and the elderly. As director of a college group work program, she was involved with students in designing T-group and leadership training programs, group dynamics workshops, and a range of group services. As Director of Field Instruction at Adelphi, Professor Glassman has written about group field instruction, humanistic education and experiential learning, and has co-chaired a national symposium on field education.

LEN KATES, D.S.W., social worker, psychotherapist, and family therapist, is Associate Professor at the Adelphi University School of Social Work. He is Academic Coordinator of the School's curriculum in social work practice. He has served as Chairperson of the Group Work, and Human Behavior and Social Environment sequences, and as Associate Director of the School's agency, the Social Services Center. He teaches and supervises the practice of social work with groups, as well as other clinical methods. He has been actively practicing social work with groups in the broad array of fields of social work practice since 1961.

Urania Glassman and Len Kates have collaborated on several publications and papers about social group work practice theory, as well as group work education. Both have been active supporters of the Association for the Advancement of Social Work with Groups.

NOTES

NOTES